THE SOCIAL WORLD OF THE PRIMARY SCHOOL

The Social World of the Primary School

Andrew Pollard
Oxford Polytechnic

HOLT, RINEHART AND WINSTON
London·New York·Sydney·Toronto

Holt, Rinehart and Winston Ltd: 1 St Anne's Road,
Eastbourne, East Sussex BN21 3UN

For Ros, Ben and Amy

British Library Cataloguing in Publication Data

Pollard, Andrew
  The social world of the primary school.
  1. Schools—Social aspects—England
  2. Education, Elementary—England
  3. Educational sociology—England
  I. Title
  372.942   LC191.8.G7

ISBN 0-03-910613-6

Typeset by Scribe Design, Gillingham, Kent
Printed in Great Britain by Biddles of Guildford.

Last digit is print number: 9 8 7 6 5 4 3 2 1

Contents

ACKNOWLEDGEMENTS   vii

Introduction   ix

1   Teaching and Learning   1

Part 1   Perspectives

2   The View from the Teachers   15
3   Childhood and Child Culture   37
4   The View from the Children   56

Part 2   Social Context

5   Primary Schools and Society   95
6   Inside Primary Schools   115

Part 3   Interaction

7   Coping with Classroom Life   149
8   Classroom Strategies   172
9   Classroom Processes and Social Consequences   198

Conclusion

10   Teaching and Learning Revisited   235

Notes for Further Reading   249

REFERENCES   254

NAME INDEX   262

SUBJECT INDEX   264

Acknowledgements

A very large number of people have helped me during the years in which the ideas in this book have been developed. I would like first to thank all the teachers, children and other staff at the schools in which I have taught and studied. Unfortunately they must remain anonymous, but I know very well that my researches could not even have been begun without their interest and friendship.

During my part-time studies at Sheffield University my tutor, John Quicke, was an invaluable source of advice, and I am pleased to be able to thank him publicly here. I am also glad to acknowledge the encouragement which was offered to me in the early stages of my work by a number of sociologists. In this regard I would particularly mention Peter Woods, David Hargreaves, Martyn Hammersley and Tony Edwards. I would also like to thank Andy Hargreaves for his help at various times.

A number of people read the whole or part of the book in draft form and supplied me with useful feedback. I would like to thank John Isaac, Ian Sugarman, John Coe, Bev Jones, Richard Border, Robin Wonnocott, Cedric Cullingford and Jan Mark for performing this service.

Dee Croft typed all my early work with great care, and that burden has been carried more recently and with equal efficiency by Greta Ilott.

I would like to thank the following for permission to draw on previously published work:

Carfax Publishing Company for permission to use parts of 'Coping strategies and the multiplication of social differentiation', *British Educational Research Journal*, **10**(1), 1984, and elements of 'A model of classroom coping strategies', *British Journal of Sociology of Education*, **3**(1), 1982.

Studies in Education Ltd for permission to use parts of 'Negotiation, deviance and "getting done" in primary school classrooms', in Barton, L. and Meighan, R. (1979) *Schools, Pupils and Deviance*.

I am also very grateful for the encouragement and practical help which has been provided by my parents. This has been of great significance to me.

   I have to conclude by thanking my wife, Ros, in whatever way I can. She has put up with the particular aberration which this book represents since I began detailed studies of classrooms in 1976. Since then she has been my closest supporter. Nevertheless, I am fairly sure that the best way I can thank her is to send this manuscript to the publisher at once.

OXFORD   ANDREW POLLARD
                                                    SEPTEMBER 1984

Introduction

In this book I have set out to describe and analyse socially important features of routine everyday life in primary schools.

Essentially the book derives from a combination of a decade of experience as a classroom teacher with some specialist knowledge of a particular type of sociology. I have used this combination to develop various analytical models about social processes in schools and I hope that these will facilitate a type of socially aware reflection on classroom practice. Since the analysis was explicitly derived from the views and perspectives of teachers and children themselves, I also hope that it benefits from a certain sense of grounded realism.

I wrote the book partly because I take the view that teachers' study and reflection of social processes in classrooms can help to develop teaching; also because I wanted to trace how teacher actions influence the quality of children's school experience itself. I would argue that the need for consideration of such issues is increasing in our complex and rapidly changing society and that self-evaluation, social awareness and analysis of classroom practices can play a significant part in professional development. Of course such arguments are not new; for instance they relate closely to the idea of practical theorising about classroom work (Reid 1978) and to the concept of reflective teaching (Zeichner and Teitelbaum 1982)—the skill of analysing, evaluating and responding effectively to new situations and demands as they occur.

The book has been written in prime expectation of a teacher and student-teacher audience. Of course, I hope that those who study the sociology of education will also find it of value, and the main analytical parts (Chapters 2 to 9) will stand alone in sociological terms. Such readers may also care to read Pollard (1984), which could be regarded as providing a sociological rationale for the way the book is presented. More detailed accounts of many elements of the analysis are available elsewhere and the interested reader should refer to the References and Notes for Further Reading at the end of the book.

THEORY AND METHOD

Most forms of research have an element of theory behind them. This supplies coherence and often provides links with the particular methodologies which guide empirical work. The present study is no exception, and draws on the sociological approaches known as symbolic interactionism and phenomenology, and on a particular type of research method known as ethnography. A brief outline of these is provided below.

Symbolic interactionism is founded on the belief that people 'act' on the basis of meanings and understandings which they develop through interaction with others. Human action is thus seen as having a social basis rather than deriving, for example, from instinct or genetics. Through symbolic interaction, be it verbal or non-verbal, individuals are thought to develop a concept of 'self' as they interpret the responses of other people to their own actions. Although the sense of self is first developed in childhood, interactionists argue that it is continually refined in later life and that it provides a basis for thought and behaviour. We shall see in other chapters how this theoretical approach can be applied to analyse processes of teacher–child interaction in primary-school classrooms.

I have used phenomenology here in a fairly limited way to focus on the simple but critical point that what people experience has a direct and powerful influence on their knowledge and perception of social situations. Again this can be applied to education: it is not often necessary to stress the importance of classroom experience when talking to teachers.

Looking then at ethnography, the main methodological approach I used, the first point to note is that ethnographers are concerned to describe the perspectives and points of view of the people in the particular social situation being studied as accurately as possible. They try to do this through careful observation of and participation in the subjects' way of life. In this respect, actually being a teacher, as I was when I began these studies, provides a flying start for anyone investigating aspects of schools.

Data are systematically collected and recorded and, building on the understandings which are gradually developed, ethnographers continually analyse their data before embarking on further rounds of data collection.

As they search for patterns of understanding they try to relate these to social factors in the situation being studied so that types of theory are generated (Glaser and Strauss 1967). In this way ethnographers attempt to classify the commonsense and taken-for-granted knowledge of the participants and try to suggest analytical concepts by which such tacit knowledge can be named and made available for reflection. As David Hargreaves (1978) pointed out, many teacher skills rest upon tacit knowledge, knowledge which is based on experience, but knowledge which is rarely made explicit because of the lack of a conceptual apparatus with which to express it. Ethnography, in combination with symbolic interactionism, can thus provide ' . . . a language for speaking about that which is not normally spoken about' (Hargreaves 1978, p.19). Clearly the existence of such a conceptual language could assist all educationists in reflecting on social aspects of classroom practice.

Knowledge about school and classroom processes based on this type of research develops mainly through the accumulation of case studies. It thus has an inherently weak claim to generalisability, but a strong claim to a type of internal validity which comes from the detailed, holistic study of particular social situations. By its very nature it is also largely dependent on subjective and qualitative sources of data rather than on objective and quantitative ones. For these reasons it is not appropriate to suggest that such work produces *verified* accounts; more realistically and positively the emphasis should be placed on the capacity of this type of work to *generate theoretical models*. If these are well grounded they can be stimulating in their own right, and it is this attribute that I have attempted to exploit in this book.

THE SCHOOLS

The analysis presented in this book was most systematically developed from case studies of three schools: an infant school, a 5–9 first school and an 8–12 middle school. However, it is right to acknowledge that it is also grounded in my teaching experience and in my contact with various other schools. The list below provides brief details about the most significant of these schools and indicates the basis of my links with them. Of course, the names of all the schools, teachers and children in the book are pseudonyms.

Netherdyke Primary School had about 300 children on its roll, and served a mixed area of private and council housing in a large village just outside a Northern industrial town. This was my first teaching post, and I taught first a reception class and then seven- and eight-year-olds.

Hawthorn Junior School and Hawthorn Infant School each had about 200 children on its roll. They were near Netherdyke Primary and served a similar village, but were generally regarded as having a more 'challenging' intake, in other words more children from the council estate. I had professional contacts and friends in both of the Hawthorn schools.

Summerlands Infant School had about 200 children on its roll and served a council estate in a suburb of a Northern industrial town. It was recommended to me by advisers as a 'good formal school' in which to work when studying for my MEd. (Pollard 1976). For this I particularly studied processes in the classroom of Mrs Rothwell, who taught six- and seven-year-olds.

Ashton First School (5–9 years) had about 300 children on its roll and served a council estate close to the centre of a Northern city. It was the second school in which I studied for my MEd., and I focused on the teaching of Mr Harman. Mr Harman taught six- and seven-year-olds.

Moorside Middle School (8–12 years) had about 600 children on its roll, of whom around half were from Asian families. The remainder were from an established working-class community within the Northern textile town in which the school was situated. It was a new school with purpose-built units for each year group. I taught ten- and eleven-year-olds who were having some difficulties with their school-work. I also researched at this school for my PhD (Pollard 1981), which was based on a detailed case study of it. For details of the methodology employed in this see Pollard (1985).

Burns Road Infant School (4–7 years) had about 140 children on its roll and served a largely private suburb of a Northern city. It was a modern, open-plan school of which I was deputy head. I taught 'rising fives' and vertically grouped classes of five-, six- and seven-year-olds.

I am well aware that serious methodological issues are raised when drawing across cases and experiences in this apparently eclectic way. However, the impression of eclecticism requires some modification, since the concepts and forms of analysis which are discussed in the book are derived almost exclusively from my MEd.and PhD studies. In listing the other schools above I am simply acknowledging the way in which my teaching and work in them complemented research by providing an input of 'subsidiary awareness', resonance and comparison. The only exception to this is the case of Burns Road Infant School, from which I have drawn a few illustrative examples.

I would also reiterate that my priority here has been to present educationists with various analytic concepts and models which seem to me to highlight important social processes affecting primary schools and classrooms. I make no undue claims about verification or generalisability, for such concerns required different types of research and more resources than I have had available. It is therefore right, proper and entirely in keeping with the spirit of this book that readers actively attempt to match the analysis offered to their own knowledge and experience. Indeed, I have adopted a rather similar procedure in this book by relating it to other published work where possible. If discussion, debate and practical enquiry are generated in this way then the book will have served one of its main purposes.

THE STRUCTURE OF THE BOOK

The analytical model which forms the core of the book is introduced in three parts—'Perspectives', 'Social Context' and 'Interaction'— each containing several chapters. However, the book begins and ends with chapters which are somewhat different because they focus on the relevance to teachers of the consideration of social factors in schools and classrooms. In these chapters I have also made my own values and opinions clear and used them to highlight certain issues, each embedded in the book, which I feel are important. The main analytical parts of the book are presented in a more conventional academic way.

The issues which are introduced in the first and last chapters include teaching and learning, social differentiation and the nature of teacher–child relationships. In particular I suggest that, as teachers in schools strive to meet the professional challenges of the 1980s, they are confronted by acute dilemmas which are, at root, caused by a discrepancy between ends and means in education. Thus I argue that, whatever the educational goals which are publicly endorsed at any particular time happen to be, they will produce only disillusion and disappointment unless they pass the test of viability in the light of practical classroom experience. Of course, my argument is that social factors of the sort considered in the bulk of the book have a great deal of influence on how this practical classroom experience occurs and is perceived. I suggest, therefore, that the study can contribute not only to our understanding of what happens in schools but also to our understanding of what is possible and of what might need to be done in the future.

The structure of the substantive parts of the book, which gradually introduce the analytical model of the book, is as follows.

Part 1   Perspectives

These chapters describe some significant aspects of the perspectives of teachers and children. These perspectives are related to the contexts in which teachers and children act and it is suggested that when interacting in the classroom teachers and children not only have educational concerns but also maintain particular interests-at-hand which are essentially pragmatic. These interests are a little different from those which educational theorists might lead us to expect.

Part 2   Social Context

This part of the analysis considers the wider context in which primary classrooms are located. One chapter focuses on the school, on the school ethos or institutional bias and on the role of the head teacher. Another chapter relates primary schools to society as a whole and traces the common disjunction between what primary schools are required to do and the provision of the means to carry policies out. Both chapters explore how these social factors can be constraining, pressurising *and* enabling with regard to classroom action, thus producing contradictions, posing dilemmas and explaining many aspects of teachers' and children's perspectives.

Part 3   Interaction

This is the most important part of the book and builds on the previous analysis. It focuses on classroom processes, and a model of teacher–child interaction is constructed. Action is viewed as a creative response by each unique individual to their structural and material position in the classroom. Thus action and constraint, biography and role are linked. The key concept here is that of coping strategy, and it is argued that teachers and children in primary classrooms normally develop a type of mutual accommodation by which they each cope—a working consensus.

The strategies of teachers and children are considered, in particular the ways in which they 'juggle' their interests and the ways in which their strategies mesh together. Finally, some social consequences of teacher–pupil interaction are discussed.

The book concludes with a review of possible applications of the model which has been developed and with a call for positive thinking with regard to primary-school practice. I argue that the commitment and philosophy of teachers offer many opportunities for socially progressive developments and suggest that we should all work to bring them about.

1

Teaching and Learning in Primary Schools

The 1980s have provided many challenges for teachers and, in a rapidly changing society, this may well be the pattern for the future. With this in mind it is appropriate to begin this book by identifying what may be seen as two of the most fundamental factors which affect educational practice. I will then use the discussion of these factors as a means of briefly introducing the social world of primary schools itself and also of indicating some of the issues to which I believe the book is relevant. In respect of the latter, I have chosen to highlight teaching and learning processes, teacher–pupil relationships and processes of social differentiation in primary schools. I hope that a preliminary discussion of such topics will provide something of an educational context in which to set the subsequent analysis.

The first fundamental issue which teachers face concerns the purpose of education itself. We lack, and perhaps have always lacked, a stable, coherent and generally acceptable specification of educational aims. Should we focus on the child or the subject, on creativity or basic skills, on independent thinking or on straightforward 'knowledge', on individual development or on socialisation into groups? The dilemmas are endless. Commitments, opinions and priorities among teachers and other educationists take many forms, just as they do among national governments, local education authorities and the public at large, and teachers have had little success in attempts to define areas of professional autonomy within which they might establish their own purposes collectively. Perhaps education is considered to be too important for that, for it is, of course, a political and socially sensitive issue. In any event, the result is that, despite the beliefs and commitments of individual teachers, the educational priorities which they are expected to endorse both

1

change over time and cover a very wide range. A teacher's 'role', if one can talk in such terms, is thus diffuse and ill-defined, but it is also subject to particular types of pressure at particular times in response both to national trends and to those with the power to influence such definitions. For example, many issues call for the attention of primary-school teachers in the mid-1980s: children with special educational needs, multicultural education, information technology, subject specialism, standards in basic skills, science, and links with industry, to name but a few. The obvious problem which this poses for teachers is that not only do they have to relate these priorities to their own educational beliefs, but to attend to one issue almost inevitably involves a relative neglect of others—a fact which often exposes the profession to public criticism. Standing back from such problems, it could be argued that an enduring solution may in fact be impossible. Schools and teachers are always likely to be called upon to respond to the social and economic necessities of the time as seen by a variety of interest groups. Flexibility and adaptability may thus be the only viable strategy in the long term.

This brings us to the second fundamental factor which affects educational practice, a factor which is related to 'means' rather than 'ends'. As all teachers know, resource provision and the issue of finance are absolutely vital to what it is possible to do in education. But any public education system is expensive and has to be paid for. For instance, in 1981–82 the UK education service as a whole cost £13 873 million, 5.4 per cent of the total expenditure by public authorities. In a sense education has always been a bottomless pit as regards finance, precisely because of the lack of clarity about aims, but on the other hand the relationship between expected ends and the means supplied seems to have been becoming increasingly out of alignment in recent years. This is of the utmost importance.

It is to their credit that, despite such difficulties, most teachers in primary schools continue to have a pride in their work and in their traditions. Indeed the primary sector has been looked to as a particular source of idealism and professional commitment for many years. However, as they strive to meet the priorities of the 1980s, most primary-school teachers will know from their daily practical experience of the difficulties which lie ahead and of the constraints within which they must work.

The 1980s are thus a time when educational ends are not quite clear and educational means are not plentiful. Such a situation may not be as unusual as we may think, but nevertheless it poses the question 'What should teachers do?'. In my view they will do precisely what teachers have done many times in the past and what anyone in any walk of life would do—they will adapt—and it is this process of adaptation which brings us to the present book.

Adaptations are, in a sense, the main subject of the book, for they are essentially social phenomena. They are patterns of actions taken by individuals or groups in response to their perceived circumstances. In other words, adaptations occur at the point where ends, means and people meet. Of course the school situation is complicated by the fact that teacher adaptations are related to, and mirrored by, children's adaptations so that neither can really be understood except by reference to the other. In fact there is a sense in which teachers and children directly 'construct' understandings and social practices through their activity and interaction together, and it is the product of these adaptations, or strategies, by teachers and children which makes up the 'social world' of the primary school.

The social world of the primary school can thus be seen partially as a manifestation of the disjunction between ends and means in education. It lies at the point where the creativity, ideas and perceptions of teachers and young children meet the practical and material realities of their situation. The teachers who develop adaptations together and the children whose peer-group culture offers them support all meet in the classroom, where further understandings of what is possible, of what is to be done, and of what is not, are negotiated.

It is worth bearing in mind here that what I have described in terms of the recent experience of primary schools, and in terms of a disjunction of ends and means, is really only a specific case of a more universal and much discussed phenomenon: that of the social outcomes of the interaction of subjective and objective phenomena, of idealism and materialism, of action and of constraint. Although there is no need to enter into the sociological and philosophical debates which have surrounded these relationships, I draw attention to them here simply to indicate that a vast resource of relevant knowledge and social analysis exists, and this could be helpful when we seek to analyse social processes in schools.

Despite such resources elsewhere, it is a strange fact that published accounts and discussion of this social world in primary schools have not been common in recent years, but perhaps this simply reflects another deep-seated problem in education: the gap between theory and practice.

The theory–practice problem has been long-lasting and has been fuelled, in my view, by many misunderstandings and a certain amount of prejudice on both sides. For instance, I would judge an assertion heard in a school that 'the academic disciplines are irrelevant to teachers' to be just as misplaced as the suggestion heard at a university that 'teachers never seriously think about what they are doing'. That both propositions are absurd is one point, but it is more important to note that such attitudes are counterproductive: they weaken both cases and the possibilities for our understanding of educational processes at a stroke.

To study the social world of primary schools is a fascinating experience with regard to this issue probably more than any other, since it appears to provide a genuine opportunity to bridge the divide. The strategies which teachers adopt in order to accommodate and adapt theory in their daily practice are one side of the coin, but an issue of much more importance for the future concerns the extent to which a socially aware and self-critical type of practical theorising, based on classroom action itself, can be constructed by teachers. I would argue that a precondition of this is a greater conceptual understanding of the 'social world of schools'—of what actually goes on in schools and of the subjective meanings and concerns that teachers and children bring to and use in the classroom.

The important point is that this puts direct attention on to many explicitly qualitative factors: subjective perceptions, feelings, values, interests, understandings. The fact that they may not be measurable or readily observable, in the way that 'behaviour' is, has undoubtedly contributed to the relative lack of prominence of such factors in educational discussion and decision-making, despite the protestations of many teachers about the importance of the 'quality' of classroom life irrespective of measurable outputs. But qualitative factors are too important to ignore, as I hope to demonstrate in this book.

Indeed, I would argue strongly that if there is ever to be any significant narrowing of the gap between ends and means, or of that between theory and practice, it will have to be based on a realistic understanding of the people involved in classrooms as people— active, social, creative and adaptive people. Without this we shall simply sustain our illusions of what is possible and are likely to continue to lurch between idealism and disappointment in future developments as we have done many times in the past. This, then, is what the study of the social world is about; it is a close look at the people in school, at their thoughts, at their creative and strategic adaptations and at the consequences of those actions.

I would like to reinforce the argument that such an analysis may usefully contribute to educational thinking and classroom practice by looking at several practical issues which are of relevance to primary education and at some aspects of our understanding of them. I shall return to consider these issues again in the final chapter of the book.

Let us begin with two very basic concerns: teaching and learning.

TEACHING AND LEARNING

For many years now the contribution of psychology to our understanding of teaching and learning processes has been very great. Studies of cognition and studies of child development have been particularly valuable and influential. While in no way decrying such work, I believe its practical utility has often been reduced by the failure of researchers to test and locate their studies in a socially meaningful analysis of the classroom situations in which teaching and learning are expected to take place. I think, therefore, that if it is possible to develop a greater understanding of the social world of primary schools it could be helpful with regard to these basic issues.

Let me take as an example the question of the 'match' between a child's knowledge and understanding and the task which a teacher might set for him or her. This is an important current issue because one of the most significant trends of recent years in primary education has been the gradual emergence of new views about how children learn and how they should be taught. The dominance of Piaget's developmental child psychology (Piaget 1959) and of the Plowden Report's prescriptions (Central Advisory Council for Education 1967), often crudely summarised as 'learning through experience', has been challenged. This challenge has grown since the mid-1970s, with some HMI support (Department of Education and Science 1978), and it emphasises the appropriateness, consistency and structure of the curriculum which is provided for a child. Of course the importance of children's experience is not ignored, but it is argued that the level of 'cognitive demand' in work tasks is particularly important and that it should be very carefully matched to the child's existing level of knowledge or skill. The example which has been chosen is thus a critical one.

There seems to me to be two aspects of this issue which are particularly salient. The first concerns what it is that has to be matched and the second concerns how matching is to be achieved in classrooms.

Regarding what has to be matched, the simple answer is in terms of the appropriateness of cognitive demand—a factor which is obviously crucial. A second factor though, is motivation, and it is to this that social, subjective and qualitative issues are important. Motivation in a classroom is not simply to do with 'stimulating the children's interests', for such a strategy is totally decontextualised. It is also about establishing a social atmosphere in which children will want to work and in which they know their efforts will be valued and judged fairly. In addition, it concerns setting tasks and providing activities which relate positively to children's social relationships, their expectations and their cultural understandings about work tasks. If this is not done the work set is likely to be regarded as 'unfair' and the children's motivation will be reduced. A task should thus be socially as well as cognitively appropriate. Both types of matching are necessary if children are to apply themselves fully to learning, and each is insufficient on its own.

The second salient issue regarding matching concerns how it is to be achieved in classrooms on a day-to-day basis. In this regard the valuable study by Bennett et al. (1984) is very interesting. Bennett and his colleagues worked with 16 teachers of 96 six- to seven-year-old children in primary and infant schools. The degree of cognitive match in the work that the teachers set was assessed for number tasks and for language tasks. In number, 43 per cent of the tasks were found to be matched, with 28 per cent being too difficult and 26 per cent too easy. In language only 40 per cent were matched: 29 per cent were too difficult and 26 per cent were too easy. The proportion of correctly matched work was thus low. As Bennett and his colleagues commented, '...although there were marked differences in the classrooms studied, tasks demanding practice of existing knowledge, concepts or skills predominated' (Bennett et al. 1984, p.213). Evidently a great deal of routine work was done despite the fact that the teachers were 'clearly conscientious and dedicated'. More specifically, Bennett et al. focused on two major problems which the teachers encountered: providing an accurate diagnosis of the child's understanding and designing appropriate tasks.

This is a sympathetic and supportive study which recognises the pressure on teachers in crowded classrooms, the need to respond to individual children when required and the need to manage crises as they occur. However, when it comes to proposing classroom solutions it is disappointing because it reveals only a limited appreciation of the subjective concerns and motivations of teachers and children which could account for the observed results. For instance, Bennett et al. suggest that teachers seemed 'totally blind' to tasks with demands which were too easy (Bennett et al. 1984, p.215) and attribute this to a tendency to equate task appropriateness with children seeming 'busy' when viewed from the front of the class. As we shall see later, many more issues are likely to have been involved. Teachers and children adapt to their classroom life together and their social strategies often mesh to produce sets of stable, routine practices which are understood and used to 'cope' with the situation. In my opinion, with class sizes of between 25 and 30 children the social understanding that a teacher 'should be' and 'does feel' fairly content if the children remain 'busy' is often a regrettable but necessary reality.

My point is that teaching and learning are processes which have social, interactive and pragmatic dimensions. The issues are not simply cognitive or organisational but involve the perspectives and practical concerns of teachers and children as they work together. An understanding of common patterns in the subjective perceptions of teachers and children is thus a necessary complement to other types of insight about teaching and learning in classrooms.

TEACHER-PUPIL RELATIONSHIPS

Establishing a 'good relationship' is commonly regarded as being fundamental to successful work with young children. For instance Yardley (1976) claims that '...the quality of relationships within the school is at the root of the discipline which pertains there...' and that '...the intimate communion between teacher and child makes the modern infant school what it is' (Yardley, 1976, p.67). Kirby (1981) suggests that the post-Plowden 'revolution' in primary education as a whole represents '...a return (from class teaching) to the more genuine meeting of two minds, to conditions more likely to produce a personal relationship between teacher and child' (Kirby, 1981, p.4). Many more examples of this concern could be cited, ranging from the early 1970s work of people like Len Marsh and Sir Alec Clegg to the more recent writings of Stephen Rowlands (1984) and John Coe, Chairman of the National Association of Primary Education. Indeed, in a very real sense, this concern is at the core of primary-school ideology and conveys values with which many primary-school teachers would wish to identify. It is more than just a set of ideas, though, for it has undoubtedly given many primary schools and classrooms a unique quality of warmth, friendship and openness, and has provided the cornerstone of their educational achievement. In addition, teachers are well aware of the satisfaction and enjoyment which they get from the close and long-term relationships which they develop with their classes during a year.

However, despite all the importance which is attached to it, the concept of a 'good relationship' has remained intangible and elusive. As Kirby put it himself, '...the teacher has to have the sensitivity of the artist to understand children' (Kirby, 1981, p.54), and many teachers would argue that it is only their spontaneous responses and intuition which enable them to initiate and maintain close and unique personal relationships with the children in their class.

I have considerable sympathy with this view, but it does seem to me to carry with it some difficulties and result in some missed opportunities. In the first place there is the problem of access to such a 'good relationship'. It is all very well for an experienced teacher to celebrate this ephemeral sign of competence, but how is a student teacher or a teacher in difficulties to be inducted into the process of osmosis by which a 'good relationship' will grow? Obviously, certain personal qualities and interpersonal skills are vital, but I believe that it may also be helpful to many people to be more sociologically attuned to the processes which may be involved. As I shall attempt to show in later chapters, it is perfectly possible to analyse a 'good relationship' as a set of understandings which have been socially constructed through classroom interaction. The critical point here is that both teachers and pupils must recognise the basic concerns of the other.

An analysis of this sort provides certain opportunities, for, if its ramifications are clearly understood, it can be a very powerful tool in classroom problem-solving and in professional self-evaluation.

For instance, I suggested earlier that such an analysis provides one way of investigating and assessing the social aspects of the classroom as a learning environment, and it is worth exploring this issue further. I have already argued that children's learning is not achieved just by providing experiences, in the Piagetian emphasis, or by a cognitive and curricular match, important though these issues may be, and I have suggested that social, interactive and pragmatic factors also apply. An additional factor, in my view, relates to the degree to which the learners *control* their own learning. The importance of this has been carefully documented by Rowlands (1984) and Armstrong (1980) in two detailed and classroom-based studies of children's thinking and learning. If they are correct then the importance of the relationship between teachers and pupils is further emphasised, and it becomes critical to identify how teachers can use their power and authority in the classroom to structure learning situations which both put children 'in control' and are practically viable. Such issues are clearly amenable to sociological work.

However, the analysis which is presented in this book is arguably even more relevant to issues of discipline, deviance and classroom order. This centrality arises because the 'social world', as I have defined it, exists as the product of a constant process of negotiation for shared understandings among or between teachers and children, with each individual having slightly different concerns and interests.

An underlying theme of the book, as with much sociological work, thus concerns the basis of social order and social control. I should perhaps make clear, however, that no 'tips' on discipline matters will be found here, and the analysis may cause us to look more towards ourselves as teachers in this respect than towards the children. As I shall try to demonstrate, classroom order, like the 'good relationship', can endure only if it is based on offering a child fairness and dignity.

I want to conclude this discussion of the teacher–pupil relationship by focusing on one further and rather important reason for attempting to make such qualities more tangible. It arises because the ephemeral character which is in a sense the strength of such relationships is also a source of weakness. A vague notion, which 'good relationships' may well seem to be, is very vulnerable indeed to those who exercise influence over resources. After all, it seems perfectly reasonable from an accounting point of view that the financial input to the education service should result in some sort of measurable output. Sometimes such evidence is provided but, conversely, resource decisions are often made in areas which, while minimising overt, objective or behavioural consequences, do a great deal of damage to essential interpersonal aspects of primary-school life.

If subjective qualities of this sort are to be protected in a harsh economic climate then we must begin to develop a means of specifying how they originate and develop and how they are sustained. From this base we may be better able to demonstrate their value and thus justify them as legitimate social costs (Mishan 1967). I am hopeful, then, that an analytic study of the social world of the primary school, however tentative, may be at least one step forward.

PROCESSES OF SOCIAL DIFFERENTIATION

Of course social differentiation is a classic sociological and political concern which, above all, raises issues of social justice. It used to be manifested in teacher education programmes by courses which documented class-based differences in educational outcomes and analysed the difficulties of achieving 'equality of opportunity' for social groups who had experienced widely differing patterns of socialisation in their communities and homes. In the public sphere of political action and debate the issue of social differentiation was particularly reflected in the 1960s in the critique of the tripartite system of grammar, technical and secondary modern schools and in arguments about the establishment of comprehensive schools. Some time has passed and the ground rules and definitions which frame such discussion in the sociology of education have now changed in a way which not only broadens the concern to class, gender and race but also makes the issue much more directly relevant to the routine daily practice of teachers and children in all schools, including primary schools.

For instance it is now recognised that social processes of face-to-face interaction in classrooms are likely to have a considerable influence on the expectations, identities and eventual life chances of children. With regard to progressive primary practice, Sharp and Green (1975) made this point to powerful effect in their study of Mapledene Infant School, and in many ways this book can be seen as a development of their work. This particular emphasis is of enormous significance to teachers, for the analysis produces a marked redirection of responsibility with regard to social differentiation. The argument that the relative academic 'failure' of working-class children can in a sense be 'blamed' on their cultural background has frequently been used by teachers (King 1978) but now seems far too crude and partial. As I shall attempt to show towards the end of this book, we ourselves as teachers are also likely to contribute to processes of social differentiation through our daily practices and classroom routines. We thus play an active part and bear some responsibility for the social injustices which can result from schooling.

However, to leave the matter there would also be crude, partial and unfair. It would be unfair because teachers have to cope with their classes in circumstances which are often far from satisfactory and over which they have little control. Class sizes, resource levels, external pressures and expectations, legal responsibilities, organisational constraints—these and many other material factors provide the structural framework within which teachers work and with regard to which they naturally develop adaptive strategies. The problem arises if these ways of coping with their situation have unforeseen social consequences, but it is quite unreasonable to hold teachers themselves responsible for the circumstances to which they react. For this we have to look outside schools at various aspects of our society as a whole. I shall attempt to do this, but without plunging too deeply into sociological findings and theories, although there is a great deal of work which could be drawn on. Interested readers will find further references to this important topic in the 'Notes for Further Reading' at the end of the book.

CONCLUSION

The social world of primary schools is created by children and teachers acting and reacting to each other within their classroom situation, and this is set within the context of their school, community and society. If we want to understand what happens in primary schools then we cannot ignore the influence of the subjective perceptions, understandings, feelings and social traditions which result, and it is for this reason that the present book has been written.

The following chapter begins the first part of the analysis itself and is intended to document not only teachers' perspectives about primary education, but also their concerns about the realities of classroom life.

PART ONE

PERSPECTIVES

2

The View from the Teachers

INTRODUCTION

It has often been said that there is nothing more significant for the quality of an education service than the teachers working in it. I thus begin by focusing on primary-school teachers and on the ways in which they perceive both their educational aims and their everyday classroom experience.

As a Secretary of State for Education once put it in his White Paper on 'teaching quality', '...the school teaching profession continues to serve with resilience and commitment' (DES 1983, p.1). In this chapter I will be concerned to look closely at the nature of the 'commitment' of primary-school teachers and at the various aims and priorities which have been articulated over the years. This is important, for primary education has been regarded as being in the forefront of educational thinking since the mid-1960s and has an international reputation of which most primary-school teachers are justifiably proud. However, the public image of any institution or profession is rarely a direct reflection of actual practice, and in the major section of the chapter I will review the results of research in primary-school staffrooms which show teachers' daily concerns more clearly and highlight an important source of their 'resilience'.

Of course sociologists have often noted differences between what people say in public and what they say and do in more private situations. Specifically with regard to teachers, Keddie (1971) coined the terms 'educationist context' and 'teacher context' to emphasise the importance of the audiences and situations in which teachers speak and act. This remains a useful distinction to make, for it

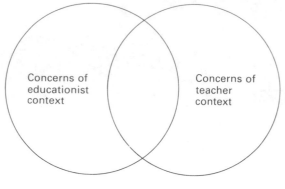

Figure 2.1

provides a way of highlighting the reality of 'doing the job' and can thus be taken as a starting point for identifying and analysing the factors that influence primary-school teachers in their work.

Fig. 2.1 provides one way of looking at this issue. The concerns of the educationist context are represented by idealism, commitment and a continuous effort to improve the quality of educational provision. The concerns of the teacher context are often represented by discussion of more personal, pragmatic and practical issues. In many primary schools the area in which these concerns overlap is significantly large, while in others the overlap is smaller. In a sense this chapter simply provides a means of discussing this relationship.

The chapter begins with a review of the influence of the Plowden Report, which is compared with evidence of actual practice.

TEACHERS AND PRIMARY-SCHOOL POLICIES

In the late 1960s, particularly after the publication of the Plowden Report (CACE 1967), primary schools developed a reputation for so-called 'progressive' and 'child-centred' teaching methods.

The Plowden Report advocated a new type of education for young children, with special stress on first-hand experience and individualised learning. As the report put it:

> The newer methods start with the direct impact of the environment on the child and the child's individual response to it. The teacher has to be prepared to follow up the personal interest of the children who, either singly, or in groups, follow divergent paths of discovery.
>
> (CACE 1967, para. 544)

Of course the philosophy on which the report was based was not new; indeed it can be traced back to Rousseau's *Emile* and had been developed by such well-known figures as Froebel, Pestalozzi, Dewey and Montessori. It had even found expression in a government report before, in the 1931 Hadow Report (Board of Education 1931), which had first coined the term 'primary' school. However, the prosperous, expansionist and optimistic 1960s provided a far more fertile ground for the ideas articulated by Plowden, and the impact of the report on teaching, thinking and practice was thought to be very great.

As a starting point from which to assess this influence there are indications that the majority of schools in the early 1960s were very different from those envisaged by Plowden, and very different too from the few so-called 'show schools' which had even then been developed in parts of the 'progressive' West Riding and Oxfordshire. For instance, a national survey of 660 primary schools in 1962 (Jackson 1964) found that no less than 96 per cent of the schools streamed their pupils into classes based on ability, a practice which was to be specifically rejected by Plowden, and it further revealed that the majority of teachers felt that academic standards and the education of both gifted and less gifted children would suffer without such streaming. The examples which Jackson drew on consistently indicated that a range of relatively formal teaching methods was the norm at the time.

Interestingly, the teachers' comments that Jackson recorded also showed a resistance to change and to new ideas from outside the 'real profession'. For instance, the teachers felt that the types of people who would oppose streaming would include:

> Head teachers who want to please certain Inspectors (Head teacher, Cumberland)
> The cranks of this world ('B' stream teacher, Plymouth)
> Ivory towered lecturers in education ('C' stream teacher, Stoke)
> (All quoted in Jackson 1964, p.41)

A total of 61 per cent of the teachers who favoured streaming identified 'people who are *not* practising teachers' as the main critics of the practice and also implied that any other type of organisation would be impractical. As one teacher put it:

> These ill-informed critics do not realise the amount of work that would be necessary in preparing and marking work for an unstreamed class: it would virtually be three or four classes.
> ('A' stream teacher, Essex, quoted by Jackson 1964, p.42)

Clearly there were many teachers in the early 1960s who were unlikely to have been sympathetic to the Plowden Report of 1967.

Given this, then, the studies of the early 1970s do appear to reveal a
dramatic change. For instance, regarding classroom organisation, a
survey conducted of 189 junior-school teachers in two local
authorities in 1970 revealed that 'the overwhelming majority of
classrooms contained children of mixed ability' (Bealing 1972). A
follow-up survey of the same schools in 1977 found a 'complete
absence' of streaming (Boydell 1981), and other studies have also
shown that a considerable organisational transition took place.
Regarding school architecture, a large proportion of the new schools
at the time adopted open-plan designs in keeping with the Plowden
philosophy. The same influence also appeared to be present in
teachers' views as indicated in 1970 by a national survey of 1513
teachers who were asked detailed questions about the aims of
primary education, which they prioritised (Ashton et al. 1975). Two
broad purposes were identified which reflected the emphasis of
teacher aims and stood in a 'kind of opposition'. The first was the
'societal purpose', which emphasised skills, had 'a strong three Rs
flavour' and 'stressed conformity to existing standards', while the
second purpose, the 'individualistic', was more concerned with
questioning and with 'autonomy and distinctively individual development'. As Ashton et al. put it:

> The societal teachers see their task as deciding upon what children are
> to learn and closely directing the course of that learning. The
> individualist teachers see teaching as a much more cooperative venture
> with children, who should have a measure of choice in what they learn
> and a much more active part in it.
>
>   (Ashton et al. 1975, p.90)

Clearly the individualistic purpose is more in line with the Plowden
philosophy, and interestingly it was shown in the study that older,
more experienced teachers tended to favour the societal purpose
while the younger, post-Plowden teachers endorsed more individualistic aims. Even if one allows for the fact that younger, less
experienced teachers tend to be more liberal, it is clear that the type
of individualist aims recommended by Plowden were nationally
established only three years after the report was published.

There are thus many indications that in the early 1970s the
progressive movement had developed to a considerable extent. The
combined impression given by organisational changes, new types of
school design, the continuing child-centred writings of educationists
such as Sir Alec Clegg, John Blackie, Henry Pluckrose, Len Marsh
and Alice Yardley, and an apparently increasing consensus among
teachers in their public utterances, was that there had indeed been 'a
primary-school revolution'.

Caution is necessary, however, for there are also indications that the realities of the classrooms in which many teachers attempted to implement the new ideas produced significant compromises. Indeed we should note that Ashton's study also showed that almost half of the teachers claimed to adopt a mixed-mode, 'moderate' approach to their teaching. In Bealing's survey of 189 junior-school classrooms she noted that, despite predominantly informal classroom layouts, there was 'much evidence of tight teacher control' and it seemed 'highly doubtful that there was much opportunity for children to choose or organise their own activities in most classrooms' (Bealing 1972, p.235). Similarly, a study by Moran (1971) of the 'integrated day', which was often regarded as the key organisational pattern for the new methods, showed that work on the three Rs still took priority over all other activities and in no case in his survey of 181 teachers was the children's choice complete. A little later Bennett (1976), in a study attempting to compare teaching styles and pupil performance, was unable to identify, even by 'generous estimate', more than 17 per cent of the classrooms within his sample which could be classified as progressive in terms of the Plowden Report's prescriptions. Bassey (1978) in his survey of 900 Nottinghamshire teachers again found a great deal of variety in teaching methods which even, perhaps surprisingly, prompted Lady Plowden, in her foreword to the book, to express her pleasure at 'the lack of gimmicky "progressive" methods'. Most recently, Galton, Simon and Croll (1980), reporting on the result of the systematic observation of 58 junior-school classrooms, concluded that '"progressive" teaching hardly exists in practice' and that, regarding the curriculum, 'The weight of evidence shows very clearly that the general pattern of the traditional curriculum still prevails' (Galton, Simon and Croll 1980, p.155).

Thus, despite all that was written, said and imagined about the impact of child-centred primary-school philosophy, it is clear that it was implemented far more cautiously by teachers. School designs did become more open and teachers did adopt more individualised methods after Plowden, but to some extent the impression created was illusionary. Teacher control remained tight and the traditional focus on the three Rs was maintained.

The main features in the development of the primary schools since the 1960s are thus reasonably clear. A progressive primary-school philosophy was articulated by the Plowden Report which appeared to have considerable influence on teachers. Indeed, so pervasive was this appearance that by the mid-1970s there were calls for more balance. However, that the reality of actual practice was much more cautious was shown by a number of studies, and was further recognised by an HMI report on primary schools (DES 1978). To an extent, then, the temporary prevalence of child-centred ideas in the early 1970s must be seen as providing part of the educational rationale of an expanding profession. In the educationist context of the time such ideas were consistently articulated despite the fact that in teacher contexts actual practice had not gone so far.

I have no doubt that it will one day be possible to document similar disjunctions between what is said and what is done in education for the 1980s; it is, after all, an entirely natural phenomenon which can be found in almost every area of social life. The point, though, is to recognise that such discrepancies do occur and to attempt to appreciate and understand why. It is now appropriate, therefore, to begin to look further into teacher contexts, to look behind the rhetoric and the survey results, and to see what issues are prominent in teachers' thinking in less public situations. Perhaps this may lead us towards an explanation of the apparent lack of fundamental change in classroom practices and towards a greater understanding of teachers' daily practical concerns.

THE STAFFROOM AND TEACHER KNOWLEDGE

Staffrooms are places where many of the issues mentioned above are aired, shared and discussed, and over the years in which I have worked in primary schools I have participated in many such conversations. I was able to record some of these using the standard ethnographic method of compiling 'field notes', particularly when I taught at Moorside Middle School. These field notes form the basis of the following analysis.

The staffroom is in many respects a place of retreat, a place to which teachers retire at playtimes and dinner-times and are temporarily insulated from the demands of the young children in their classes, a place where coffee and tea are made, sandwiches are eaten or perhaps cake is consumed on birthdays, a place for jokes, anecdotes and conversation, a place where many head teachers feel uneasy and into which parents seldom venture. In short, it is the territory of the classroom teacher and a critical area in which confidences are exchanged, tension is released and the staff culture of the school develops. Thus, despite the variation which will undoubtedly exist in the views of each individual, the primary-school staffroom often provides a place from which a degree of cohesion in teachers' views of school life emerges.

For instance, at Burns Road Infant School there were many shared understandings about such things as the quality of work which was hoped for and ways of relating to the children. Examples of 'good work' would often be brought into the staffroom for other teachers to see and, conversely, difficulties experienced in class would sometimes be aired. The staff regularly worked together at lunchtimes to plan curriculum-development projects and school events. This collaboration was much appreciated:

> *Teacher at Burns*   It really is nice when we get something going
> *Road Infant*   together. This topic (a project on Africa
> *School*   across the school) has stimulated a lot of
>   interest and, apart from anything else, I've
>   enjoyed being part of it.

The shared understandings which were built up to form the staff culture of the school could also be used as a defensive resource against the occasional parental complaint or an unpopular request from the head teacher. More routinely, though, it provided a simple, but essential, source of friendship, company and everyday conversation.

Moorside Middle School also had an established reputation for having a happy staffroom. As one of the most experienced teachers explained:

> *Mrs Jones*   The basis is happy and whoever comes into it
>   is welcomed in and sort of 'come and join us
>   and muck in and you'll be all right' sort of
>   thing.

The atmosphere was open and often a high-spirited sense of humour was directed towards any particular problems that came up. For example, in discussion of David Brown, a child whom many teachers found difficult to control, the joking went like this:

> *Mr Mitchell*   I know, we'll have to get him certified.
> *Mr Smith*   But we won't get the support of the psychologist
>   unless we can prove he's disturbed or something.
> *Mrs Linford*   He keeps ripping his trousers.
> *Mr Jackson*   Well, try and get a photograph!

Again, humour would often be generated in response to external threats such as the visits of managers, parents or advisers, or in ways which asserted the solidarity of the staff. When an adviser failed to keep an appointment at the school, among the comments were:

> *Mrs Hunt*   He's probably been drinking too much coffee on the
>   way round.
> *Mr Rose*   No . . . he's either tripped over his pay cheque or
>   his tongue!

When a Help the Aged representative was due to call:

Mr Jackson	There's somebody coming to talk to the kids in assembly next week. I don't know if she's from War on Want, bibs and bobs or what. Something like that anyway.

Through humour, much of the potential threat of both external and daily classroom pressures was allayed, a process which simultaneously asserted a communal sense of the true 'reality' of the staffroom perspective.

Of course there will be variations in teacher perspectives based on the unique biography, personality and background of each individual. However, in sociological terms, it is the nature of the *similarities* in perspectives which is of more significance. These similarities, even between schools, derive from the fact that classroom teachers in primary schools share virtually identical structural positions. This will be discussed in detail in later chapters, but in simple terms I would argue that most teachers face relatively large numbers of children on a long-term, day-to-day basis, with relatively few resources available to them. In my view these simple facts produce enduring problems and a potential for conflict which is structurally inherent in classroom life. Waller expressed this point in particularly graphic terms in his classic (1932) analysis:

> The teacher–pupil relationship is a form of institutionalized dominance and subordination. Teacher and pupil confront each other in the school with an original conflict of desires, and however much that conflict may be reduced in amount, or however much it may be hidden, it still remains. The teacher represents the adult group, ever the enemy of the spontaneous life of groups of children. The teacher represents the formal curriculum, and his interest is in imposing that curriculum upon the children in the form of tasks; pupils are much more interested in life in their own world than in the desiccated bits of adult life which teachers have to offer. The teacher represents the established social order in the school, and his interest is in maintaining that order, whereas pupils have only a negative interest in that feudal superstructure. Teacher and pupil confront each other with attitudes from which the underlying hostility can never be altogether removed. Pupils are the material in which teachers are supposed to produce results. Pupils are human beings striving to realise themselves in their own spontaneous manner, striving to produce their own results in their own way. Each of these hostile parties stands in the way of the other; in so far as the aims of either are realised, it is at the sacrifice of the aims of the other.
>
> (Waller 1932, p.195)

At the same time as facing this potential conflict teachers are subject to a wide range of expectations and prescriptions about what should and should not be done for the children's educational benefit. These are often articulated from outside—for instance by parents, the local education authority, the government or industry—but may also take on further force as elements of teachers' professional concern. Nor are these expectations, prescriptions and aspirations necessarily consistent; indeed many of them are just the opposite and pose constant dilemmas (Berlak and Berlak 1981). Should the teacher or the child exert the most control in learning? How should the curriculum be 'balanced'? What teaching methods should be adopted? How should resources be allocated? How should the needs of individuals be balanced with the needs of the class as a whole?

In order to cope with such enduring problems and dilemmas, teachers, while knowing what their educational goals may be, also develop a strong sense of what is possible. Indeed, the existence of this sense of reality, and of teachers' confidence in it, provides the main thrust of the analysis which follows.

We can note at once that the basic foundation of commonsense knowledge is 'essential actual experience'. This is the terminology of Schutz (1970), a phenomenologist, who asserted the importance of experience: that which is subjective, spontaneous and continually developing through everyday processes such as those which occur in classrooms. In addition we should note the important role of discussion, in places such as staffrooms, in the reflection and organisation of this experience into patterns of coherent meaning. Here, then, is a source of teachers' practical realism and of the assertion that a major criterion by which to judge knowledge is whether it works. Of course it is by just this test that much educational theory, based on the disciplines of psychology, history, philosophy and sociology, has often been found wanting. The phenomenological analysis relates closely to common teacher views that abstract theory is often peripheral to action. Of far more importance in the immediacy of dynamic classroom situations are the range of particular and practical issues with which a teacher may be concerned. As a significant element in the model of classroom processes that this book seeks to construct I shall refer to such immediate concerns using the technical concept of 'interests-at-hand'. I shall argue that these critically influence the ways in which teachers perceive classroom situations and decide on their actions. The focus, then, is on factors which teachers are concerned about in the immediate situation.

Because the staffroom is a retreat, it is a place where such concerns are often openly expressed and, over time, patterns in these interests become apparent. It is an analysis of such patterns which forms the subject of the next section.

TEACHER INTERESTS-AT-HAND

The most salient point to emerge from staffroom discussions in the schools in which I studied and worked was that teachers voiced a strong desire to *control* their work situation, particularly with regard to how it affected them personally. There are several facets of this concern, and I shall describe four in particular: those of enjoyment, workload, health and stress, and autonomy. These relate to a fifth and even more fundamental concern, which is the maintenance of self-image.

Enjoyment

Teaching has always provided reliable jobs, but it is not a highly paid profession. It is not perhaps surprising, then, that those who are attracted to it are people who particularly enjoy working with children and who experience a sense of fulfilment from teaching. This enthusiasm often came over in staffroom conversation:

Teacher at Burns Road Infant School	I've just read my lot *The Enormous Croco-dile*. You should have seen them! Their eyes were *wide* and they got *so* excited when the elephant threw it into the sun they burst out cheering. It was great!
Teacher at an Oxfordshire primary school	Phew, I enjoyed that! We've been preparing all week to get ready to show the parents, and the children have worked so hard . . . it went really well, didn't it? . . . everyone worked together . . . smashing!

The interest and enjoyment of the teachers were also often related to particular emphases in the curriculum:

Teacher at Burns Road Infant School	We do a lot of music. That's what I really enjoy doing with them.

There was plenty of evidence too that many teachers enjoyed having a laugh in lessons. Humour and jokes seemed to provide opportunities for the relaxation of roles, and clearly teachers enjoyed relating closely with the children on these occasions, provided of course that they controlled the humour rather than becoming its butt. They also enjoyed the unusually 'genuine' motivation which a good 'red herring' can produce in class discussion:

Teacher at Moorside Middle School	I had a long discussion with the fourth-years this morning, all about women's lib. We didn't get any French done, but they seemed really interested; they're great when they're like that.

The desire to get personal enjoyment and fulfilment from their work was thus shown to be an important day-to-day classroom concern among the teachers in the schools studied, and it was apparent that classroom activities would often be adjusted to make adequate provision for this concern. On these occasions games of 'hangman', 'Simon says', 'sleeping lions' or just humorous banter could provide interludes of light relief in the working day.

Workload

The issue of workload is important to people in all walks of life, but primary schools often benefit from having particularly dedicated staff. For instance:

Teacher at Burns Road Infant School	I work as hard as I can for these kids. There's always something to do in the classroom and I often take things home . . . my family have got used to that! But I wouldn't have it any other way.

Nevertheless a discrepancy was often revealed in the staffrooms between what teachers thought they 'should do' and what in fact they were prepared to do. The question of commitment is the important one here and quite naturally some teachers took a reflective look at the problem and decided to 'draw a line' regarding how much effort to put in. As one infant teacher commented:

Teacher at Burns Road Infant School	The trouble with teaching is that the job is endless. There's nothing definite, no final result, so you can't say, 'right, now we're finished'. When a child has mastered one thing there's always something else. Sometimes I wish I was doing something straightforward like working in a factory or a shop.

A middle-school teacher took refuge in staff work-norms from her more 'professional' concerns:

Teacher at Moorside Middle School	I used to do a lot, plan my lessons, bring things in, take clubs at dinner times, things like that. Now I don't bother. I used to feel guilty but nobody else seems to do much—anyway, when I get home I'd rather do the garden than mark books or plan things.

The same concern is apparent at a more immediate level, which reveals the importance of the amount of work involved in the planning, preparation, teaching, clearing up, marking or mounting of particular lessons or activities. Generally speaking, of course, the simpler and more routine the task the less effort is required of the teacher. A simple task may thus be sought out:

| Teacher at Moorside Middle School | (on entry to staffroom) God, I'm knackered. We'll have to crayon some maps this afternoon. I don't feel like anything else. A nice quiet sit down, that's what I need. |

Some activities, such as using clay and water with young children, are commonly avoided partly because of the work which is thought to be involved in clearing up. In some cases this tension between what may be felt *should* be done and what any teacher is in fact *prepared* to do is resolved increasingly pragmatically as teachers 'gain experience'. As one teacher put it:

| Teacher at Moorside Middle School | It's all right for these young ones straight from college and full of ideas. When you've been teaching as long as I have you have to settle down to something more realistic. |

A very real interest thus often emerged from staffroom talk relating to conserving energy, getting through the week and controlling the workload.

Health and Stress

Another aspect of concern which was frequently discussed by teachers in the schools studied was that of their health. On a day-to-day basis the health of teachers obviously does affect their work. They discussed getting particularly tired towards the end of the week and at the end of term; they sometimes had colds, headaches or other minor ailments; and they sometimes had more serious health problems. These factors formed a teacher-interest which would be defended even in the classroom. For instance:

Teacher at Moorside Middle School	I just didn't feel like it today, I think it's that 'flu, so we've done some stuff off the board.
Teacher at Ashton First School	Gosh I'm tired. I think we'll have to do some crayoning . . . then at least I can sit down . . . I can hear a few readers too.
Teacher at Moorside Middle School	You'd better take it easy; your voice sounds a bit ropy. Get them to do some worksheets or something.

A relatively common problem like backache could have significant consequences too. For instance, in infant schools the question of whether to see children's work at the teacher's desk or whether to circulate often focused on the issue of how particular teachers could manage bending down for long periods. Signs of stress are also common:

> *Teacher at Moorside Middle School*
> This is the second day I've got a headache. I'm fed up with all the noise. I'm just glad we can do silent reading now.

Indeed this problem of stress has attracted attention among teachers' professional associations (NAS and UWT 1976) and researchers (Kyriacou 1980) and there is no doubt that the avoidance of stress was an important influence on what teachers did in their classrooms. Turning a blind eye occasionally is not just a class management technique: it also relates to whether the teachers feel able to assert themselves at particular signs of mischief or distraction. They may decide to conserve their energy for more serious crises.

Autonomy

Another important concern of the teachers was the protection of their personal independence and autonomy. As I mentioned earlier, the teachers wanted to control their work situation, and classroom autonomy was jealously guarded, particularly where the school itself was seen as lacking in cohesion. As one teacher commented:

> *Teacher at Moorside Middle School*
> This place is sometimes such a muddle . . . I just reckon to shut my door and teach my class in the way I know works best. I have tried working with some of the others but it just doesn't work . . . teaching is so personal. It's just much easier to get on with it yourself.

Two main threats to classroom autonomy routinely emerge: the head teachers and parents. The activities of head teachers tend to be a regular topic of conversation among classroom teachers. A head teacher is the formal authority figure in a school and has a considerable amount of power to influence each teacher's work experience. Of course the degree of tact and negotiating skill of head teachers varies considerably, and their visits to the classrooms could be seen as intrusions:

> *Teacher at Moorside Middle School*
> He came straight in—I was just explaining about doing some maths—and he interrupted and started going on about Harvest Festival and who would be bringing things. It makes a complete mess of the lesson and I have to pick it all up again after he's finished . . .

Teacher at Ashton	If she goes snooping in my stock-cupboard
First School	again I'll tell her straight . . . she's got no
	right.

To the extent that head teachers are responsible for overall school policy, a potential conflict with individual teachers is inevitable unless the school is extremely cohesive. I would suggest that such levels of cohesion are relatively rare, and the concern of classroom teachers to protect their independence is thus evident in much that they say and do.

Parents are the other main source of potential threat to teacher autonomy. The structural source of the problem here is that, while parents are concerned for their particular child, the teacher has responsibility for all the children in the class. Furthermore, given the resources available, teachers cannot always provide the quality of education which they might like. They are thus vulnerable to parents who wish to make specific observations or complaints or to question policies. The fact that parents are likely to know a lot more than the teacher about many aspects of their child in a sense only aggravates the situation.

Teacher at Moorside	Mrs Biggs was in again . . . she keeps coming
Middle School	to tell me about Andrew's hearing . . . you'd
	think I'd got nothing else to do but worry
	about him.
Teacher at Burns	You've got to watch those Appletree Close
Road Infant School	parents . . . they all get together at some
	coffee morning and find something to moan
	about . . . then one of them'll be down here.
	They can be a real nuisance . . . just talk to
	them if you can or send them to me.

Of course the best defence against criticisms which could adversely affect teacher autonomy is to be seen to be good at the job. Being good at the job is also a means of satisfying other concerns such as obtaining enjoyment and managing stress and workload, and it also relates to gaining the respect of colleagues. In a large number of ways, then, performance in the classroom is of direct personal importance to a teacher. Perhaps the most important teacher concern, though, is a more global one: the maintenance of self-image.

Maintenance of Self-Image

Every individual, and thus every teacher, is different. He or she has a unique personality and a unique biographical background. Upbringing, social class background, age, sex, race, work experience, professional training: these and many other personal factors influence 'the person they are' and lead towards the construction of their particular self-image. When teachers enter a classroom it is fundamentally this self-image that they draw on when they project their personality and take action decisions. Self-image is thus a classroom concern which is drawn on, is fostered and has to be protected: it provides an interest-at-hand. Let us take some examples.

Consider Mrs Jones, a 'unit leader' at Moorside Middle School. Mrs Jones liked to have an ordered atmosphere in her classroom and she demanded high standards of work and behaviour. She linked these concerns directly to 'the type of person' she was. As she put it:

> *Mrs Jones*   I couldn't work under a system that wasn't relatively speaking, ordered . . . er . . . where everyone knew what was expected of them and where they were going . . . not necessarily that it was laid down in rules but . . . you see, I'm not that sort of a person that can just take it as it comes . . . I'm a mathematician at heart and . . . things fit in little boxes y'know . . . I mean that sums a lot up . . . and if you're going to do a job you do it and finish it and that's it and that's my attitude to life and everything . . . I like it neat, ordered and under control . . . basically I like it neat and tidy and inevitably it comes through; it's bound to do.

Mrs Jones had been born near Moorside and had attended the local grammar school. Her parents had come from nearby villages and had lived nearby throughout their married life. Her father had been a local primary-school head teacher and this had influenced Mrs Jones:

> *Mrs Jones*   I always wanted to be a teacher . . . I wasn't consciously following my Dad but I suppose it must have been there . . . he's had a lot of friends who were teachers . . . I was used to having teachers all around me . . . I never wanted to do anything else.

Her father had also influenced her perspective on teaching:

> *Mrs Jones*   My father's teaching style was much the same as mine . . . I don't think much got past him, y'know, I think he was pretty strict . . . and I suppose I follow in his footsteps . . . I'm organised . . . I like to know where everything is . . . sort of get everything planned . . . I like to be organised and to have everything neat and tidy . . . and things to be taken care of like he did.

Providing some contrast, Mr Matthews, also from Moorside, adopted a more relaxed teaching style which again was related to his sense of 'self':

Mr Matthews   The way you teach reflects a lot on your character, 'erm . . . it isn't my way of working to work in a strictly rigid set-up with absolute silence and everybody gets on—no 'cos that'd drive me mad as well just as much as I think it would drive them mad . . . I think with the stresses on the teacher as well, using a little bit of a lighthearted approach can relieve tension both for the teacher and for the children. I think it's very much something of your own, for your own well-being, for your own peace of mind and to make you feel more relaxed . . . as much as it is for the children.

I think if you're sort of sitting there and you've got children at you all the time . . . there are a lot of people outside who don't realise that once you are shut in your little room in the morning then bang wallop that's it, no matter how you feel you are there, you can't sort of relax like in an office job and have a cigarette or p'raps a cup of coffee or just have a quick glance at the paper . . . once you are in that room that is it until the bell goes . . . there's no sort of release unless you can introduce a bit of a lighthearted approach occasionally as a means of releasing tension.

Mr Matthews related these classroom strategies to his own upbringing:

Mr Matthews   I was allowed a lot of freedom at home and I could more or less please myself on various things, *but* on the other hand, I knew where to draw the line, I knew when I would be pulled up . . . my Mum and Dad would make that clear, they were quite clear in what their own values were . . . it was more or less a situation of letting anything go, providing that it doesn't interfere in a harmful or detrimental sort of way with other people . . . even . . . and that what I was doing wasn't going to sort of damage my future prospects or get me into any real sort of trouble . . . and make it pretty clear to me whatever situation had arisen. It was quite a free, sort of informal, sort of atmosphere, 'erm providing I knew where the boundaries were . . . looking back on it I suppose what I'm doing now in my teaching is a bit of an extension of that . . .

Of course the majority of primary-school teachers have a very strong sense of commitment to their work and to the children in their care. This could be seen as part of the professional socialisation begun in teacher-education courses and developed thereafter, or it could be seen as a more free-standing type of idealism. In many cases such commitment forms an element of self-image. For instance:

Teacher from Burns Road Infant School	I try to do my very best for these children. I really feel satisfied when I know things are going well. I may get exhausted but if the children are benefiting then it's all worth while. I wouldn't feel true to my own beliefs if I did anything different. You can't compromise on children.
Teacher from Moorside Middle School	Most teachers here reckon to shout at 'em or belt 'em. I don't believe in that because they've got to learn self-discipline and frightening them doesn't help. I'd feel I'd let myself down if I hit one.

Other teachers may have more pragmatic concerns, and a very common dilemma is based on the question of maintaining a particular aspect of self-image or belief compared with a more pragmatic adaptation to specific pressures or necessities. In a way it is a question of commitment to an ideal self or acceptance of more pragmatic interests. This occurs a lot with teachers who are particularly conscious of the discrepancy between educational ideologies and practical realities. For instance:

Teacher from Moorside Middle School	I don't really like doing this type of lesson (class art, design being copied from the blackboard) because it's not very creative, but I don't find time to organise other things and we've got a lot of paint left and not much else.
Teacher from Moorside Middle School	I'm sure we ought to go on more visits outside, get out of school, see what life's really like, but it's terribly difficult to get that sort of thing organised. The kids like it but they always mess about when they get out, so it makes it difficult to deal with. Then the Head's not very keen; he seems much happier if everyone is neatly inside their classrooms.
Teacher from Moorside Middle School	I started off trying to be child-centred and doing all the stuff that they teach you at college. I still believe in that but it's very hard to do when you've not got much equipment and the kids aren't used to it, so I've compromised quite a lot.

Of course whatever the basic biography and commitment of a teacher the experience of working in classrooms also *develops* their self-image and calls for adjustments to the ways in which they present themselves. This is often something of a difficulty, particularly for

probationers. At Moorside Middle School a young teacher called
Miss Newsome was appointed. She was in her first year of teaching
and she had some problems which were a great challenge to her sense
of self. As she explained:

Miss Newsome	When I started I had terrible trouble with the children talking, and interrupting when I was speaking, shouting out . . . with the maths group I felt I was losing all the way along the line. From coming in they'd sit down . . . blah, blah, blah . . . I'd explain things . . . they'd listen for five minutes . . . and as soon as I'd stopped explaining that was the end of it . . . that was the end of the lesson as far as they were concerned . . . they'd start talking about what they were having for dinner, who they'd played football with, all that sort of thing . . . I couldn't stop them . . . it would be a case of—'yes miss all right, we'll stop miss'—and next minute you'd turn round and they'd have started again. I thought—I'm in the wrong job here, I just can't do it—I'm never going to succeed at this . . . what I ought to have done was to have had a bit more about me . . . and made them work the way I wanted to . . . but the whole situation was so different to what I wanted that *it was difficult to be somebody that I wasn't at the time* . . . I mean what I should have done to start with was turn round and really made them do what I wanted instead of just expecting them to do what they were told . . . you know this 'silly little attitude' that I had . . .
A.P.	What do you mean by that?
Miss Newsome	Well, I'd never come across anybody really that was never going to do what you said . . . you know that'd say—'Oh well, that's what you think, but we're going to do it' . . . I hadn't really come across anybody who didn't want to learn, yeah, it's true to say that I'd never come across children before, like I have done here, I just haven't experienced how significant learning difficulties could be, and . . . when you go through a fairly easy, country grammar school background, you go to college . . . even if they show you poor schools it doesn't really *mean* anything . . . but you come here and you've got to cope with it face to face and you know what they were talking about—before you can just 'glide' through it and it doesn't hit you. I didn't start learning about this until I walked into that classroom and met it face to face.

Miss Newsome had been brought up on a farm in Cheshire, had
attended a small village primary school and the local grammar school

and had then gone to college to become a teacher when positive alternatives were not obvious. She described what she felt the effects of this background had been on her and in particular the ways in which it hindered her in asserting herself in the classroom:

> *Miss Newsome* If you're easy-going, you're easy-going, you can't suddenly become very forthright can you . . . I had a very easy home background, very easy relationships at home . . . I know you can go into a lot of homes which are very argumentative—which it wasn't . . . no particular struggles through life . . . everything was fine . . . a very easy, carefree life . . . I've never been a leader, even all through school with friends, it's never been me who made the decisions to do things, or go somewhere . . . I'd rather follow anybody than lead anybody, and to stand up in front of the children and suddenly become this horrible person who had to be nasty to get control . . . it wasn't me in the first place which is why I found it difficult to do.

Miss Newsome's self-image clearly jarred with the strategies that she felt she needed to adopt in order to establish herself with her first class. Subsequently as she gained more skill and experience she was able to relax the assertive front which she had used. In her view her true personality then became more evident and her enjoyment increased. Her teaching began to reflect her genuine self and to bear the hallmarks of her identity. She had the skills to protect her self if it was threatened and thus her self-esteem and her confidence grew.

What Miss Newsome illustrates, in addition to the developments in self-image that often occur, is that teachers must, above all, be *competent* in order to satisfy the various facets of their fundamentally *personal* interests-at-hand. This is of considerable interest because the idea that classroom competence is particularly significant has been arrived at in many academic analyses by considering teachers' roles as ascribed by external social expectations. In essence there are two aspects of this postulated role: ensuring that the children are learning and keeping control. For instance Hargreaves (1972) argued that the roles of instructor and disciplinarian are 'almost impossible' for a teacher to avoid and there have been many analyses of it (e.g. Wilson 1962; Westwood 1967). The basic argument has been that social expectations define the role. Of course the importance of such influences cannot be denied, but to augment this emphasis, the point which I want to make is that the concern of teachers with order and instruction has a much more direct source in their experience of classroom life. Indeed order and instruction can be seen as 'enabling interests' by which the various facets of the more 'primary interest' of self can be satisfied. As one of the middle-school teachers put it:

| Teacher at Moorside Middle School | It's simple really, there's a lot of them and if you don't keep them under control they'll run all over you. The easiest way to do that is to keep them interested and keep them working. |

Staffrooms are full of such talk:

| Primary-school teacher | They're getting a bit 'high' today aren't they . . . all the rain and indoor playtimes . . . I'm going to introduce my stuff on birds I think. If I can get them going on that they'll probably settle down. |

| Teacher at Burns Road Infant School | Has anyone got a Roald Dahl or something good to read . . . I want something that they'll *all* like. I can't stand reading to them when they start to lose interest. |

Sometimes the unexpected priority even becomes overt:

| Teacher at Burns Road Infant School | I'm going to do some more creative writing with them, I think. They've done quite a bit this week but it keeps them quiet. |

Order and instruction are thus very important, but in my view they are only secondary interests-at-hand when it comes to the classroom and should be viewed as enabling interests. To take just a few examples: without a satisfactory level of order and instruction a teacher's autonomy and independence are likely to be threatened by criticism; the avoidance of stress is closely linked to maintaining order; maintaining self-image may well be linked to particular instructional methods and objects; controlling workload may be linked to long-evolved formulas for instruction and to routines which are tried and tested to suit a particular teacher's level of enthusiasm. Many other concerns could be considered to illustrate the point made here: that many aspects of teachers' disciplinary or instructional goals are adopted as a means of achieving ends which are much more personal and immediate to the teacher. Table 2.1 summarises the argument to highlight this distinction between primary and enabling interests-at-hand.

Thus teaching the children and 'keeping them under control' are not undertaken *just* because that is what teachers are committed to doing or are expected to do: they are also undertaken because it helps the teachers to 'survive' and defend their concerns in the classroom. Of course this fact has a significant effect on the *ways* in which children are taught and the ways in which discipline is maintained. To

Table 2.1

Primary interests-at-hand	*Enabling interests-at-hand*
Self	Order
self-image	Instruction
workload	
health and stress	
enjoyment	
autonomy	

'an extent it also explains, in my view, why the child-centred 'primary-school revolution' never took off in quite the way it appeared to and why it remains to be seen how the new prescriptions of the 1980s will fare. It is one thing to articulate a new philosophy, but quite another to implement it in inherently difficult situations.

CONCLUSION

In this chapter I have reviewed some basic elements and developments in the public articulation of primary-school philosophy and policy since the Plowden Report. We saw that what went on in the classroom was related to what was talked about outside the school in an educationist context, but it was *not* the same. In almost every respect the differences could be accounted for by the more down-to-earth practical and pragmatic realism of the teacher in the classroom. The structural position of classroom teachers was considered and this was related to their direct experience of classroom life and the types of relevant knowledge which are characteristically developed in order to accomplish it. The staffroom was seen as a relatively private situation in which this knowledge was refined.

I suggested that by analysing the themes which are most commonly raised in staffrooms the particular interests-at-hand of the classroom teacher could be identified. The *primary* interest-at-hand was postulated, using a tenet of symbolic interactionism, to be 'self', and it was suggested that it has various facets—enjoyment, workload, health and stress, autonomy and maintenance of self-image. These interests are satisfied through two *enabling* interests: keeping order and instructing the children.

Government reports and writings by educationists are necessary and important, but they often ignore the realities of classroom life.

The stark facts are large class sizes, limited resources and the structurally inherent possibility of teacher–pupil conflict. In situations which are framed by those factors it is no wonder that teachers have to balance their educational and professional concerns with more personal interests; nor is it any wonder that on many occasions instruction and the maintenance of order seem important primarily because of the way in which they enable immediate concerns to be satisfied, and only secondarily because they reflect what teachers are ostensibly paid to do.

3
Childhood and Child Culture

In many ways this chapter parallels the preceding one on teachers. It begins with consideration of how adults conceptualise children and childhood. From this it is suggested that there are many contradictions in the child role as socially ascribed and that children face numerous dilemmas when attempting to decide between various courses of action. The specific context of the primary classroom is then considered and I argue that it is powerfully influenced by basic structural features such as the teacher–pupil ratio, resource levels, educationist and parental expectations, school design and legal constraints. The daily realities that children face are thus those of the 'crowd' of others in their class, of teacher power, of frequently being evaluated and of being expected to learn whatever curriculum is chosen for them.

As with teachers who have a need to interpret, adapt and reconstruct the meaning of classroom experience and develop various pragmatic ways of coping with daily events, so it is with children. The second half of the chapter is therefore devoted to a consideration of the nature of child culture with particular reference to schools. This culture, which is most evident in the playground, is seen partly as representing a defensive resource for children against teachers and other adults. Thus children do not go alone to face the classroom conflict which Waller believed to be structurally inherent in schooling.

The chapter, then, is about the nature of childhood and classroom life and about children's cultural resources.

VIEWS OF CHILDHOOD AND THE CHILD ROLE

To understand the modern Western conception of childhood it is necessary to relate it to particular social, economic and cultural developments (Aries 1962). At one time, before the industrial revolution, young people were given much more independence than they have now. Indeed, the gradual increase over the years in the length of compulsory schooling which has been deemed necessary for children can be closely related to developments in technology and changing requirements made of the labour force. Anthropological studies of how other societies treat their young people also show us the relativism of our own expectations.

Throughout the period of development of our concept of 'child', and particularly since the seventeenth century, certain contrasting themes have been present, and indeed they remain evident today. I refer to the conceptions of the 'child as evil' and the 'child as good'. Perhaps for us these ideas reflect contradictions in our view of children, but at one time the issue was more about basic assumptions. The 'child as evil' assumption found graphic expression in some of the writings of Thomas Martin, an influential seventeenth-century Methodist minister who argued that children need to be 'scourged for their salvation'. As he put it:

> As we bring with us into the world a nature replete with evil propensities, and as these propensities begin to manifest themselves as soon as the mind is capable of expression or action, so the first emotions of a mind will be emotions of evil, and the first effects of powers so depraved will be evil.
>
> (Cited in Kessen 1965)

Thus childhood was seen as an age of imperfection and children were seen as needing moral guidance to lead them into adulthood. In many ways they were thus regarded as being 'deficient'.

In complete contrast we have Rousseau's work. As he argued in *Emile*, first published in 1762:

> Let us lay it down as an incontrovertible rule that the first impulses in nature are always right; there is no original sin in the human heart, the how and why of the entrance of every vice can be traced.
>
> (Rousseau 1972, p.56)

Thus in Rousseau's philosophy evil is seen as the creation of people and it is only the intervention of teachers and parents which prevents the inherent goodness of children from blossoming.

It is arguable that a modern derivation of these arguments is reflected in the societal and individualistic priorities which Ashton's studies of teacher aims (Ashton et al. 1975, Ashton 1981) have documented and to which reference was made in Chapter 2. The societal aims emphasise what it is deemed that the child *needs* to be taught for the benefit of society, while the individualistic aims stress personal growth and self-expression. We can also see the nature of the contradiction in the modern view of children by looking at the perspective of parents. Sometimes children are seen as warm, innocent and fulfilling and on other occasions as selfish, manipulative and a drain on energy and resources. Teachers' views are similar. On the one hand there is the expectation and enjoyment to be derived from children's natural growth, curiosity and learning, guided by the teachers' professional skills. On the other hand, the children are the most pressing daily source of threat to the classroom teacher, and staffroom talk leaves no doubt that they are sometimes seen as being potentially disruptive and anarchic.

A deeply ambiguous conception of children thus exists. Children are believed to be immature, irresponsible, delicate and dependent. They are therefore of low status, but at the same time they carry adults' hopes for the future. They are thus also regarded as being valuable and their nurture is thought of as being very important.

The social expectations which exist about children can be analysed using the concept of role. I should clarify, however, that the use of the term here is not meant to imply that there are homogeneous expectations to which children necessarily conform; rather it is used to describe common sets of mostly adult assumptions which provide part of the social context to which children must respond. Of course the child role reflects the ambiguities which exist in the way childhood is conceptualised. As Calvert (1975) puts it:

> ... children are important and unimportant, they are expected to behave childishly but are criticised for this childishness; they are supposed to play with absorption when told to play, and not to mind stopping when told to stop; they are supposed to be dependent when adults prefer dependence and responsible when adults prefer that; they are supposed to think for themselves, but they are criticised for original solutions to problems.
>
> (Calvert 1975, p.19)

There are also a variety of social expectations which impinge on children. For instance, various professional groups such as social workers, teachers and doctors each have conceptions of normal child behaviour and of children's needs. Various branches of industry also have interests in particular types of child behaviour because children are mass consumers. Thus children will be encouraged by advertising to eat particular sweets, buy particular toys, wear particular clothes, watch particular programmes on television, listen to particular records, etc. Indeed, the media and industry have had considerable success in penetrating child culture.

The child role thus contains contradictions which are likely to present acute dilemmas for children and which are potentially highly confusing. Of course many of the ambiguities of their role will be particularly pointed in the highly evaluative context of the classroom, and it is to that specific context that I now turn.

THE STRUCTURAL POSITION OF CHILDREN IN THE PRIMARY CLASSROOM

Clearly there are important differences between the school experiences of children of different ages, sexes and background, some of which will be explored in Chapter 4. Although these variations are significant it is, in my view, even more important to understand the basic structural similarities in the classroom situation and experiences faced by children in primary schools. As we have seen, Waller (1932) suggested that an 'original conflict of desires' exists in schools between teachers and children, but this potential conflict is only a *result* of more fundamental factors. The first of these is the fact that schooling is compulsory. Attendance can be enforced by law and children soon learn that they have to go to school and have to do what the teacher says. Second, despite recent falls in teacher–pupil ratios, actual class sizes remain high, with an average of between 25 and 30 pupils a class. A child is thus always one among many others in the class. Third, primary schools are designed, used and resourced in particular ways. The majority of classes remain closed and, even where more open teaching-styles are adopted, links with the community are often very slight. Schools are essentially closed institutions to which children are 'sent'. In addition, the normal level of resourcing of primary schools means that there are always limitations on what can be done in them and on the range of experiences which can be offered to children. Fourth, teachers in primary schools are subject to particular types of external expectation and pressure about what and how they should teach. This is reflected in what they then ask the children to do, and this educational concern pressurises children at almost every stage of their school career.

These structural facts impinge on children from nursery to the upper end of the primary school and beyond, and we shall consider their origin in more detail in other chapters. The point to consider now concerns the ways in which they are reflected in the daily classroom experience of children, and we can look at this in more detail by following Jackson's (1968) identification of the most salient facts of life in classrooms: those of crowds, praise and power. I will add a fourth to these: that of the curriculum.

Crowds

The first fact of life identified by Jackson was that of the crowd. From a child's point of view their experience as one of a crowd in schools is likely to be in stark contrast to their experience at home. For instance, it was shown in the ORACLE study of junior-school classrooms (Galton, Simon and Croll 1980) that children interacted with their teacher for only 2.3 per cent of the time as individuals and only 15.8 per cent of the time as a member of a group or of the whole class. These are dramatically small overall figures, but ones which are perhaps inevitable given the teacher–pupil ratios which are deemed to be acceptable in primary-school classrooms. The problem is further exacerbated by the uneven distribution of contact between teachers and children (Garner and Bing 1973). Studies have shown that those receiving most attention tend to be either 'active, bright and personable' children or 'active, duller miscreants', while some children have very little individual contact with their teacher. Many studies have also shown that girls tend to receive less attention than boys (e.g. Evans 1979).

Being one of a crowd is thus not a uniform experience for children, but there are certain common features. Jackson described these as delay, denial, interruption and social distraction. There is delay because the teacher is busy and because of the management needs of the school. Thus children spend time waiting: waiting to be told what to do, waiting to ask questions, waiting to use resources, waiting to have work marked, waiting in lines, waiting for bells to ring, etc. The denial of desire is closely related to these delays. Because of the crowd and the limitations of material resources, children have to fit in with the procedures, routines and activities which the teacher develops in order to manage the situation. It will be regarded as impractical to develop the individual interests and desires of many children in such situations, while those which are developed may well be interrupted and frustrated as classroom routines necessarily roll on. Jackson also draws attention to a strange contradiction in that, despite the crowd of children available to talk and play with, each individual is often expected to concentrate alone on their work. As Jackson puts it:

> They must keep their eyes on the paper when human faces beckon. These young students . . . must learn how to be alone in a crowd.
>
> (Jackson 1968, p.16)

Children in the artificial setting of the classroom thus have to learn how to manage social distractions and how to chart a course between the influence of their peers and the expectations of their teacher. This is a crucial dilemma for children in classrooms and one to which we shall return.

Praise

Praise is the second fact of life identified by Jackson, and I want to link it here with children's conceptions of themselves. Classrooms are highly evaluative settings: that is made almost inevitable by the relationship of schooling to the wider social structure and by the power of the teacher. Because of this classrooms are always potentially threatening for children: children are routinely evaluated and often feel vulnerable. Nor are classroom criteria simply academic. Praise and evaluation are used by teachers as a means of obtaining classroom control, as Hargreaves (1972), using exchange theory, and O'Leary and O'Leary (1972), advocating behaviour modification, have shown. In a sense praise is the currency of the classroom, by which a teacher can exchange extrinsic rewards for compliance. The point which follows is that, whatever their purpose or character, praise and evaluation are experienced very directly by children and thus have a significant impact on their self-image and self-respect.

Self-image, of course, has a social origin. For each child it is the product of their unique biographical experiences and the social backgrounds, cultures and interactions in which they have participated. In the classroom when they take on the socially ascribed role of pupil they have to present their 'self' and to manage the impression which they create in the particular context of school. The ambiguities, contradictions and dilemmas of social expectations combine with the basic weakness of the child's structural position to make this concern of paramount importance for children. Self can thus be taken to represent the primary interest for children in classrooms. As Calvert (1975) put it:

> To survive in the classroom children must find a way of interpreting their occasional or regular failures so that they retain their self-respect and the respect of others who matter to them.
>
> (Calvert 1975, p.31)

Clearly children can never ignore this evaluative pressure which permeates their daily lives at school.

Power

Of course pupils' greatest weakness is their relative lack of power compared with that of teachers, and it follows that their ways of coping with classroom life and their knowledge about it are likely to be highly refined defensively. On the other hand, teachers who can rely on a power advantage may tend to take it for granted. In Schutz's terms (Schutz 1970) the actors in different structural positions and with different interests develop separate systems of relevance based on their own direct experience. This perhaps explains why the use of power is so little acknowledged in educational writings, despite its being an endemic feature of classroom life. For the teacher it is a multipurpose tool which is often taken for granted; for the child it is always a potential hazard.

The Curriculum

The curriculum is an additional fact of life which I add to those identified by Jackson, for clearly it is very important. The basic rationale for the presence of the occupants of classrooms is that there are bodies of knowledge and cognitive skills which children should learn about and acquire. In psychological terms these are very complex issues and a range of learning theories are available to assist analysis of the processes involved. However, learning is also a social process, as Barnes (1969) made clear:

> the teacher initiates within his frame of reference; the pupils learn in theirs, taking in his words, which 'mean' something different to them, and struggling to incorporate this meaning into their own frames of reference.
>
> (Barnes 1969, p.29)

Indeed, according to Esland (1971), teachers are employed simply to 'transform the child's reality'. The seemingly objective curriculum is thus experienced and interpreted differently by the teachers and the taught. In sociological terms the meaning which the curriculum is to have, and which is expected to be accepted by the children, *has* to be negotiated. The curriculum thus has implications for the goals and experience of the classroom participants. The teacher will attempt to negotiate acceptance of the explicit knowledge that she is employed to teach, and may use a variety of strategies in order to do so. The experience of the children will vary, first according to their degree of acceptance of the teacher's curricular aims, and second, if they do accept them, according to their ability to carry those aims out. Their success or failure may have great importance in terms of their developing identities and ultimately of their chances in life.

The curriculum thus represents the explicit terrain over which children's school competence is tested. In primary schools there is a basic core of subjects and skills, which are taught in a variety of ways. The range of other subjects and topics which make up the curriculum is considerable, and varies from school to school and from teacher to teacher. From each child's point of view this variation is a mixed blessing. It is an asset because the chances of identifying with particular subjects or topics at some point are increased; but it is a difficulty in that the variety makes it necessary to be constantly aware of the changing frames of reference of different topics, teachers and curricular areas. However it is regarded, the curriculum, the explicit content of which classroom processes are supposed to revolve around, can never be ignored in any account of classroom processes.

The structural position of children in classrooms is thus not a strong one. Their role is ambiguous and they are subject to a variety of often contradictory expectations. They have to manage their self-image in the face of the dilemmas which result and in the face of the structural aspects of classrooms which stem from their position within our particular schooling system. Each child is one of a crowd, is routinely subject to teacher power and is required to perform in terms of the particular curricular areas and pedagogic approaches which are regarded as being appropriate for young children. It is not surprising that not every child likes school, and the next section will consider the strong defensive resources which thus tend to be developed in the form of child culture.

CHILD CULTURE

Many aspects of the culture of young children in Britain have been charted in the classic studies by Opie and Opie (1959, 1969). In particular they document the history and regional variations of children's rhymes and games, which provide oral and behavioural evidence of their culture. As Opie and Opie put it:

> the anthropologist can, without travelling a mile from his door, examine a thriving unselfconscious culture which is as unnoticed by the sophisticated world as is the culture of some dwindling aboriginal tribe.
>
> (Opie and Opie 1959, p.1)

Opie and Opie observed that teachers and other adults 'tend to deride' children's culture. This occurs, they suggested, not only because adults 'know very little about it', but also because in schools it is sensed as being in opposition to the teacher's requirements of order, concentration and learning. =) Teacher preorder

Some of the playground rhymes that Opie and Opie found confirmed this oppositional element and showed the ritual expression of hostility. For instance:

> Twelve and twelve are twenty-four
> Kick the teacher out the door.

> Sir is kind, and Sir is gentle
> Sir is strong and Sir is mental.

(Opie and Opie 1959, p.365)

However, this overt, almost propagandist type of rhyme does not convey the most distinctive source of the children's dependence on their culture or of the teacher's general unease and lack of understanding of it. The most important point is that children's culture is their own.

> It is not intended for adult ears . . . it is at once more real, more immediately serviceable, and vastly more entertaining, than anything which they learn from grown-ups.

(Opie and Opie 1959, p.1)

Davies (1982) also studied child culture, using the accounts of Australian children about their life in playground and classroom. She argued that the form that child culture takes is in many ways a reaction to their structural position of weakness in relation to adults. As she puts it:

> . . . Even without the rights enjoyed by adults, and despite the expectations placed on them as members of the institution of childhood, children busily get on with the business of constructing their own reality with each other, as well as making sense of and developing strategies to cope with the adult world as and when it impinges on their world. This reality and its related strategies I refer to as the culture of childhood.

(Davies 1982, p.33)

The existence and form of this culture can be briefly illustrated by some observations which I made in the playground at Summerlands Infant School. In that school's playground numerous games were played and rhymes chanted some of which were known about and encouraged by teachers and dinner ladies, and others which were not allowed or not known. It seems that some of the children's games were acceptable within adult definitions while others were not. Those which were accepted included most skipping rhymes, 'ring-a-ring-o'-roses', 'down by the river', 'I'm a little sandy girl', hop-scotch, 'Lucy Locket' and 'Scottish bluebells'. However, there were certain playground areas which the teachers found hard to supervise, and these tended to attract games outside the adult definition of acceptability which, at this infant school, were played mostly by boys. These areas included behind the bushes, through a hole in the fence, down the drive, and round a corner. Games played here included 'gangs', 'battles', hide and seek (the only places to hide were out of bounds), football (balls were not allowed so pebbles were used) and an unnamed game involving creeping up on available innocents and pulling their pants down. Such games also sometimes occurred in other playground areas, but would ebb and flow according to teacher proximity.

Inside the school some games continued and had been evolved to be played when 'working' in the classroom. There were several under-the-table games including shoe-swapping and playing with small toys such as plastic cowboys. The greatest refinement was 'Boogie Thomas', which was a game of tig played with pieces of paper torn from a wax crayon: the child hit by the paper was 'on' and would then throw the next piece of paper. Clearly these types of activity very much reflect the children's own collective strategies for making school fun in their own terms, despite the 'sensible' injunctions of adults.

It has been suggested by Woods (1983) that there are three particularly common themes that are embedded in such cultures: those of relationships, competence and status. I shall consider them in turn.

Relationships

Regarding relationships, Woods suggests that ' . . . friendship groups form the structural basis of the child's extra-curricular life from a very early stage' (Woods 1983, p.96). Giving some indication of why this should be so, Rubin (1980) has argued that for people of all ages friendship denotes 'relationships which are likely to foster a feeling of belonging and a sense of identity' (Rubin 1980, p.37). Clearly this definition links well with the concern of symbolic interactionists with self. Rubin further suggests that there is a major distinction between the friendships of young children in the primary-school age range, which are based on physical accessibility, and those of children in their early teens, who emphasise a greater need for psychological compatibility. The basis of young children's friendship in accessibility is reinforced by Davies' (1979) work, in which she argues that, above all else, friends are seen by young children as people who should 'be with you' and who 'should not pose' or 'show off'. In more detail she found that appropriate behaviours for friends were that they:

Play with you, play properly, play nice, take turns.
Help, do things for you, are good at schoolwork.
Stick up for you, be tough, tell the teacher what he/she thinks.
Know your feelings, share.

(Davies 1979, p.21)

Conversely, she found that inappropriate behaviours were that they:

Leave you on your own.
Pose, show off, are too full of themselves.
Want everything their own way.
Pick on you, tease you.
Act stupid.
Are 'piss weak'.

(Davies 1979, p.21)

Davies has also argued that the concerns that friends should 'be with you' and 'not pose' relate to children's sense of vulnerability at school. As she puts it:

To be alone in a new place without friends is potentially devastating. To find a friend is partially to alleviate the problem. By building with that friend a system of shared meanings and understandings, such that the world is a predictable place, children take the first step towards being competent people within the social setting of the school.

(Davies 1982, p.63)

Competence

Competence is the second theme of children's culture which was identified by Woods, and as he sees it children are concerned to be seen as competent in order to 'carve out acceptable identities for themselves' (Woods 1983, p.100). Again the interactionist issue of 'self' is evident here. A number of social skills are involved, including how to gain entry to group activities, how to express oneself and act when with one's peers and how to manage conflicts appropriately—in short, how to be a 'member' of a group of friends who can maintain and act on the shared meanings and understandings which have been constructed. Sluckin (1981) has provided a fascinating account of these conventions based on a detailed study of children's activities in the playgrounds of a first school and a middle school in Oxford. He found ritualised patterns of behaviour which were cued by terms such as 'bagsee', 'pax', 'crucems' and 'mercy', as well as innumerable examples of the protocol involved in playing playground games and in 'being friends'.

Taking this a little further Davies (1982) has suggested that embedded in such detail there are certain critical constructs which have to be understood and acted upon if behaviour is to be acceptable. Reciprocity is perhaps the most important, and can take both positive and negative forms. Thus the negative action of one child to another would provide clear legitimation to the second child's 'paying it back', as in 'you pushed me first'. In a related way the understanding of what a friend should be like implies a direct reciprocity of trust—sharing, playing properly, being with you, not showing off. Such commonly held constructs obviously result in a degree of continuity between forms of child culture in different areas, and indeed Opie and Opie (1959) described many nationally established forms of children's protocol. They even suggested that these amounted to a 'code of oral legislation'. Thus issues such as becoming friends, making bargains, swapping, testing truthfulness, gaining possession of things and keeping secrets were seen to be ordered and rule bound. If social awareness of such rules does not exist, or where children are disliked for other reasons, then a range of nicknames, jeers, torments and tricks may be drawn on to exclude them. Examples of such are:

> JOE BLOGGS is no good,
> Chop him up for fire wood;
> When he's dead, boil his head,
> Make it into ginger bread.
>
> If I'm soft, you're hard,
> If I'm butter, you're lard,
> If I'm treacle, you're cheese,
> Mind Your Own Business, Please.
>   (Opie and Opie 1959, p.184)

For adults to understand such social conventions within child culture is something akin to attempting to appreciate the rules of disorder (Marsh, Rosser and Harré 1978) among groups, such as football crowds, which are often regarded as being simply anarchic. The reality of being 'childish' is far from the state of irrational simplicity or foolishness which is sometimes implied by adults. All the evidence shows that it is a stage of life which is highly structured by social rules and conventions and that to negotiate it successfully requires considerable social sophistication and competence.

Status

Status is the last of the themes which Woods identified. To some extent it cuts across the questions of friendship relations and of social competence and in a sense it summarises their social outcome. In particular it relates to the particular identity which is attributed to and developed by each child. Thus a popular child who is able to take on a leadership role in social situations such as solving disputes or playing games is likely to have a high status almost by definition. However, status is something that can be competed for, and it is not at all uncommon for relatively unpopular or socially incompetent children to try to gain status in forceful and competitive ways. I well remember a five-year-old boy in my infant-school class who, although overweight, ungainly and somewhat shunned by the other children, took great pleasure in lifting off the ground all the seven-year-olds that he could catch. His status as the strongest boy in the school was soon established and he often paraded it further with his 'Incredible Hulk' T-shirt. Sluckin (1981) documents a similar example of a child called Neil who established himself as 'boss of the playground' at an Oxford first school, and at Moorside Middle School, in which I made a particular study of child culture, the position of 'cock of the school' was regularly fought for.

These examples perhaps reflect the particularly graphic manifestations of children's concern with status and identity which are provided by the macho boys. Girls are no less concerned, however, and indeed disputes within girls' friendship groups, which can be related to establishing status, were noted as a particular feature of such groups by Meyenn (1980). On a national scale Opie and Opie (1959) document many of the chants and procedures by which a pecking order is established within the playground. 'Buying a way in' with sweets or birthday-party invitations is evidently a much less satisfactory strategy than competence at telling jokes, playing marbles or football, doing pop-song routines, skipping without faltering, arm-wrestling, etc.

As we shall see in more detail in the next chapter, children's culture develops within an informal social structure of friendship, hierarchy and status. This is very important to children and provides a social context which runs in parallel with that of the official academic and organisational structures of the school. To enjoy their school days to the full children must cope in both spheres at the same time—a point which has been recognised with regard to secondary schools for some time (Hargreaves 1967).

In child culture, then, we have a social phenomenon which orients itself in two directions at once. Looking externally, it develops within the adult-directed structures of the school and community, and it offers children a source of support, security and positive esteem which is to a great extent insulated from the often threatening experience of teacher-dominated classroom processes or of parental strictures. It is developed largely from the children's territory of the playground while the grown-ups drink their coffee. It also offers a means of defining and reinterpreting the meaning and relevance of the contradictions, dilemmas and expectations which impinge on children because of their structural position. Thus within children's friendship groups commonsense knowledge, shared values and collective strategies will be developed to cope with the world of adults. On the other hand, if we look internally, child culture acts rather differently to provide norms, constraints and expectations which bear on its members. Thus although it is enabling in one respect, it is constraining in another, and we have seen that the social system of children is itself structured and represents a context in which children seek to establish their competence and a positive identity.

This issue of the structuring of children's social systems is very important, for it would be inaccurate to give an impression of homogeneity in the detail of the cultural forms that are adopted. In any particular context, differentiation processes must be taken into account. Thus, within a school, friendships might be developed based on the chance factor of which class a child is placed in, levels of academic achievement or types of group organisation within the classroom. Children at different positions in the structures thus created are likely to form more enduring relationships (Bossert 1979). In this way groups are formed and begin to act as reference groups with which the children make sense of their experiences.

An illustration of the perspectives of a friendship group may be helpful here, and one is provided by data on a group of eleven-year-old girls from Moorside Middle School. I studied this group as part of an attempt to document and understand the structure of the children's social world and the variations in the perspectives of the different friendship groups within it, more details of which will be reported and analysed in the next chapter. The girls' group used in this example was an exceptionally outspoken group. Despite what I judge to be an element of bravado in their comments, the group has been deliberately chosen here to illustrate the argument that girls' views and actions can be very different from those which common assumptions about passivity and conformity would suggest.

'JANINE'S TERRORS'

The members of the group were Janine, Penny, Margaret, Judith, Lorna, Jenny and Barbara. They were of moderate ability and were mostly in the same class groups for maths and English. They all lived in the same part of the school catchment area and saw a great deal of each other outside school. Within school they were inseparable.

Their favourite playground activities were often consciously provocative. As they explained:

Lorna	We like to cause trouble with people and we all stick together.
Judith	We have to do something so we cause trouble. We have to do this because there is nothing in the playgrounds to play at. We like other groups because we can cause trouble with them. Sometimes we cause trouble with Inson or Whitey but nobody gets hurt, just them.
Barbara	We all like playing at fighting and causing bother but if somebody starts [name calling] they get a fist in the mouth.
Janine	We have lots of fun together. We play at teasing all the boys. The boys we tease most are Jim and Paul White. We like to play at chains. We all get hold of each other and Lorna is the leader of the chains and pulls us. It's great 'cos we all go flying down the banking and get done by the silly-cow dinner ladies.

As well as teasing games, Janine's Terrors enjoyed tremendous rivalry with another girls' group, led by Samantha. As Janine and Margaret explained:

Janine	I don't like Samantha and Tracey's gang. They are always causing trouble with us, like name calling or sticking their tongues out 'n that. If we bash them we get done. I think they are rubbish and Samantha is soft.
Margaret	The group that I don't like is Samantha's gang. Samantha and Liz are stupid; just because we start calling people names like 'squarehead' and 'ferret-face' then they had to too.

Fights and insult-exchanges between these two groups to establish which was 'best' were common. In fact Janine's group distinguished themselves from other gangs:

Judith	We are not really a nasty type of gang. We don't like gangs that go around and smash windows. Some people

in gangs think they are just good and they get too big for their boots.

Barbara   Gangs are good except for them that go around throwing stones at people, ringing doorbells and things like that.

Given the rivalries and favoured activities of the girls it is not surprising that they were conscious of the protective function of their close-knit group within the playground.

Janine   Our gang is fantastic; we have lots of fun and if somebody was going to bray [attack] me then all my gang would join in and fight. Then we would be able to bash them. I would never be able to part with my friends.

Lorna   We all stick together. We line up together and sit together if we can. We play together and stick up for each other.

Judith   We stick up for each other and we share things. If one of us is having a fight we cheer them and make sure they win.

One of their activities, which the girls felt distinguished them from 'rough, nasty' groups, was their practice of giving 'shows' to children in the playground. The shows involved carefully choreographed and rehearsed dancing and singing routines, usually of current pop songs.

One of the few things about the school which the group liked was the occasional discos:

Barbara   The discos are great when we have them. We all had a great laugh when Mr Matthews was dancing with Janine and he held her hand.

The group were more attuned to teenage culture than other girls' groups, with both a greater interest in pop music and dancing, and a concern about fashionable clothing and make-up. On this they faced difficulties with their teachers:

Janine   We ought to be allowed to wear make-up and bring our clothes what we want. Sometimes we wear a bit of eye-shadow and the teachers don't notice, but we can't wear rings. Mrs Jones told me to take mine off.

Lorna   Teachers can wear what they like so I don't see why we can't. They just say . . . 'It's not sensible for school'.

In their attitudes to various aspects of school, Janine's Terrors were extremely outspoken and militant. For instance, respect for teachers and their authority was small:

Judith	I think teachers are not fair because they are bloody rotten to us. They never listen to what we have to say. Like if we get done [told off] and we said to the teachers that we did not do it they would still do us. It's because they are smelly gits and they don't listen to a word we say.
Jenny	The teachers are always telling us what to do—you can't do this, you can't do that. They won't even let us have a bloody gonk on the end of our pencils.

The group felt they were often picked on by the head teacher, teachers and dinner ladies:

Jayne	Why does Mr Smith play heck with you in assembly?
Janine	He's always blaming it on to us. He never says 'owt to the others—he just picks on us 'cos he's a bit round the bend.
Jenny	At dinner-time, he was sitting near our table and he says 'here you are, take my plate back'. Well, we couldn't say that to him could we? He's just using us as mugs.
Lorna	Teachers are always playing heck with us lot, they split us up a lot, but they don't split up the others.
Margaret	That Mrs Dover [dinner lady], she always picks on us lot, she never picks on nobody else—ever since I've come to school it's only us what get done—nobody else. The first time we came in here that Mrs Dover thought, 'right, we've got it in for that lot'.

Getting 'done' by teachers was disliked by the group:

Jenny	I get scared when they shout at me 'n that.

But the group provided a great deal of solidarity by which to neutralise such effects:

Margaret	The one thing I do when they play heck with me is I don't listen, then get back with my mates.
Jenny	They always threaten us with going up to Mr Smith.
Lorna	They reckon he'll scare us.
A.P.	Well, doesn't he scare you?
Lorna	Yeah, of course, he does me.
Jenny	If Smith touches me just once my Mum'll be straight down here with her umbrella, and we'll all go and sort him out.

In fact the solidarity and cohesion of the group had enabled 'getting into bother with dinner ladies' to become a favoured activity at dinner-times.

Margaret   We run down the banking or cheek them off or
                something and when they tell us off we just laugh; we
                don't care.

The group were not entirely against school-work and they were not unsuccessful academically or unaware of the significance of school for their futures:

Jenny   School-work is too easy. You've got to do your work.
                I'd rather have a school because it gives you a good
                education, and when you leave school you've got a
                good education to get a good job. If you don't go to
                school and you skive off you're not going to know
                anything.

Janine   I'll be glad when we leave school, 'cos I'm going
                straight into a job . . .

They also distinguished themselves from slow-learning children, whom they termed 'thickos' and who were taught in remedial groups in 'Unit 5':

Janine   I think this is a good idea though—Unit 5 y'know for all
                them not right brainy, to go in it to learn a bit more.

However, lessons were generally felt to be boring and laughs were felt to be essential:

Margaret   Sometimes school is a complete bore. I like to have a
                laugh when we do a boring lesson and I can't be
                bothered to write or do anything.

Judith   Having a laugh is great. We should not be silent and no
                talking; we need to have a laugh at school.

Lorna   When I'm with my friends we can have a laugh any
                time, whenever we feel like it. It takes your mind off
                your work and it's good when you need cheering up.
                What would you do if you didn't have laughs?

Although the girls recognised the need to control their laughs to avoid punishment, they were well prepared to laugh at, rather than only with, a teacher:

Janine   A good one was when Judith said that the flies would
                use the top of Mr Matthews' head for a skateboard
                rink. [Mr Matthews was balding.]

When laughing with a teacher they were also aware of the breaking down of barriers and tensions which such laughs can produce:

Judith   When the teacher makes a joke or something it's good,
             'cos you feel that the teachers might like you a bit and it
             makes you feel happy. It makes you feel you can speak
             more freely.

The group were regarded by both teachers and other children as a
tough and formidable group of troublemakers. The name 'Janine's
Terrors' was given to them in the playground and, as we have seen,
their solidarity, cohesion and articulation of opinion were such that
they were able to maintain hostile attitudes to many aspects of school
and provocative activities in the playground without suffering the
consequences which for less organised groups or individuals would
certainly have followed. The group, meshed as it was within child
culture, offered a means of defining school and the adult world in the
children's own terms and thus of making sense of it. At the same time
it provided security, identity and status within the social system of the
playground. It represented the means by which the girls coped with
school.

CONCLUSION

This chapter has reviewed the way childhood is conceptualised, the
structural position of children in primary classrooms and the nature
of child culture. The discussion of these issues provides the
precondition for introducing more complex questions about variations in children's perspectives and about the nature of children's
social structure as such. Thus, where this chapter has treated children
and child culture in a relatively homogeneous way, the next chapter
attempts to identify some of the most significant *variations* that can
be found in children's perspectives.

4

The View from the Children

INTRODUCTION

This chapter focuses on variations in children's perspectives about school, and I shall suggest that these variations are related to the structural position that each child occupies. The most important factors that I shall consider here are social class and gender, together with the relative degree of success in school that each child experiences.

The chapter draws predominantly on a study of children's social structure and perspectives which was made when I taught and researched at Moorside Middle School, and it thus has a case-study base. In this respect we should recall that the age range at Moorside was eight to twelve years, it was a large school with just over 600 children on its roll and it had a significant Asian intake, particularly in the younger year groups. I focused my studies on the perspectives of 80 eleven-year-old white children, who formed 58 per cent of the fourth year; 43 were girls and 37 were boys. Unfortunately it was not possible to study the perspectives of the Asian children to the same extent because of time constraints (see Pollard 1985), and I have not reported on them here.

As with all case-study work, the concern in this chapter is to highlight issues which emerged as being significant during a detailed study of particular groups and situations rather than to claim a typicality or precise representativeness. In this regard I hope that the analysis of children's friendship groups and of their main classroom concerns will stimulate comparison with the perspectives of children in other situations. I myself found very similar attitudes among nine-year-old children at Moorside during a pilot study, and have identified the same tendencies in infant classes. In my view this occurs because, despite the uniqueness of each situation or case, the classrooms in which children of all ages are placed in school share the same fundamental structural features (ratios, resources, time constraints, curricular expectations, etc.). Comparisons between cases will thus tend to show up similarities as well as differences and this is, of course, the fascination of case-study work.

My concern to understand children's perspectives meant that I had to find a way of collecting data which minimised the possible distorting effect of being seen as a teacher, albeit a teacher of younger children. The ways in which I attempted this have been described elsewhere (Pollard 1985), but the key procedure which I adopted, of working with a team of child interviewers, requires a brief description here. The crucial initiative was to start a dinner-time club for fourth-year children concerned with 'finding out what children think about school'. The children who came to the club regularly called it MID, the Moorside Investigation Department, and it seemed to capture their imagination. Club members invited other children to be interviewed, initiated discussions and emphasised the 'top secret' and confidential nature of the activity. After a period in which confidence and trust developed I became more involved and worked alongside the child interviewers. Interviews were recorded on cassettes and later transcribed. The children also discussed many elements of my analysis with me as it emerged.

I also collected sociometric information about friendship groups and various types of quantitative data concerning academic achievement. Towards the end of the study written views about various specific aspects of school life were collected across the whole year group in another confidential exercise. This was administered by the children but was done within lesson-time and with the endorsement of the teachers.

In reporting the results of this inquiry this chapter develops the themes about child culture which were raised in Chapter 3 and continues to parallel the earlier analysis of teacher perspectives. Above all it confirms a desire by children in schools to control their classroom experiences and render them predictable and personally 'safe', even though they are likely to set about achieving these goals in different ways.

GOODIES, JOKERS AND GANGS

When I began my work at Moorside three basic cleavages in the children's social system were immediately apparent, based on age, sex and race. Sociometric analysis and playground observations showed this clearly, though for each factor there were instances where the generalisation requires qualification. For instance, older children might 'look after' or 'entertain' younger children, girls might sometimes chase or tease boys or vice versa, and the Asian and white children would often integrate when playing football or other active playground games. Such instances occurred around particular activities, but the tendency to gravitate towards friendship groups based on the child's age and unit, cultural background and sex was always present.

During the year in which interviews were conducted it became apparent that certain *types* of friendship group existed and, since the

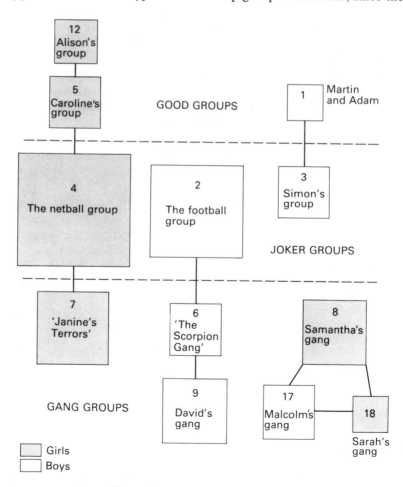

Figure 4.1 *An inter-group sociogram.*

differences between these types of group came to have considerable significance in my subsequent analysis, I have highlighted them here. In this respect it should be noted that this analytical device, although necessary for the development of clear categories on which to base further reflection, has tended to simplify some aspects of the complex relationships which existed among the children.

For two of the three types of group the children had their own names—'good groups' and 'gangs'—and I coined the name 'jokers' to highlight a particular quality of the third type. Eventually I was able to produce an inter-group sociogram to show the relationships between the groups at the time of the study.

In Fig. 4.1 good, joker and gang groups are shown, and the size and sex of each group are indicated. The numbers refer to the ranked academic position of each group across the whole year group (using the mean of combined group scores on various indicators of achievement). I have also used these numbers in the chapter to show the group to which quoted individuals normally affiliated.

I want now to begin to illustrate the main differences between these types of group by considering their perspectives on various issues: their views of themselves and their attitudes to each other, their favoured activities both in the classroom and outside in the playground, and their attitudes towards teachers and education.

View of Themselves and Each Other

Good Groups

The good groups (1, 5, 12) saw themselves as sensible, honest, quiet and friendly. They tended to distance themselves from other children and from the more common activities of other children in the school. For instance, Martin, who with Adam made up the only good group of boys (1), commented on one of the gang groups:

> Martin (1)   They act as if they were the Moorside Mafia; they're not very fair, they're stupid and they're always fighting or playing soppy games of football.

Members of the two good groups of girls (5, 12) held similar views; they valued the companionship and reliability of their 'small, friendly groups'. They greatly disliked gang groups and felt threatened by them:

> Mandy (5)   I think gangs are not at all nice because they are rough and I am nearly always getting bashed in so I have to stay clear of them. I don't think it is fun at all.

Their attitude to joker groups was a mixture of disdain and admiration:

> *Linda (5)*   Some people that we don't like are Paula and Julie (of group 4)—they talk too much and are show-offs. Some of that lot dress too old for their age . . . but they are all in the top groups for everything.

Joker groups were also regarded as 'playing with boys too much'. The girls and boys in good groups preferred to keep apart.

Joker Groups

The boys and girls in joker groups (4, 2, 3) also thought of themselves as being sensible. They felt that good groups were far too boring and 'didn't do anything'. In contrast joker groups liked to be active both in school and in the playground. They thought very little of gangs:

> *Peter (2)*   I think that gangs are daft because they only cause bother. Robert thinks he's great with his haircut and that leather band that he wears round his wrist. Plus he wears Dr Marten's boots which make him think he's great. But he is not. He is really just acting like a silly kid.

> *Colin (2)*   Gangs are rubbish. They're like big-headed farts that think they are big and go around kicking in little lads and old folk.

> *Heather (4)*   Gangs are rough and they shout their gobs off. They think they're tough and they go round knocking on old people's doors and picking on people. That lot of Neil's (6)—they're disgusting in manner and speech. Why can't they be kind and sensible?

Gang Groups

The children who were members of gang groups (7, 6, 9, 8, 17, 18) reciprocated the insults. For instance, Samantha (8) regarded the largest group of joker girls as a 'rubbish group of bigheads', and many of the other children were regarded as being privileged:

> *Carly (8)*   Lots of people act as if they are posh, just because they go on holiday each year and buy expensive things for their homes and make their kids look nice and take them to school in the car thinking one of the teachers should see her, and try to see how her child is getting on at school. Most people act as if they were posh but they

just put it on an' show off about something new. They ask their Mums if they can have this, that and the other. They try to get the nicest present for a party. But them who are not that well off, they act normally. They admit that they do not get very much but they are still thankful for what they have got. If you have a lot you can't have very much more so I don't care really.

While the joker groups were regarded as 'show-offs' and 'bossy noses', the good groups were thought of as being completely beyond the pale:

Samantha (8)   They're no good; they just play and do what they're told; some of 'em are teacher's pets. We like causing bother.

Malcolm (17)   Them goody-goodies? Well, they're just pathetic, aren't they?

However, there was considerable evidence of inter-gang rivalry; indeed, chasing, 'gobbing', stealing secrets and getting others into trouble were the main playtime occupations of these groups. In-group solidarity was thus important. As some of the children put it:

Tracey (8)   Our gang is good 'cos we can get our own back and it's great braying people back.

Kevin (9)   Our gang has got ways of sticking up for people . . . it's great.

	...good groups are...	...joker groups are...	...gang groups are...
Good groups think...	sensible, quiet, honest, fair and friendly.	nice, but they show off too much.	stupid, rough, unfair, unkind, troublemakers.
Joker groups think...	quiet, boring, and they just wander about.	good fun, friendly and sensible, good to play with.	rough, thick, bossy, disgusting, silly, stupid babies, and they cause trouble.
Gang groups think...	goody-goodies, pathetic, soft, and they just talk and do what they're told.	big-heads and show-offs, posh, rubbish.	(own gang) great, fantastic, rough and tough. (other gangs) cocky, rubbish, soft, stupid, thick, smelly, horrible, daft.

Figure 4.2 *Patterns in inter-group attitudes.*

Gang groups thus thought very little of good or joker groups. Despite the fact that they would frequently fight or trade insults among themselves, they respected the 'toughness' and 'roughness' of other gang groups; indeed, establishing a pecking order on those criteria seemed to be one of their main concerns.

The matrix in Fig. 4.2 is one way of summarising the patterns in these inter-group attitudes.

Outside the Classroom

Good Groups

The good-group children tended not to join in mainstream activities in the playground and were clearly in a marginal position within the children's social structure as a whole. For instance, among the boys neither Adam nor Martin (1) was good at football, which was the high-status sport among the boys, but, with very different associations, they were the only two children to take violin lessons. As Adam put it:

> *Adam (1)*   I don't like doing anything in the playground much . . . I think indoors is better than outdoors 'cos you can sit down and read books and finish work, y'know, 'cos there's more things to do . . .

The two good groups of girls felt similarly. Caroline (5) liked to 'wander around' and enjoyed 'just talking and being together', while the less academically successful group, led by Alison (12), played 'with others who have no-one to play with'. As Kirsty and Linda (5) put it:

> *Kirsty (5)*   We like to sit in the classroom and talk. We talk about fashion and animals or what we have been doing in lesson times. In the playground we play letter tig. We like to do ballroom dancing together.
>
> *Linda (5)*   We like to sit around and talk to each other. We sometimes all play games in the middle playground.

The good groups were not as inactive as other children thought them to be. For instance, Adam and Martin often met outside school and had generated a style of weekend activities of which they were proud. Martin was particularly keen:

> *Martin (1)*   Other groups make up secrets but none is better than ours. We have a motto—'Adventure comes before girls'—and that's what we have—adventure and exploration.

In sentiment the motto seems to be almost drawn from the traditional values of the *Boy's Own Paper*, and indeed Martin and Adam saw most of the common playground activities as being 'silly'. Thus in school they quietly conformed to the archetypal image of the studious pupil while reserving adventure and exploration, often on their bikes, for weekends and evenings. Caroline's group (5) also met regularly out of school, with visits to each other's homes to 'listen to records and talk', and some of the girls went on regular shopping trips together. Alison's group (12) had once even tried to form a 'friendly gang' in the playground. They had equipped themselves with codebooks, passwords, secrets and invisible-ink pens, but the game was not sustained after their codes were 'pinched' by a gang of younger children, which perhaps in itself showed the group's weakness.

Joker Groups

The joker groups were much more obviously active. The main boys' group (2) was centred around the school football team, and they spent most of the time in the playground playing that game. However, they also enjoyed meeting together outside school:

> Stephen (2) We usually play together or work together as a group. We all like much the same things like football or swimming and we usually do this in a group. Last night I went to the baths with three of my best friends, Peter, Smit and Philip. Most of us go to a football club called the Sporting Milltown Boys Club where we all play soccer. We often go to each other's houses to play as well.

> Alan (2) My most enjoyable moment was when I joined Milltown Skateboarding Club with some of my friends. We had to tell him our names and addresses and how old we were. In the club they test your skateboard and we can go to places like Scarborough and Blackpool. I have fallen off my skateboard twice and got two grazes on my leg. My skateboard is called a superflyer. We have all got elbow pads and helmets but I still need some knee pads and some gloves.

Activities of this sort clearly bonded the group together. At indoor playtimes or dinner-times they would often draw pictures, play noughts and crosses, password or hangman or write rhymes about each other. For instance:

Paul (2)   Now Moonshine lives up Parkstone Road, And according
to Pod is a slimy toad. But Moonshine doesn't care
anyway, he just keeps goal for the school team, And
supports Man' United, they rule supreme.

The drawing of pictures was a source of considerable amusement; for
instance this is one of the headmaster:

The large joker group of girls was centred on the netball team. In the
playground they were disadvantaged by the lack of a court and by the
dominance of football. While a few of the girls had taken to football
and had become better than many of the boys, the majority of the
joker girls varied their activities between 'going around together to
see what's going on', helping teachers do jobs, and more active
games:

Gill (4)   We like playing with a ball and skipping and playing out in
the playground. We like to talk and have a good laugh.
Sometimes we play chasing with the boys or watching
them playing football.

The game of chasing with the joker boys was common and, from
observation, involved considerable degrees of excitement and
flirtation. 'Steady' liaisons were set up and revealed in inscriptions on
tables and in rough notebooks by both girls and boys. For instance:

Peter (2)

I will always love
Tessa and never
chuck her to go
out with anybody
else!

The girls tended to be more romantically inclined, as is shown in a poem by Carol:

> *Carol (4)* February the 14th 1978,
> St Valentine's Day,
> Everyone is in a good mood,
> Love letters are sent,
> Hearts are drawn,
> Kisses are blown,
> Kiss chase is played.
>
> Love at first sight,
> Eyes meet blue as blue,
> The romance of it all,
> See you tonight darling,
> The scent of your perfume,
> The colour of your lips,
> I love you so truly.

Teasing and speculation were a part of this game among the joker children, but it was defended:

> *Paul (2)* Well . . . it's like . . . we play chasing and they come and watch us play football. Some people say it's soppy to go out with girls but I like them.

And the girls had a clear conception of the limits of respectable behaviour with boys. For instance, here is a comment on the activities of two gang members:

> *Becky (4)* Last night I saw 'em necking in the corner. It's getting out of hand. It's disgraceful.

The girls also had reservations about wearing fashionable clothes at school:

> *Jayne (4)* Oh no, we shouldn't come in trousers like Bay City Rollers trousers and things like that; after all school's only to learn at, not to be so smart and be a fashion show.

The existence of these activities and perspectives is particularly interesting when one realises that in the classroom the girls regularly gave the impression of not mixing with boys at all.

Gang Groups

The gang groups were easily identified by their activities. The 'rough gangs' (8, 17, 18) were mostly made up of children who were relative failures in academic terms; indeed many of them had been allocated to remedial groups in the school. The boys (17) and the girls (8, 18) in these gangs mixed together a great deal and shared many perspectives. Some quotations will give the flavour of their activities.

Samantha (8)   Carly is good fun. Every time we go in for dinner she always puts her foot in the mud and kicks it in our hair and sometimes on our clothes. One day Louise got it right up her skirt and all on her face. Then we try to do it back to her but it's hard to get her.

Sarah (18)   We get all sorts of fun y'know; someone'll say come on we'll go and beat so and so up and get into trouble. Sometimes we'll just be friends but we'll start playing rough again.

Robert (17)   Like yesterday I were getting somebody. I went for the football in the playground and him who was playing, Kevin, says 'Oh it's our ball' so I went to get the ball off him and he kicked me, so I goes 'Right, I'm going to bray you' [beat you up]—so I did, at four o'clock.

Nigel (17)   In the playground we like to spoil people's games. It's great fun. Samantha's gang (8) are a load of rubbish because they are soft. I think gangs are great because when we start kicking everybody in I join in; that is the best part that I like about gangs and we are not soft like everyone else.

Thus the fun of 'causing trouble' was one major type of activity. Another was fighting within and between the groups. Among the girls in particular there was a rivalry over friendships. For instance Tracey commented:

Tracey (8)   I have a good group of friends when I don't fall out with them. Katherine is always falling out with me and going off with Carly. If that happens, like, she has pinched my friend, then Carly is a fat cow. When I am friends with Sarah, just because I am small for my age, she always pushes me around and blames me for things, but Lucy, if we are friends and we play hitting one another it's good fun. But if I hit her too hard she will not play at all. She can be a baby sometimes.

Sometimes fighting produced rapidly changing groupings and alliances, often of great intensity while the issue which brought them about was current. Sometimes outside assistance would be brought in; for instance, a letter from Sarah to her secondary-school neighbour, Anthony, read:

Dear Anthony,
    Some boys at school have been braying me. Will you come over and bray them for me. They are Robert and Malcolm.
    Thank you.
      From
        Sarah.

There was also some activity and teasing about who was going with who. Malcolm and Sarah were paired by repute, although Sarah sometimes wished to refute the rumours of 'goings on' in the woods:

Sarah (18)   Well, we was in there and y'know . . . anyway we didn't do nothing and now I don't like him. It said on telly if you hit 'em on the nose you love 'em—but I don't love him I just want to hit him.

Many of these activities seemed to be concerned with establishing status within the groups, the ultimate route to which was by fighting. For instance, on an occasion when both the boys and girls were acting together, they commented:

Sarah (18)   Malcolm's the leader 'cos he's cock of our gang, but I'm in charge of the girls because I can bray Diana, and Julie if she comes with us.

A.P.   How do you decide who is leader? Does it have to be the biggest?

Malcolm (17)   No, it depends who goes in first. I go in first and the rest follows—when we're fighting I'm the toughest.

For disputes both inside the groups and outside there was a rhetoric of the fight preliminaries, such as 'smashing their teeth in', 'pulping their nose' and 'gobbing their face'. However, there was also an unwritten code of conduct which governed many of their activities. For example a fair fight was considered to be between children of the same age and sex, and would generally be watched by others without interference and ignoring differences in size or strength. However, people were rarely badly hurt and the fights only went on until submission was acknowledged by crying or 'giving in'. In this way not only were disputes solved but the pecking order of toughness was established. Most children seemed to know or have an informed opinion about who could 'bray' who. Interestingly, in the 'sensible' footballing joker group (2) a similar degree of knowledge existed, but about in-group abilities at arm wrestling.

The handshake was another convention which was honoured, but this was not the usual shake, which in fact was used only 'if you didn't mean it really'. At Moorside a 'true' shake had to be 'broken' by someone else, and then the trust remained and was respected.

Loyalty and help were also given to members of the groups who were in 'dead trouble'. For instance, Nigel had been in a lot of trouble with the headmaster:

> *Nigel (17)*   I've been in trouble so if I bray anybody I get whacked by Mr Smith.
>
> *Sarah (18)*   So we bray 'em instead 'cos he knows if he brays anybody again he'll get done so he tells us and then we bray 'em for him.

Outside school in the evenings and at weekends the groups were also active together:

> *Sarah (18)*   Me and Malcolm and Diana went exploring. We went to the valley of the 5000 dreams—we found it up on the tops. We've never been before and there's bats and danger.
>
> *Malcolm (17)*   Sometimes we go past the old people's home and ring the bells, then we have a good laugh in the bushes.

The children also acknowledged scrumping apples, breaking windows at a local mill, pinching sweets from a shop, smoking and 'nicking stuff' from school, and Robert and Malcolm had been in trouble with the police.

'Having a Laugh' in Class

Good Groups

With the good-group children it was immediately noticeable that they consistently tried to please their teachers and were unlikely to risk any sort of trouble. For instance, when I asked Adam (1) about having a laugh in lessons he was very hesitant:

> *Adam (1)*   Well, sometimes I do laugh but only if it's very safe to.
>
> *A.P.*   How can you tell?
>
> *Adam (1)*   If the teacher is in a good mood, well, then, maybe it's safe.

The girls of Caroline's group (5) also explained their concern:

> *Kirsty (5)*   You should only laugh really when the teacher is laughing, then it's all right, but some of the lessons we get people messing about all the time. Having a laugh is a good thing 'cos it brings out the happy side of you and makes you cheery and bright, but we shouldn't do it too much at school or we'll never get any work done.

| Mandy (5) | We don't like getting into trouble because when we get told off we get upset. It's not very nice 'cos you don't know what to do. Usually we try to keep out of trouble then it's OK. |

Joker Groups

The joker-group children took a very different view and indeed the name 'jokers' is itself intended to highlight their perspective, for while good groups tended to remain 'good' and gangs, as we shall see, tended to 'cause bother and muck about' with shades of oppositional intent, the joker groups directed their efforts at 'having a bit of fun' or 'playing about', often with the participation of their teachers and within the context of their overall 'sensible' behaviour. As they explained:

| Donna (4) | Children should be good in school, but not good all the time because we can't all be goody-goodies. |
| Paul (2) | Children, I think, can never be good all the time. It's like men being shut up in Colditz. But as long as they finish their work on time it doesn't matter what they do. |

'Having a laugh' was seen as an essential counter to boredom:

Alan (2)	I think having a laugh is a good thing because it makes the day pass quicker, and when you laugh you are very happy and you stay happy all day.
Stephen (2)	Having a laugh in school is a good thing because if you couldn't have a laugh you would be miserable and bored. For instance in religious education Mr Rogers is nearly always in a bad mood so it is boring; the only laugh is when the sun comes out when he wants us to watch a film. (There were no blackouts in that classroom.)
Becky (4)	It's boring being in general studies, when we have to stop and think; you're looking around the room, you've nothing to do, thinking, wondering what to do, run out of ideas, looking at the paper, sighing and can't think properly, thinking of something else and can't concentrate on what you're doing—you need a laugh.

The critical aspect of the joker groups' perspective which linked 'being sensible' with 'laughs' was that it took account of teacher perspectives and, as with good groups, they were aware of the safety of laughing with or at the initiation of the teacher.

Alan (2)   The lesson which you can have a laugh in is science because Mr Matthews always makes jokes about people. You can tell if it is safe to have a laugh because Mr Matthews laughs with you and so does Mrs Jones. We had some good laughs last time when he said that Paul goes out with Penny.

Peter (2)   When a teacher tells a joke I think they are probably in a good mood so it is probably safe for us to laugh.

Thus the joker-group children were concerned not to prejudice their learning or their relationships with teachers, but they would also, as Stephen (2) put it, 'do 'owt for a laugh'. Their concern represented a non-threatening, non-malicious attitude to teacher authority which was qualitatively different from the 'messing about' and 'causing bother' activities of gangs in the classroom.

Gang Groups

As with joker groups, the gang-group children sought a laugh in lessons when they got bored or 'couldn't be bothered to do any work', but they were much more prepared to laugh at or despite a teacher. Members of Samantha's group explained:

Anna (8)   If we have a laugh and the teacher's in a bad mood well that's hard lines; we don't care.

Lucy (8)   You can have a laugh about something and then if someone gets told off you can have a laugh about that 'cos it's only a warning. That gives you a laugh too when you get into the playground.

Carly (8)   When Mrs Jones caught us fooling about and my boot wouldn't come off, she said, 'you two are making fools of yourselves' and I was laughing all the time when I bent down to put my boot on and then she said 'Let's hope you come in a better frame of mind tomorrow', and we was laughing all the way home.

The children in these groups had difficulty with much of the work which they were expected to do and they often felt 'bored stiff' by teachers in lessons. Some of the children in groups 9, 17 and 18 told me:

Andrew (9) Being bored is being unhappy; you get miserable; like when Mrs Linford's talking and you start fidgeting and you get bored and start throwing things about and then you get into trouble. They just stand talking. They talk too much.

Nigel (17)	When the work's hard I feel sad; if I can't do it I feel sad and because of you've spent hours trying and all of a sudden you've forgot so you get fed up and you just kick out or flick a pencil or hide someone's pencil or hit someone. Sometimes you have a laugh at anything.

Robert expressed a particularly clear view on doing work:

Robert (17)	If we *have* to, I do it—that's if we *have* to. If we don't have to, we don't have to, and I don't—it's as simple as that.

Bearing these concerns in mind, the gang-group children had developed many ways of evading work or subverting a lesson:

Malcolm (17)	You can waste time anytime, like breaking your pencil or hiding the rubber or writing on someone's book.
Robert (17)	We always like to come in late. After playtime we go in the toilets and then we come into the lesson when the teacher is talking. We get right noisy.
Diana (18)	I don't like PE so I usually pretend to lose my pumps. It was good with Sarah 'cos we pretended I'd lost an earring so we went round all the classes looking for it.
Andrew (9)	We can say we want to get something so we walk across the classroom then I might, say, hit Malcolm on the way. I might be getting a rubber or a dictionary and the teacher doesn't notice and Malcolm gets mad.
Sarah (18)	Sometimes we try to go to the toilets at the same time, then we can have a talk and mess about.

Other acknowledged activities included deliberate shouting out, hand-farts, talking, kicking battles and flicking paper at people. There were also conscious tactics:

Andrew (9)	If a teacher has a joke with you and then you do summat silly then she can't touch you as much, 'cos she's done things with you.
Sarah (18)	With talking, we start low and then someone talks louder so you've got to talk louder to talk to your friends and so on—till you're shouting. It just gets louder until the teacher stops it then we have to have silent talking for a bit again.

The children were skilled at cheating in tests. Tactics which were acknowledged included writing spellings on hands, using notes kept under books, leaving a book open, copying from the next person, 'filling in' when answers were given and altering an answer after marking so that the mark could be disputed.

Teachers and 'Getting Done'

The children's views on teacher behaviour revealed clear differences between the three types of group, differences which particularly related to the opinions held by the children concerning 'fairness' and the use of power by teachers. Of course fairness is a critical issue to children because, while perceived justice enables them to retain their dignity and protect their self-esteem, perceived injustice demeans it. The problem is that justice and fairness can mean different things to different people.

In the first place, though, almost *all* the children interviewed were quite clear that 'getting done' (told off) for no apparent or justifiable reason was unfair, arbitrary and destructive:

> *Michael (3)*   Sometimes Mr Smith comes in and he's right mad right from the start. He thumps his books down, shouts at everyone and gets really angry if anyone asks a question. Then he gets angry if you get the work wrong, so it's awful.

> *Paul (2)*   He was really stupid and unfair; we were walking down the path and he rang the bell. Then he came out and started shouting. He said we'd have to stay in at four o'clock. We didn't know exactly when the bell was going.

Good Groups

Despite this, members of good groups indicated strong support for teachers' 'getting mad when gangs get acting daft 'n that' because:

> *Mandy (5)*   Well, the teachers are here to help us and children should be good in school 'cos if we aren't we won't get a good education, and then we might not get a job later. Anyway when gangs start messing about they disturb everyone and nothing gets learnt.

> *Martin (1)*   There's lots of things that we have to learn and teachers do their best to teach us but they can't do it if they're always having to deal with nutty people like Carl or people telling jokes 'n that.

This deference to perceived teacher authority and clear disassociation both from the activities of the 'noisy, selfish gangs' and, to some extent, from jokers clearly distinguished the good-group members. Nor, in general, were they confident with teachers, for their concern to please often seemed to prevent open relationships. As Kirsty commented:

Kirsty (5)   Talking to a teacher is very hard. If you know what to say before you still get so nervous that you just mumble something out and hope for the best and to get it over and done with. At home it is more relaxed but at school it's easy to get the words all jumbled up which is very embarrassing and it's very hard to show that you are not that way really. It's horrible, and you feel as though you are going to cry about it any time, but you can't.

Joker Groups

The children in joker groups were not as deferential to or as consistently supportive of teachers. In a more sophisticated way it appeared that they assessed the legitimacy of each teacher act in the particular situation which arose. Thus when asked to comment on the fairness or otherwise of certain teacher actions they gave replies such as:

June (4)   Well, it all depends on what's been happening . . .

Stephen (2)   Sometimes it's fair and sometimes it isn't . . .

Tina (4)   It's right most times but not if the teacher has done . . etc.

Sometimes when teachers acted in ways which the children judged to be unfair they were criticised and condemned. For instance the head teacher was often regarded as being inconsistent and unreasonable:

Stephen (2)   If we are having RE no-one is in the mood for a joke or anything as Mr Smith would not have it. He just wants to get the information straight into your head and keep it there. It seems as if he doesn't want us to enjoy ourselves. He's unfair too, always shouting at people. He gives us work and doesn't tell us how to do it. He expects us to finish in seconds—it's miserable.

The children also clearly rejected the right of a teacher to 'pick on' or 'go mad with' people with no justifiable reason:

Jayne (4)   I think when teachers pick on people and go mad it's probably because they've been arguing with their husband or wife at home, or there's been summat happening at home, and they take it out on the children; they come to school because it's the law. It's not fair that some kids get upset by teachers when they're just in a bad mood.

As we saw in the previous section, the joker-group children would 'do 'owt for a laugh', but they took their laughs 'sensibly' and usually *with* their teachers. It was evident that the teachers often enjoyed such incidents too, and the children appreciated the closer relationship and the breaking down of barriers which they felt resulted. The 'joking about' was felt to have a humanising effect:

Philip (2)	In science with Mr Matthews, he jokes about who's going out with who—he says 'how are you getting on with her' an' that, and 'don't get too close to so and so or you might catch summat'. He jokes you off.
Stephen (2)	Teachers like that . . . they can blend into . . . y'know . . . you get on well with them, they can be your friends like any of your other friends like.
Simon (2)	Yeah, it's like that when you're having a joke with 'em, and at the School Gala, you could just talk to 'em as if they were another person, and not as a teacher.
Hazel (4)	Yeah, we like it with Miss Newsome because she lets us tell jokes sometimes and she's OK, we've, like, got to know her.

However, despite the movement towards closer relationships which laughter was felt to bring, the 'sensible' parameters were carefully perceived. As the children put it:

Michael (3)	One of the best times to have a laugh is when I'm not doing any work that is important.
Stephen (2)	I like to have a laugh but I also like to get on with my work and if I think it will interfere with my work I will stop. I also think that having a laugh in school makes you enjoy your work so you do it better.
Jim (2)	We couldn't come to school and play about all the time or we'd never learn anything.
Dawn (4)	I like teachers who makes things interesting so you learn; you can have a laugh a bit but you still learn—that's the best.

Some teachers were even regarded as joking about too much themselves:

Julie (4)	You haven't to joke about as much as Mr Matthews does sometimes; he doesn't let you get on with your work sometimes.

Here we see the children's concern to learn effectively and develop their knowledge, but also their desire to balance this with the right amount of enjoyment and diversion. In most cases, when the teachers provided this balance in a consistent way the children respected their authority and understood the parameters of acceptable behaviour.

Jo (4)	Teachers can joke with us and it's good fun. The school rules are for our own good and they're usually fair. In these ways school helps you, learns you all it can so that you grow up well educated.
Tessa (4)	Like Mrs Graves. If you've been really naughty she'll give you the slipper but otherwise she'll just shout at you—or sometimes she'll just leave you, but if you carry on after a period she'll give you a smack or whatever. I think that's right. Teachers can't be patient all the time; they have to teach us.
Philip (2)	Anna [Group 8] actually swore at the teacher.
A.P.	And what happened?
Philip (2)	Well, I think that's unfair to the teacher 'cos if you do something wrong you need punishing.

Gang Groups

The children in gang groups often felt that they were misunderstood and treated unfairly:

Nigel 17)	You can't do anything in this school without getting into trouble; we're not supposed to run, not supposed to talk, not supposed to play games in school. It's daft.
Jonathan (9)	Mr Taylor, he's a miserable git, he tells us lot off whenever we start messing about, even if we're just having a bit of fun. Some people don't mind him but I don't see why he should tell us what to do—he talks when he wants to so why shouldn't we?
Lucy (8)	Teachers are always telling us off. I don't see why they should; it's just bloody boring in school.

Although their attitudes to teacher authority and school rules might acknowledge a degree of well-meaning intent, they were clearly unfavourable in many other ways:

Anna (8)	I think some teachers do try to be fair but most are stinking ratbags and are always on to you. The school rules are not fair because if someone starts trouble and you bash them up then teachers interfere and you get into big, big trouble. The school tries to help you sometimes but they treat us like dirt so at other times they don't try to help us one little bit. If we were good in school there would be no fun at all.
Tracey (8)	If you can't spell they learn you how and if you can't write properly they will learn you how to do it but when we get done and they shout at us it's not fair.

Gang-group members felt particularly incensed if they were 'picked on' by a teacher:

Kevin (9)	One teacher I don't like was Mrs Burke; she was always saying 'Shut up, you gasbag' and she kept making me do my drawings again; she said they weren't good enough. I don't like her. She used to pick on me and Jonathan (6) and Carl (6), just us few. She'd get in good with them such as Anne (4).
Samantha (8)	Sometimes they tell us off for nothing, so then we should not be good, we should get our own back on them, not let them get us into trouble for nothing.
Liz (8)	I hate Mr Smith; he shows off too much and he shouts too much and he's always picking on us.

The result of this perception of teachers as being unfair and biased in their dealings with gang-group children was that respect for teachers was very limited. As Liz (8) said:

Liz (8)	Our gang just doesn't care what Mr Smith says, like Sarah, she just told him to f . . . off. If he hits me I'll just walk out. I don't care. He's a stupid, bog-eyed berk!

The children would also sometimes actively resist the teachers, and the comments of Robert (17) and Sarah (18) below are not pure bravado:

A.P.	What do you think when a teacher gets mad?
Robert (17)	Well I look at him, like in a mad voice—'I don't like him'.
Sarah (18)	Yeah, we think to us 'sen, 'Oh, he's in a right narky mood; he's going to be mad . . .'
Robert (17)	And then them such as I, they say, 'Right, *I'll* be mad, then, if he's mad'.
Sarah (18)	And then you start and you might say such as 'ahh' [said insolently] to him or 'F . . . off' and that lot.

School and Education

Good and Joker Groups

The children in these groups generally had positive attitudes towards school and were prepared to balance some aspects of their daily experiences against long-term benefits. For instance, Martin (1) was particularly clear about the value of school and had absorbed a very externalised adult reason for 'being good':

Martin (1)   I think school tries to help you because you will need to know everything you can when you grow older, and I think children should be good too because it would give the place a better name.

Other children had similar views and regarded education as important both for personal and for career reasons:

Caroline (5)   I think school helps us a lot because if there was no teachers we would never learn anything and when we were up to the age of getting a job we would not know a thing about it or what to do, or if you worked in a shop you would not be any better off because you would get shown up.

Stuart (3)   I do think school tries to help us, so that we will have a good education—and when we get older when we look for jobs they might like to look at school reports to see if we are a good person or a bad person.

Anthony (2)   I think school rules are very fair because they only stop us from doing things we shouldn't do. School tries to help you in many ways. It educates our small minds to help us get jobs when we leave school and get 'A' and 'O' levels in different subjects. I think children should be good in school as it helps their education but in being bad like some gangs it will get less and less each day.

Gang Groups

Gang-group members were far more concerned with the immediate experiences of school and the direct personal effects on them. They were particularly resistant to what they saw as posh teachers trying to help them, but only by changing them in the process. As the girls in Janine's gang expressed it:

Barbara (7)   Sometimes school tries to help us but most of us don't want to be helped. We want to stay how we are. We don't want to be all posh like them; they don't understand at all.

Jenny (7)   I am the person that I am and I will not change my mind and I will not change my ways just for them.

In interview Malcolm (17) reluctantly acknowledged some value in school but showed an overall lack of concern about the future:

Malcolm (17)   Well, I suppose it'll help us a bit like when we want to get a job, but I can get a job anyway. I've done some in the holiday so I'm not bothered.

And Nigel's (17) view appeared to be the prevalent one among the majority of gang-group members:

> *Nigel (17)*   Coming to school is a waste of time: I wish this school would burn down and there would be no more school. I don't like school, I never have and I never will.

THE STRUCTURAL POSITION OF THE GROUPS

Having identified the three types of groups from interviews and from observation, it was interesting to relate them to slightly more quantitative data. For this purpose simple indices of social class, school achievement and school involvement were adopted.

Regarding social class, the housing type in which the children lived was investigated. The results, which are shown in Table 4.1, revealed a striking pattern of good-group and joker-group members coming from private housing while gang-group members tended to come from families in council housing.

Table 4.1   *Types of housing and friendship group.*

Friendship group	Private housing	Council housing
Good-group children	7	2
Joker-group children	30	8
Gang-group children	3	25

Looking at addresses, it was also noticeable that some of the groups lived in particular parts of the catchment area. For instance the members of Janine's Terrors (7) and Samantha's gang (8) were mostly centred on adjacent roads in one council estate, while the joker members of groups 2 and 4 tended to live in a particular area of semi-detached private housing. It thus seems very likely that structural factors relating to social class, income and employment which affect housing tenure were also influential in the formation of friendships and attitudes in school.

Within the school, differences in achievement of the members of different types of group were also evident. On NFER (National Foundation for Educational Research) tests for maths and English the mean scores were as shown in Table 4.2. The academic success of

Table 4.2 *Mean maths and English scores by type of group.*

Friendship group	Maths	English
Good-group members	96.6	97.5
Joker-group members	103.6	103.5
Gang-group members	90.0	89.5

the joker-group children and relative failure of gang-group children were thus confirmed.

Regarding the children's involvement in other aspects of school life, a similar pattern also recurred. Information on those involved in the following activities was collected:

(a) house captains
(b) members of the Road Safety Quiz team
(c) in the school play
(d) editors of the school magazine
(e) answering the school telephone
(f) helping teachers with dinner-time jobs
(g) learning to play musical instruments
(h) members of the choir
(i) going to the school camp
(j) members of the football team
(k) members of the netball team
(l) members of the rugby team
(m) members of the inter-school sports team
(n) members of the swimming team

Good-group members and gang-group members were involved on average with one of these activities each, compared with an average involvement in three activities for joker group members—a very great degree of difference.

Regarding gender and type of group, it was interesting that no significant differences between boys and girls emerged for social class, academic achievement or degree of school involvement. However, it was notable overall that, despite the absence of friendship groups of mixed sex, there were close links between some groups of different sexes. This was particularly so in the case of the joker groups and the gang groups, with the good groups being more reserved. This is interesting, because it has sometimes been argued that boys and girls of this age will tend not to interact because of their emergent sexual awareness. Observations at Moorside would support that view for children in relatively formal situations and with a teacher or peer-group audience. However, it appeared that in more open contexts the boys and girls interacted a lot precisely because of their emergent sexual awareness. Chasing, teasing, speculation and 'romance' were very much part of the children's games and culture.

Undoubtedly the boys took on a prominent role both inside and outside the classroom and would more often take overt initiatives in having laughs and in games. For the most part the girls seemed to accept this. It was an established pattern in the community and the wider society and was even replicated in relationships between the teaching staff of the school. This traditional female role was accepted most by good-group members. For example, one girl's New Year's resolution was:

> Linda (5)   My New Year's resolution is to help my mum by keeping my bedroom tidy and as well to help my mum to do the shopping and to help her to do the washing because I like washing.

On the other hand, some girls were very much aware of the inequalities which they experienced. For instance, members of a joker group talked with me:

> Jayne (4)   My Dad, he says . . . 'Look, you'll get a chance for choice when you grow up, so you'll get the chance to wash up when you grow up but you've got to do it now'—and my brother, he always gets out of stuff like that; all he has to do is fill the coal hod and then he can go out and play as long as he wants, and he could do that when he was our age and that's all he had to do. Now we're our age we have to clean up, wash up and all sorts.
>
> A.P.   And why do you think that is?
>
> Jayne (4)   It's 'cos he's lazy.
>
> Tessa (4)   It's 'cos we're girls.

Perhaps the views of the girls' gang groups were even more significant. As we have seen, Janine's Terrors, Samantha's gang and Sarah's gang were conscious and aware of their position; they had developed clear perspectives and activities which seemed to be far removed from the traditional image of their role and indeed showed an active resistance to many aspects of it.

There were thus some very significant differences in the experiences, activities and perspectives of the boys and the girls. What is also of great interest, though, is the *similarity* of the perspectives regarding school and teachers of children of the same structural position irrespective of sex. The Moorside case appears to indicate that the responses of girls and boys of a similar structural position may take a characteristic form because of gender influences, but they are likely to be equally active.

CHILDREN'S INTERESTS-AT-HAND

The previous section of this chapter has been largely descriptive, and it is necessary, in order to establish a potential for generalisation, to introduce a more analytical framework by which to interpret the children's perspectives. As in the earlier discussion about teachers, this will be done through the concept of interests-at-hand, which represents an attempt to establish the children's most significant and immediate concerns in the ebb and flow of classroom processes. In doing this we must remember the crucial fact of the social situation within a classroom: that two relatively distinct social systems exist beside each other. The official system of the school, with its hierarchy, rules and particular criteria of evaluation, exists alongside the children's own social system, which may appear to be less formal but which also has its own hierarchy, rules and particular criteria of judgement. In lessons the official school system is represented by the teacher, while the children's own social system is represented by each child's peers. To which party and to which social system should each child refer his or her actions, and with what consequences?

I would argue that the most important factor in each child's solution to these dilemmas is his or her structural position within the school and class, and therefore that their solutions can be seen as being patterned around the goody, joker and gang distinctions. In Fig. 4.3 typical tendencies for reference groups in lessons are shown. The figure shows goodies conforming to teachers and the official school system during lessons, while gang members tend to direct their actions more to their peer group. The success of jokers lies in their

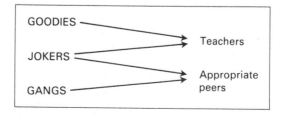

Figure 4.3 *Tendencies for reference groups in lessons.*

skill and flexibility in bridging both types of social system. I am thus arguing that jokers are able to square their reference groups in both systems in ways which goodies do not attempt and which gangs would not attempt.

Following the same arguments that were used in Chapter 2 with regard to teachers, it is possible to identify particular issues which were salient to the children and appeared to be bound to their instrumental concern with prediction and control in their classrooms. The concerns can thus be grouped by purpose, which makes it possible to infer interests. In the case of Moorside this procedure yielded six groupings, and again it seemed analytically useful to draw a distinction between the primary interest of 'self', which has several facets and by which the personal coping of any child in class may be

Table 4.3 *The interests-at-hand of children in classrooms.*

Primary interests-at-hand	*Enabling interests-at-hand*
Self	Peer-group membership
maintenance of self-image	Learning
enjoyment	
control of stress	
retention of dignity	

defined, and more secondary interests, which are enabling interests in an essentially means–end relationship. These interests are shown in Table 4.3. As we shall see below, it can be argued that all children within primary schools share these interests-at-hand in classroom contexts, though the prominence and the exact nature of each vary depending on the child's structural position. I shall consider them in turn.

Self-image

As has been reported, the children at Moorside had clear images of their own identities. These were related in many ways to their friendship groups and thus had gender, race and social-class links. Good groups thought of themselves as kind, quiet and friendly, the joker groups believed themselves to be clever and good fun, but sensible, while the gangs regarded themselves as tough and rough. These identities were further defined by their contrasts, which were highlighted by denigrating concepts such as reference by joker groups to gangs as 'thick, silly yobs' or by gangs to joker groups as 'snobbish, creeping pansies'.

Such identities were significant and could be seen as representing identification with forms of possible careers which the children anticipated, thus providing links from school processes into the outside world and the occupational structure. That issue aside for the moment, though, it was quite clear that when interacting in their classrooms the children would act to maintain their self-image vis-à-vis their peers, often even when other interests were threatened. Perhaps the most regular and obvious instance of this was the number of boys in gangs who would assert their toughness by defying teachers and 'taking' the punishments and sanctions which followed.

Very similar findings on the significance of self-image and peer-group values have been found by other studies. For instance Meyenn (1980) identified the friendship groups among girls in a Birmingham middle school and found that one group had:

> . . . accepted their placement in the bottom sets and the definition that they are 'thick' to such an extent that they see this as preferable . . .
>
> (Meyenn 1980, p.140)

Clearly children have to manage their self-image in ways which are advantageous to them, and this presentational problem can be acute in the classroom, when the expectations of peers and the teacher or parent may clash. Maintaining their self-image and sense of identity in this context is an ever-present concern.

Enjoyment

'Enjoyment' here refers to the degree of intrinsic self-fulfilment to be obtained from interaction with other people. Children will hope to experience a sense of positive reward from interactions so that they are supportive of self.

Of course there are many forms which such enjoyment can take, but one which stands out in the literature, as at Moorside, is that of 'having a laugh'. As Woods (1976) put it:

> . . . pupils have their own norms, rules and values and . . . their school lives are well structured by them . . . In their lives, laughter has a central place whether as a natural product or as a life-saving response to the exigencies of the institution—boredom, ritual, routine, regulations, oppressive authority.
>
> (Woods 1976, p.185)

However, not all laughs are oppositional. Humour in the classroom also often enables teachers and pupils to step out of their role and to express themselves and to communicate in less guarded ways than they might usually adopt. As such, humour can also be seen as a source of reinforcement and development of teacher–pupil relationships, in that to share and 'get the joke' reasserts and constructs the culture of the classroom (Walker and Adelman 1976) and thus gives security to all members within that setting.

Stebbins (1980) has noted that for teachers humour is both a strategy used for control and a form of self-expression. Having a laugh can be seen in similar terms for children. It can be a strategy of opposition which challenges teacher control or it can be enjoyable as a form of collective relaxation. At Moorside the different types of friendship groups had characteristically patterned aspirations. In the case of gangs, their greatest enjoyment appeared to come from forms of action which were essentially oppositional to teachers. Thus they emphasised incidents of 'causing bother' and 'mucking about' as highlights of their experiences and they liked the excitement of such activities as 'cheeking off' teachers or playing at 'dares' in lessons. Joker groups also enjoyed excitement, but appeared to derive it in lessons from less disruptive actions such as sending notes or drawing in jotters. Rather than 'act daft' and 'cause bother', they would derive their greatest enjoyment from 'having a laugh', with teacher participation, and they also reported enjoying lessons which were particularly interesting. Good groups also emphasised enjoying interesting lessons and mentioned enjoying lessons sometimes when teachers told jokes. In most instances, however, their great desire to avoid stress meant that they felt most relaxed in ordered, routine and predictable lessons.

The references to enjoyment from interesting lessons of course relates to the other main source of positive reward for children: the sense of self-fulfilment produced by success and achievement in learning. At Moorside many children, particularly in joker and good groups, wanted to succeed in academic terms; after all, these were the official, adult criteria by which they would be evaluated and by which to some extent they evaluated themselves. The key to this, though was balance, as Davies (1979) also found. Children wanted teachers who would 'have a laugh' *and* 'teach things'. The degree of emphasis placed on each element by each type of group is crudely shown in Fig. 4.4.

For each type of group enjoyment can be seen as occurring through the existence from time to time of situations which were supportive of each type of group's reference-group values and each individual's

enjoyment ⇒ Supportive of type of groups ref group value
⇒ each individuals self-image

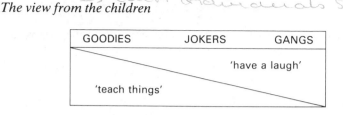

Figure 4.4 *The balance of enjoyment.*

self-image. Clearly some groups derived more enjoyment from
school than others, and the nature of such enjoyment also varied
considerably.

Control of Stress

The main source of stress for children in classrooms derives from
teacher power and the evaluative context of schooling. For good
groups at Moorside, stress avoidance seemed to be a particularly
prominent interest-at-hand, largely, I would argue, because their
self-image as quiet, studious and conformist was undercut with few
defences if rejected by a teacher 'getting mad' with them. They were
also vulnerable and relatively defenceless if in conflict with other
groups of children. Thus they tended to be wary and to concentrate
on avoiding trouble. In contrast, gangs almost needed stress to assert
their toughness. At the same time, though, I found few children who
actually sought out, say, a severe telling-off from a teacher. If such a
thing occurred, then it was used to build the tough identity but it was
not enjoyed in itself. Joker groups were also concerned to avoid
stress, be it from academic failure or acts of deviance. They very
much disliked being told off because it negated the type of
relationships which they tried to establish with teachers. At the same
time, though, it is clear that a lot of their good fun and enjoyment was
derived from juggling with the risks of 'getting done' by teachers. If
their judgements were correct, then routine teacher reactions would
not result in much stress. Indeed, spice and zest would be added to
classroom experiences from such exploration of the limits without
serious sanctions resulting.

Stress is thus a double-edged interest-at-hand. Usually children
seek to avoid the potential stress to which they are permanently
subject because of teacher power and because of the constant
evaluation of their learning. However, there is no doubt that other
sorts of stress are wilfully introduced by children from time to time as
a source of enjoyment and as an antidote to routine or boredom.

Acceptance of such risk varies between different groups and individuals.

Retaining Dignity

This was one of the most important interests-at-hand for all groups of children at Moorside, being crucial for the preservation of self- and peer-group esteem, and of course such concern has been shown in studies of pupils of all ages. For instance Rosser (1976) identified an 'offence of depersonalisation' felt by sixteen-year-olds when treated with contempt by teachers. She wrote:

> Good teachers, in essence, were those who . . . were seen [by children] to treat them as equals and [who] tried to understand them. Recognition of self as individual and of value was a central concern and teachers who offended against this principle were strongly resented.
>
> (Rosser 1976, p.22)

Similarly, Woods (1975) has shown the deep sense of humiliation felt by children who may be 'shown up' by teachers. Blishen's (1969) study of pupil views of their ideal teacher concluded that:

> They should be understanding . . . and patient . . . should listen to pupils and give their pupils a chance to speak; should be willing to have points made against them, be humble, kind, capable of informality, and simply pleasant; . . . and, above all, should be warm and personal.
>
> (Blishen 1969, p.131)

The same concern comes from Nash's data (1976) on pupils' expectations of teachers and also from Meighan's (1978) review of the issue. Children do not like teachers who threaten their dignity, for such a threat represents a direct attack on their self-image. Children resent teachers who forget their names (Morgan, O'Neill and Harré 1979) or who use offensive nicknames, teachers who show them up or mock them when they have difficulty with work, and teachers who reprimand them unfairly.

There is a close relationship between dignity and perceived 'fairness', and this was particularly clear at Moorside. Thus teacher actions and censures would be constantly assessed by the children for legitimacy. 'Getting done' could therefore be accepted without loss of dignity if it was fair, but if the teacher 'went mad', and particularly if he or she started shouting at and denigrating a child, then this would be regarded as a most unfair assault by all the children. Other, more specific threats to dignity came from being picked on or teased by teachers, as well as from having one's name forgotten. Being picked on was felt particularly deeply as a personal attack by the gang groups. It was regarded as unfair because it was seen to arise from unusual levels of teacher surveillance and from particular attention being directed towards them. Similarly, being shown up was recognised as a specific act of depersonalisation intended to set an example. For instance:

> *Malcolm (17)* He only showed me up like that in front of everyone just to make me look stupid . . . and just to try to make us all learn the notes better. He's always getting on at us for it and just 'cos I couldn't answer his questions he picked on me.

On the other hand, being teased was something which the joker groups seemed particularly conscious of. The girls related that one teacher often teased them about boyfriends, which in some cases upset them because it made them 'go all red and look silly'. The relatively quiet members of good groups were the main group of children who reported having their names forgotten. They clearly regarded this as insulting and resented it.

With regard to retaining dignity vis-à-vis the other children similar issues seemed important. The inter-group rivalry at Moorside was reflected in mild forms of teasing and in more serious episodes of name calling or fighting similar to those recorded by Sluckin (1981) in Oxfordshire primary schools. In all cases, though, the children's comments on such incidents revealed both defensive and aggressive actions to be forms of assertion of particular self-identities with particular group associations. The defence of personal dignity thus seems to be a very prominent interest-at-hand for children in all school contexts.

Peer-group Membership and Learning

I earlier suggested that peer-group loyalty and learning should be seen as enabling interests rather than as facets of the primary self-interest. They thus take on the same role for children as order and instruction do for teachers, in that they articulate between the social ascriptions of respective reference groups and facets of the primary interest-at-hand of the participants. In the case of teachers, order and instruction can be seen as the two main aspects of their role expectation which they have to come to terms with if they are to avoid external pressure. However, they are also the means of achieving satisfaction of more personal interests. In the case of the children, peer-group membership and learning seem to relate to the social ascriptions of the child culture and social system and of the adult educational culture and wider society respectively. As such they reflect the ambiguity of each child's structural position and of course to some extent they offer alternative means of enabling the primary interest-at-hand to be satisfied. They also pose severe dilemmas for the children when they come to make strategic decisions about action and to juggle with their interests in the dynamic flow of classroom processes, decisions being required between the strategies of the 'swots' and those of the 'dossers' (Turner 1983).

Peer-group Membership

At Moorside, peer-group membership was linked to both the assertion and the defence of self. Enjoyment, laughs and 'great times' almost exclusively derived from interaction between the children and their friends with or without the positive participation of the teacher. A supportive audience was thus crucial and could be guaranteed only by the secure membership and solidarity of a peer group. Peer-group competence, similar to the competence required of teachers (Denscombe 1980a), sometimes had to be proved if a child were to avoid being rejected as 'wet' or 'stupid', but of course would vary in its nature depending on the type of group. Group membership was also of defensive value against the threat both from teachers and from other children. The solidarity which existed within groups provided a powerful resource for individuals in exposed situations both in the classroom and in the playground. Group members were expected to 'stick up' for each other, and certainly one of the worst actions imaginable was to 'snitch' or 'tell tales' on a friend. Peer-group solidarity was a particularly important interest for gang groups because of the consequences of their frequent rejection of teacher authority.

As we saw in the previous chapter, Davies (1979), in her study of primary-aged children's friendship groups in Australia, found very similar results and reported children's concerns that friends should 'be with you' and should not 'pose'. As she put it:

> [Those concerns] both relate to the vulnerability experienced by the children if they find themselves alone at school—vulnerability in terms of not knowing how to operate alone within the system of the school and vulnerability in terms of defencelessness in the face of other children who may be posing.
>
> (Davies 1979, pp.20–21)

The study by Sluckin (1981) of first-school and middle-school playground cultures also shows the importance, sophistication and order of children's informal social systems. It emphasises the learning and growth of social competence which emerge from peer-group interaction and also the pragmatic necessity of friendships for coping with playground life. Clearly peer-group membership is important for children in terms of gaining support both in the classroom and in the playground. Children's concern to be seen as full and competent members of their peer group can thus be seen as an enabling interest in the context of their primary concern to protect their self and survive the variety of situations which they encounter at school.

Learning

While the enabling interest of peer-group membership responds to the children's social system, the interest of learning is clearly a primary means of coping in the adult evaluation systems of teachers and parents. Teachers and parents expect children to learn. Thus one way of satisfying them and of negotiating their power and influence is to do just that. However, within children's social structures there will be considerable variation in the degree of commitment to this strategy. For instance, at Moorside the children would constantly assess the cost of trying to learn by evaluating how interesting or boring the lessons were. Of course there were variations not only in those judgements but also in the responses then made. Good groups might consider a lesson as boring but put up with it anyway, accepting it as good for them and not wishing to compromise their identities with their teachers. Joker-group members would be more inclined to attempt to direct the lesson into more fertile activities, while gang members would be likely to attempt to subvert the lesson directly. Good-group and joker-group members reported far more intrinsic satisfaction from lessons than gang members. The latter were far more likely to see lessons as a waste of time or time spent 'doing nothing' unless a direct link with future work possibilities was drawn. They thus generally had a more exclusively instrumental approach than the other, more academically successful, types of group. Obviously their perceived academic failure meant that learning did not seem to provide anything more than a very limited means of enabling them to cope with their situation. On the other hand, for joker-group members their success at learning earned them the credit with teachers and parents with which they were able to relax and cultivate laughs. For the good-group members the studious sincerity of their attempts to learn enabled them to accomplish lessons without incident.

The existence of children's concern with learning is well documented elsewhere. For instance, research on the types of teachers that children like best has consistently shown that they value teachers who set clear, attainable and interesting learning goals (Nash 1976, Meighan 1978).

Of course academic achievement feeds back directly to the development of each child's identity and self-concept (Nash 1973), so that to learn in lessons is not an interest-at-hand simply by virtue of the need to cope with the particular situation. It is linked to the maintenance and development of self-image, to enjoyment, to stress avoidance and to dignity—facets of self which, though experienced with immediacy, accumulate over time into more established identities. Thus not only teachers but each child him or herself comes to know who is 'thick' and who is 'bright', and of course so do other children. This last point is of considerable significance. Clearly children have developed notions of who is 'clever' and who is a 'a thickie', and this influences their friendship groups and the nature of their interaction considerably. Learning is thus a significant interest in terms of developing a particular identity for some children within their peer group, for such ability is part of the competence required of members. However, its main significance as an enabling interest clearly stems from its articulation with teacher concerns and with the official curriculum and purposes of school.

CONCLUSION

The data which have been reported in this chapter clearly show the influence of factors such as gender and social class in patterning the Moorside children's experiences and perspectives regarding school life, and yet, at the same time, they also assert the importance of the relationships which existed *within* the school between children and their teachers. In this respect it is appropriate to draw particular attention to the consequences of children's experiencing a sense of failure and rejection in school or of children's failing to establish a close relationship with their teacher.

The types of group which have been identified may cause readers to recall children they have taught, although it should be remembered that the types of group have been deliberately highlighted for analytical purposes and that at younger ages types of child strategy may be more exploratory and less polarised. Even so, they do appear to be identifiable in other situations. For instance, Sluckin (1981) used the terms 'attention seekers', 'leaders' and 'teasers', with their obvious similarity to goodies, jokers and gangs, to summarise extensive observational work on children in nurseries by Manning, Heron and Marshall (1978) and Montagner (1978).

I would suggest that the tendencies which lead to this type of crystallisation are very rarely absent from school classrooms, a fact which is an inevitable consequence of the structures within which classroom life takes place. The situation is difficult for children, just as it is for teachers. Some will seek to cope with it by conforming and seeking to 'please the teacher' as much as possible; some will reject the whole experience, treat it as an attack on their self-esteem and resist it; some may try to negotiate their way through the situation by balancing their concerns with those of the teacher. Thus we have the strategies of the good groups, the gang groups and the joker groups.

As we have seen, children share immediate concerns and interests in lessons, though they interpret them differently. These interests relate directly to the social situation in which each child acts and also to the structural, organisational and material context of the community, school and classroom. As we saw in Chapter 2, the interests of teachers also relate to such factors and indeed can be seen as a pragmatic response to them. The wider social context in which classroom life takes place is thus of enormous consequence and it is therefore the subject of Part 2 of this book.

PART TWO

SOCIAL CONTEXT

5

Primary Schools and Society

INTRODUCTION

The first part of this book has described the perspectives and daily concerns of teachers and children in primary schools. It has been suggested that in many respects these can be seen as pragmatic responses to circumstances, particularly to direct classroom experiences. This is typical of the type of explanation which symbolic interactionist studies tend to produce: the perspectives of the participants in a social situation are related to their immediate context. Despite the value of such an analysis, it has to be recognised that it has certain limitations because of its small-scale 'micro' focus. For instance, in itself it cannot tell us very much about what *produces* the context in which action takes place. In this respect we might very well want to know the origins of factors such as teacher–pupil ratios, school designs, levels of school resourcing, the legal framework of schooling, government and local education authority policies, and parental and media attitudes and expectations. These things structure school experience itself and thus are relevant and important in a sociological analysis of even a micro topic such as processes in classrooms. Similarly, it would be inaccurate to imply that the knowledge and perspectives of teachers and children in schools derive solely from their classroom and school experiences. Clearly, ideas, attitudes and beliefs are developed by each individual within a much wider social, cultural and ideological context and are only then taken into the classroom to be moulded further. Thus 'macro' factors are important to the micro situation in many ways.

Attempts to trace, understand and explain the links between schooling processes and the wider society have occupied sociologists for many years, and have necessarily taken them into the realms of history, politics and economics, and also into cultural and ideological analysis. Of course it is far beyond the scope of this book to deal with such issues in depth, even with regard to primary education; however, the issues are also far too important to be omitted. I thus aim in this chapter to review very briefly some aspects of historical development and of present structures which influence the social world of primary schools today. The notes for further reading at the end of the book provide some references for those who wish to explore the issues further.

The chapter begins with a simple account of differences in the distribution of wealth, power and life chances in British society and raises the issue of the way in which schooling relates to such an unequal society. The second section continues this theme and traces the historical development of primary schools through the elementary and developmental traditions to show how politics, ideology and educational policy have interrelated from Victorian times right up to the 1980s. The third section documents the structures and powers of the present education system. It identifies the institutions at various levels of decision-making and influence, such as the Department of Education and Science and local education authorities, and it traces recent tendencies towards the centralisation of control. A fourth section considers the influence of the social beliefs which stem from Britain's being a capitalist society and attempts to trace these social values within schools. The chapter concludes by suggesting that there are contradictions between what teachers are expected to do and the resources which are made available for them to do it, and that this is reflected in the pragmatism of their classroom practice.

SCHOOLING IN AN UNEQUAL SOCIETY

A basic but fundamental point which must be made is that primary schools exist within a society which exhibits considerable differences in wealth, status, power and life chances. The main factors which pattern this distribution are those of social class, gender, race, age and, increasingly, the region of the country in which people happen to live. For instance, according to statistics from the Royal

Commission on the Distribution of Income and Wealth (Diamond 1979), the richest 10 per cent of the population own almost two-thirds of the total wealth, and while the average level of male earnings was £4800, the comparable figure for female earnings was only £2700. Other examples show further features of these material realities, such as the fact that unemployment among West Indians is approximately twice that of whites (Labour Force Survey 1981) or the fact that most indices—proportion of private housing, unemployment levels, income levels, car ownership, etc.—show the South East to be better off than other regions (Regional Trends 1984). Such factors often cluster together to form layers of advantage or disadvantage. Thus a person who is black, female and unskilled in the north of England is statistically likely to have relatively little wealth, status or power and few prospects of improvement compared with someone who is white, male and professionally qualified living in the south of England. People in such positions create and live their lives from completely different structural starting-points.

It has sometimes been suggested that such differences are the product of an open and meritocratic society in which opportunities for advancement are freely available. Thus social differences are seen as the result of some amalgam of people's intelligence and their effort, with the education system providing the first opportunity for people to demonstrate their capacities. This argument is attractive in a democratic society, but unfortunately it defies many facts, for sociological research has consistently shown that the achievements of people are related to their social class, gender and racial background as much as to their 'intelligence' or 'effort', however these may be defined (e.g. Boudon 1974, Halsey, Heath and Ridge 1980).

In other words, a position in society reflects where you start from as well as what you have done. In this respect the education system and primary schools within it have been shown to have relatively little influence on an already divided society which tends to reproduce inequalities from one generation to the next.

Because of these facts sociologists have developed theories which largely invert the meritocratic arguments about education and suggest that the schooling system may more accurately be seen as reproducing social inequalities from one generation to the next. The detail of this process is the subject of a great deal of research and theoretical discussion, part of which relates to how classroom processes may contribute to social reproduction.

This, then, is the first and most vital element of the wider social context within which teachers and pupils in school act today. Of course such inequalities have existed for many years, and the response of people to them has also influenced the development of primary schooling and thus has contributed to many of the things about it which are now taken for granted.

THE DEVELOPMENT OF PRIMARY SCHOOLING

The historical development of primary schools can be seen as the product of the struggle for influence of two traditions, both rooted in the early part of the nineteenth century (Blyth 1965, Whitbread 1972). The elementary tradition was essentially one of pragmatism, economy and centralised control. It originated, before working men and women were allowed to vote, from governments which saw schooling for the majority of children almost as a regrettable necessity. The developmental tradition, on the other hand, was one of idealism, of trust in the child and of individualised, autonomous initiatives. Originating in the work of people like Robert Owen, Pestalozzi and Froebel, it developed, with the reinforcement of psychologists such as Isaacs and Piaget, to become a received wisdom by the time of the Plowden Report.

The two traditions are still evident today, and in simple terms it is possible to argue that, while the assumptions of the elementary tradition continue to frame the material, resource and legal structures of primary schooling, the developmental tradition has been the source of most modern educational theory and of teachers' professional beliefs. Let us look at the traditions in more detail.

The Elementary Tradition

The elementary schools which existed prior to Forster's Education Act of 1870 were based largely on charitable foundations or on the educational societies of particular religious denominations. The largest of these, the National and the British, had been founded in 1811 and 1814 respectively, and were responsible for a steady increase in the number of elementary schools for the poor from the early part of the nineteenth century. These schools based their teaching on monitorial systems in which nine- or ten-year-old children instructed small groups of less advanced pupils under the general supervision of a master. Such schools provided a generally poor quality of education. As Bagley and Bagley (1969) put it:

Almost all schools, run on gifts and penny-fees, were very short of furniture and apparatus. Many taught nothing beyond elementary reading and a mockery of religious knowledge, and, because they knew no other way, most teachers inevitably used the mechanical, brain-numbing method of monitorial teaching to control their crowded schools.

(Bagley and Bagley 1969, p.14)

From the 1830s this voluntary school system received a steadily increasing amount of government aid, recognition and control. This had begun with building grants in 1833, and government influence was extended with the introduction of systems for inspection and for the training and registration of teachers. Capitation grants became payable under certain strict conditions in the 1850s.

This government involvement was entered into reluctantly, for it was against the *laissez-faire* philosophy of the times. However, changes in English society from its old agricultural base to a new industrial economy were attended by considerable social dislocation, and education came to be seen as providing a means of maintaining social order (McCann 1977). As Johnson (1970) put it:

. . . the early Victorian obsession with the education of the poor is best understood as a concern about authority, about power, about the assertion of control . . . Supervised by its trusty teacher, surrounded by its playground wall, the school was to raise a new race of working people—respectful, cheerful, hardworking, loyal, pacific and religious.

(Johnson 1970, p.119)

Clearly if Johnson's analysis is correct then sociological models of the relationship of schooling and society are offered considerable empirical support from the example of provision in the early nineteenth century, and they derive even more support from a consideration of the system of payment by results which blighted the later part of the Victorian period. This system was introduced by Robert Lowe in 1862. Six 'standards' were set, based on the three Rs, on which children between the ages of six and eleven were examined annually. Each school received payment from the government based on the number of passes obtained in each subject and on attendance figures. This system put enormous pressure on teachers to cram their pupils with knowledge and skills as determined by the national code, to train them for the inspector's visit at exam time and to make sure that they attended regularly. As Grace (1978) put it:

The social world of the elementary school frequently witnessed the death of idealism, of spontaneity and of humane social relationships. Constrained as it was spatially, temporally and pedagogically and created essentially to 'domesticate' the urban working class, it became

a real context for alienation . . . For both teachers and pupils the
'real' world was external and constraining and characterised by
hierarchy and order.

(Grace 1978, p.38)

Payment by results was phased out in the 1890s, by which time it had
firmly proved the principles of its founder, for in 1861 Lowe had
declared to the House of Commons:

if the new system will be not cheap then it will be efficient, and if it will
not be efficient it will be cheap.

Thus in Victorian England the minimum education necessary for the
development of the skills needed by industry and for the
development of a suitable sense of respect and morality was regarded
by those in power as both proper and sufficient. Anything more
would have been thought of as wasted on the poor. In my view it is
from such a starting-point that our present assumptions about
teacher–pupil ratios, levels of resourcing, legal structures, etc. have
been derived.

The Developmental Tradition

The developmental tradition can also be traced from the early part of
the nineteenth century. Industrialisation and the increase in factory
work, in which working-class women were heavily involved, created a
problem with regard to young children which was initially catered for
by *ad hoc* arrangements for child supervision and through the growth
of dame schools. The 1820s, however, saw the development of an
infant-school movement, again based on voluntary societies, which
was considerably influenced by Robert Owen and his school at New
Lanark. As Whitbread (1972) explained, Owen:

. . . tried to provide social training in an educationally stimulating
environment suited to the age and interests of the children. By
contemporary standards his school was child-centred.

(Whitbread 1972, p.10)

Whitbread cites the instructions which Owen gave to his teachers:

. . . they were on no account ever to beat any one of the children, or to
threaten them in any manner of word or action, or to use abusive
terms; but were always to speak to them with a pleasant countenance,
and in a kind manner and tone of voice. They should tell the infants
and children that they must on all occasions do all they could to make
their playfellows happy. The schoolroom was furnished with paintings,
chiefly of animals, with maps, and often supplied with natural objects

from the gardens, fields and woods—the examination and explanation of which always excited their curiosity and created an animated conversation between the children and their instructors.
(Whitbread 1972, p.10)

Despite Owen's principles, the infant schools which developed around the country were influenced pedagogically by their position prior to the elementary stage, and this became particularly marked after the introduction of payment by results. However, the effect of payment by results and of teacher–pupil ratios of up to 1:60 even in infant schools was almost to squeeze the developmental tradition out of the state system. Thus, when Froebel's ideas became influential in the later part of the century, they had most influence on the private schools of the new middle classes.

In the early part of the twentieth century, and particularly in the period of reconstruction after the 1914–18 war, the idealistic influence of Dewey came to be felt and to have an impact on elementary schools through the development of co-operative activities, projects and the integration of some subject areas. This was combined with a gradual improvement in resources, and with an increase in diversity deriving from the new system of local education authorities which had been introduced in 1902. Child psychology was also becoming influential at this time (Isaacs 1933) and in addition there was a gradual development of the collectivist ideas which eventually were to underpin the welfare state (e.g. Tawney 1931), in which education was to play a significant role. When the Hadow Report on primary schools was published in 1931 it represented a bold reassertion of the developmental tradition, with statements which have now become classic such as:

The curriculum is to be thought of in terms of activity and experience rather than in knowledge to be acquired and facts to be stored.
(Board of Education 1931, p.93)

Thereafter the basic tenets of the developmental tradition were gradually adopted within teacher training institutions and among educationists, leading to their strong articulation by the Plowden Report in 1967. Developmental ideas had become almost synonymous with professional beliefs.

The situation in the 1970s and early 1980s illustrated the continuation of the two traditions. In the early 1970s the dominance of the developmental ideas legitimated by Plowden received a sharp critique from the publication of the so-called 'Black Papers' (Cox and Dyson 1969, 1970, Cox and Boyson 1975), which asserted that educational standards were declining and that progressive practices in comprehensive and primary schools were responsible for a deterioration in the moral standards of young people. Discussion of such issues was taken up by the media while at the same time the end of the period of fairly steady economic expansion since the war was signalled by the 1974 oil crisis. The cost and productivity of education began to assume importance in public debate. Scandal over so-called 'progressive excesses' at William Tyndale Primary School and controversy over the results of Bennett's (1976) study of the efficiency of different teaching styles used in primary schools added to public disquiet and made education a political issue. James Callaghan, the Labour Party Prime Minister, began a 'great debate' which focused on the relevance of the school curriculum to industrial needs, on standards in basic skills, and on school accountability. The primary concern had thus noticeably shifted in the decade since Plowden from a focus on the development of the child to a concern with *efficiency*. As the 1977 Green Paper (DES 1977) put it:

> Underlying all [the criticism] was the feeling that the education system was out of touch with the fundamental need for Britain to survive economically in a highly competitive world through the efficiency of its industry and commerce.
>
> (DES 1977, p.2)

Questions were raised about the need for a 'core curriculum'.

After 1979, with the return of a Conservative government, pressure for centralised control increased further. For instance, in 1980 a document entitled *A Framework for the School Curriculum* was published (DES 1980). It asserted the Secretaries of State's 'inescapable duty to satisfy themselves that the work of the schools matches national needs' (DES 1980, p.1). It set out certain aims such as 'to help pupils to develop lively minds, to apply themselves to tasks and to have religious and moral values' and it defined the 'common core' curriculum in terms of subjects: English, maths, science, modern languages, religious education and physical education. This was followed by a paper on the curriculum (DES 1981) which defined 'overriding responsibilities' and 'key areas' for primary schools to attend to and which was sent to all schools in England and Wales. Such moves towards centralised control were accompanied by a cut of almost 12 per cent between 1978 and 1984 in the proportion of public expenditure spent on education and by a dramatic increase in the control of local-authority spending by central government. The parallels with the concerns with cheapness, efficiency, control and morality which characterised the Victorian elementary schools are noticeable here.

These developments were seen not only as an attack on the quality of the education which it was possible to provide with scarce resources (NUT 1982) but also as a direct attack on the autonomy of teachers. This was itself bound up with the developmental tradition and with professionalism. As Roy (1983) put it:

> This attack on teaching has its roots in a philosophy resting on the belief that it is central government, its ministers and civil servants, that must determine not only the shape of the school system, but of the curriculum, and the methodology of the teaching process. Teachers must therefore be subordinated to a political will based on the notion that only an all powerful state knows what is best for its citizens; the individual counts for less and less because the assertion and the development of individuality, which is an essential task of the education process in a free society, gets in the way of political aspirations and systems which require both uniformity and conformity . . . The accountability of the teaching profession . . . is . . . replaced by controls removing from the teacher the professional freedom to shape the curriculum to meet the needs of the children he knows.
>
> (Roy 1983, p.2)

The 1980s thus began with the developmental tradition in retreat, though strongly defended by associations such as the National Association for Primary Education and by some educationists (e.g. Kirby 1981), and with the teaching profession facing considerable difficulties.

Again, these debates and events are of great long-term significance to classroom life, even though they may seem distant at times. The ways in which a teacher can act are crucially affected by social expectations, legal structures, resourcing and their degree of autonomy, and this brings us to another feature of the present education system—that of its structure—and it is to a slightly more detailed look at powers and control within that structure that we now turn.

THE STRUCTURE AND POWERS OF THE EDUCATION SYSTEM

The British education system has been regarded as one of the most decentralised in Europe. This decentralisation, which was greatly facilitated by the Education Act 1902, is based on the existence of local education authorities and on a precedent, gradually established after 'payment by results' had ended, of giving head teachers very great autonomy over many aspects of teaching processes and curriculum decisions. This was further enhanced by the continuing development of school-based governing bodies drawn in its most recent form from teachers, parents and representatives of the particular communities which schools serve. Overseeing all these, though, and with considerable powers, remains the Government, through the Secretary of State and the Department of Education and Science. The present governing structures for schools in England and Wales can thus be represented diagrammatically as in Fig. 5.1,

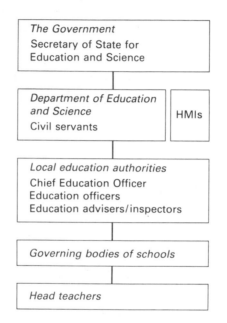

Figure 5.1   *The governing structure of primary schools in England and Wales.*

though few of the relationships implied are as simple as they appear, and there is no formal hierarchical line of accountability. We might also note that Her Majesty's Inspectors, although technically independent of the DES, have become increasingly identified with it in recent years (Salter and Tapper 1981).

The role of central government in the education system is not clearly defined in law. Until the late 1970s it was accepted that governments should be concerned with the overall organisation of the school system, with finance, with the supply of teachers and with various economic controls, for instance over building programmes. Direct government pressure regarding the curriculum or regarding issues involving the teaching profession's expertise was very unusual. As Kogan (1971) described that period:

> The only controls are, in effect, constraints on the actions of local authorities, with whom most of the initiatives lie.
>
> (Kogan 1971, p.18)

Central government thus exerted its educational influence indirectly through the DES, through educational reports such as Crowther and Plowden, and through organisations such as the Schools Council. In addition, of course, it controlled the overall level of the rate support grant to local authorities (about two-thirds of their budget), although it had no power to determine how such money was spent.

In the early 1980s control by central government tightened considerably. The proportion of local government expenditure provided by central government fell, yet at the same time a system of 'cash limits' was introduced to control expenditure by local authorities. One inevitable result was massive cuts in the resources allocated to education. Other changes which indicate the increasingly intrusive stance taken by central government included the abolition of the Schools Council, the rise of the Manpower Services Commission running educational courses, the start of a process of restructuring higher education, the setting-up of an accreditation body to monitor teacher education, the publication of reports by HMIs after school inspection, and the centralised collection of information on the curriculum taught in all schools. Thus central government began to exert *pressure*, a radical departure from the previous style of structuring by the use of constraint. Furthermore, much of this pressure was directed to the heart of the teaching process and towards the curriculum. The extent of decentralisation thus began to diminish as the Government asserted the necessity of education serving 'the nation's industrial needs' as they defined them.

These developments make crystal clear the fact that education is political. As Kogan (1978, p.15) put it, education is 'concerned with what *ought to be* rather than what *is*' and it is therefore an issue about which a variety of different views are advocated and over which power is exerted.

Politics is important at other levels also, but tends to result in increasing diversity rather than in pressure for uniformity. For instance, when decisions have to be taken at LEA level, educational policy emerges from the complex process of local political parties vying with each other in council chambers. The result is considerable variation among the 108 local authorities in England and Wales regarding policies and provision. Thus we have a great many different types of school and age ranges, and levels of such things as capitation, staffing, in-service training, books and nursery provision vary greatly in different parts of the country. For instance in 1983–84 the London Boroughs of Brent and Haringey spent £1003 and £1007 respectively on each of their primary-school pupils, compared with figures of only £610 for Cornwall and £615 for West Sussex. Similarly, their pupil–teacher ratios at 17.02:1 and 17.52:1 respectively were far below those of Hereford and Worcester, at 25.65:1, or Oxfordshire, at 24.22:1 (figures from the Chartered Institute of Public Finance and Accountancy, *TES*, 20 April 1984). The LEA level within the educational system is thus a very important one. The policy and resourcing decisions that are made by local councils are responsive to the influence of central government, yet themselves yield the detailed structures of provision within which teachers have to work.

The local education authorities also work closely with the governing bodies of each school, who may, with the guidance of LEA officials, decide on staff appointments and many other matters of specific school policy. The scope and representation of school governors was extended after the Taylor Report of 1977 in a way which represented a decentralisation of control from the LEA to those with more direct involvement in the schools' affairs. Thus although day-to-day management of schools remains in the hands of the head teacher, accountability of schools to the community is gradually increasing.

To summarise this discussion, it could be said that the structure of the education system is one which has provided for some autonomy at each of its levels, but it is increasingly necessary to point out that this freedom is used within the constraints set by the level above. In the schools and classrooms which provide the *raison d'être* for this structure, teachers and children tend to take for granted the policies and provision with which they work. Classrooms provide the final stage in the structure from the centre to the periphery and teachers and children are the people who actually have to use the materials provided and try to make the policies work. As they struggle to cope with the realities of classroom life it is thus really very important to remember the layers of social context which fundamentally structure the situation in each school. They collectively affect such things as whether specialised remedial or music teaching exists, when the annual paper and pencil supply runs out, how thoroughly schools can be cleaned and maintained, how often books can be replaced, how many in-service courses are available, etc.

These material realities influence both the quality of the education provided and the nature of the 'essential actual experience' of teachers and children—experience which, as we have seen, is a starting-point in the development of their knowledge of and perspectives on school life. However, the wider social context also influences knowledge and perspectives more directly and it is to this issue that we now turn.

EDUCATION AND SOCIETY

The way in which social and cultural values and beliefs influence schooling processes is both a very difficult area and too significant to ignore. I offer a very simple account of it here, first by considering some commonly held ideas about our economic system and then by introducing the concept of hegemony to illustrate how such ideas both spread to and can be generated from the micro situation of the classroom.

Our present economic system is perhaps best described as a form of 'state capitalism' in which large public industries, multinational corporations and financial institutions predominate. They are supported by the various agencies of the welfare state, of which education is one. Underpinning the economic system in a fundamental way are two necessities: high levels of consumption and high levels of production. The importance of these factors is constantly stressed in both public and private spheres, for instance through advertising and 'conspicuous consumption' in the case of the former and through acceptance of the work ethic and the need for industrial efficiency in the case of the latter. I would argue that this concern for consumption and production can be seen as elements of a hegemony—the dominant set of ideas which support the existing social and economic system and which permeate the thinking of the people living within it (Gramsci 1978). Thus even a system which is grossly divided and has an unequal distribution of wealth, such as British society, is legitimised and accepted because the ideas upon which it is based have become taken for granted as 'common sense' and are even regenerated in everyday practice.

This particular power of the hegemony lies in the fact that an immediate action by an individual in response to a particular situation is likely to draw on commonsense thinking which, though it 'works' in the short term, also has the long-term effect of reproducing the values on which the system as a whole is based, and to which, ironically, the initial action was responding. There is thus a continuous dialectical movement between the macro and micro levels in which the social and economic structure and individuals in interaction together generate and regenerate the hegemony. Examples of this phenomenon are readily available in schools.

For instance, in my study at Moorside I collected examples of many forms of teachers' talk—instructions, comments, questions, etc. In the general area of school-work I identified examples which seemed to relate to productivity and efficiency. For example:

Effort	'You're not trying at all.' 'That's very poor.' 'Don't be so careless.' 'Let's make a really big effort today.'
Perseverance	'Try once more.' 'Concentrate.' 'Hard luck, you'll have to do it again.' 'Try a bit longer.' 'No, you've not quite finished yet.'
Neatness	'Make it look good.' 'Do it carefully.' 'That's a nice, neat page.' 'God, you look a mess.' 'OK, tidy up now.' 'Yeah, that's nice.' 'Print it neatly'. 'Leave the classroom straight.' 'Your writing's a mess.'
Regularity	'Is that your best work?' 'I don't think you're trying today.' 'I know you can do better than that.' 'Which side of the bed did you get out of?'
Speed	'Hurry up!' 'Get a move on.' 'Who's going to finish first?' 'Has anyone finished yet?' 'Be quick.'

There is nothing unusual about these concerns. They would be found in most of our schools and many people would applaud the fact that such values are encouraged. In my view, though, they also form part of the dominant hegemony; they can be traced to the 'Protestant ethic' first documented by Weber (1976), are regularly articulated by governments and industry at a national level, and are also regarded as the main means of 'getting on' by millions of people. Concerns such as these form a major part of the dominant values of our society, and teachers working in schools within that society tend to reinforce them. However, it is crucial to note the significance of these concerns for teachers at the practical level of their day-to-day work. In this regard values such as these are directly linked to teachers' immediate concern with *instruction* as an interest which enables them to cope with their working conditions. 'Keeping their noses down' is common sense for teachers in many classroom situations, but it also reinforces the hegemony.

A second set of social values also existed at Moorside, grouped around issues of behaviour and social relationships. For instance:

Self-control	'Stop being silly.' 'Don't be a baby.' 'Don't shout out.' 'Don't just rush.'
Obedience	'Do what I tell you.' 'Behave yourself.' 'Did you hear what I said?' 'Any more acting daft and there'll be trouble.'
Politeness	'Good morning, children.' 'What do you say?' 'Please?' 'That's not a very nice thing to say, is it?'
Quietness	'Stop talking.' 'OK, quieten down.' 'Shut up.' 'Silence now.'
Respect for authority	'Hands up if you want something.' 'I said so.' 'Don't argue with me.' 'Ask me first.' 'Don't be cheeky.' 'Stand aside when I come through.' 'Listen to me when I'm talking.' ' "Yes *sir*" is what you say.'
Truth	'Let's have it straight now.' 'I don't believe a word of it.' 'Are you lying to me?' 'That's a good story, isn't it?' (said doubtfully)

Again we see here the emphasis of attributes which could be said to meet industrial needs in terms of preparing a productive and compliant workforce. However, the grouping stems more immediately from teachers' practical concern with sustaining *order and discipline*. Several of the social values identified—politeness, respect for authority, quietness—derived from teacher strategies designed to pre-empt trouble, while others—obedience, self-control, truth—emerged primarily during attempts to recoup situations.

At the same time there is evidence of concerns in schools which reinforce the expectation of mass private consumption. A simple but direct example is the common ritual in infant schools of cataloguing birthday presents in assembly before the child receives his or her 'claps'. More significant, though, is the routine stress on individualism and competitiveness. For instance:

Achievement	'Have you got that right?'
	'Well done; that was good.'
	'Good, that's right.'
	'No, that's wrong.'
	'You've got them all right. Excellent.'
Individualism	'Don't copy.'
	'Don't help each other.'
	'Do it yourself.'
	'Do your own work.'
	'Stop cheating.'
Hierarchy	'Who got ten out of ten?'
	'Who got most?'
	'That's not so good as Neil's.'
	'How many did you get?'
Self-reliance	'Well, look it up.'
	'Go and find out.'
	'You *can* do it.'
	'Everyone should be able to do it on their own now.'

Once again these values are both commonly accepted as being important in society outside schools and seen to have a degree of commonsense justification within them. Competition has always been an excellent means of achieving simultaneous productivity and control in a classroom, as elsewhere, and encouraging self-reliance often results in some immediate pressure being taken off the teacher. Interestingly, recent observational studies have shown that, even when teachers organise their classes for group work, the children in fact work as individuals for most of the time (Galton, Simon and Croll 1980). Control, noise levels, diagnosis and assessment may well be eased by this, but it is also significant that it promotes the individualism and the competition which underpin mass consumption.

Classroom practices thus 'make sense' at more than one level. Drawn by teachers from the cultural and social values of their society, they have also to be seen to 'work' in the reality of classroom life. To the extent that they do, then teachers will tend to reinforce such values and contribute to passing on the hegemony to a new generation.

Other points seem striking when considering the general absence of certain values which might be seen as potentially challenging the status quo and the prevalence of those which in fact can be seen as tending to support it. Thinking historically, the social values which were part of the taken-for-granted understandings embedded in daily practice in primary schools do appear to be similar to those which were explicitly articulated as a key part of the elementary tradition and of the rationale of educational expansion in the nineteenth century. Such values appear to remain despite innumerable changes in other aspects of schooling. Although few teachers would recognise themselves as playing a role in processes of social control, most of the teachers interviewed at Moorside acknowledged the importance of 'preparing the children for life' and expressed aspects of that task in terms which were at times reminiscent of nineteenth-century educators, in content if not in style. For instance, Mrs Jones, commenting on neatness and tidiness, explained:

> I think both neatness and tidiness are important. I think they've got to be. You've got to think about the fact that you're basically preparing them to be adults, to be acceptable adults in society with rules which have been laid down not necessarily by you or by anybody else, they've just grown that way, it's just the way society is and what society dictates. If they are neat and tidy people they'll get on much better themselves and perhaps contribute more too.

And Miss Newsome, commenting on respect for teachers, stated:

> I think it's good for the children to have respect for any adults, whoever they are. There has to be a certain distance if we're going to get on at school and they'll find this anyway when they grow up and leave school to get jobs . . . so it's a good thing for them to learn to understand it now. It wouldn't do if they waltzed up to their boss on the first day and said 'hi' as if he was one of their friends, would it?

What we have here, then, are social values being propagated which do relate to the skills and attitudes that are necessary for the reproduction of a capitalist system. Indeed, in my opinion there is no doubt that Moorside Middle School, as an institution derived from and existing within a capitalist society, did reflect values which were generally supportive of the status quo within the taken-for-granted assumptions of both teachers and children. As I have suggested, that fact can partly be seen as reflecting the penetrations of the dominant hegemony into the sense of purpose and reality, particularly as held by the teachers. However, it is important to note that, while this conclusion suggests that certain latent tendencies of schooling exist, it says nothing about reactions to such tendencies, and, as we saw in Part 1, children's reactions take many forms, including rejection.

Grace (1978) has put the argument which I am making here very clearly. He suggests that, despite many changes in the surface structure of education (pedagogy, curriculum, building design, etc.), the deep structure is characterised by continuities with those existing in the nineteenth century. This is so because:

> The teachers themselves . . . remain in the same essential position in the matrix of class relations as did their Victorian predecessors. They find themselves at the meeting point of classes, at the point where 'official' culture with its understandings, values and world view meets alternative realities, where middle-class prescription meets working-class resistance.
>
> (Grace 1978, p.53)

This concept of resistance introduces a new, but very important, complexity. The point is that no hegemony is ever total or all-embracing. Because of the creativity and uniqueness of people there is always the potential for resistance to it, and for attempts to build alternative sets of values and assumptions. Thus the imagery of struggle and contest may be employed to describe events as people strive to overthrow or change a dominant hegemony which fails to serve their interests or fit in with their beliefs. Such attempts to penetrate the existing social order and to build a new one can originate at any scale—even in a classroom, staffroom or play-ground—and it is arguable that some of the teacher and child perspectives which have been discussed in previous chapters could be seen in this way (Apple 1982). What happens in a micro situation can affect the development of society as a whole.

CONCLUSION

In this chapter I have attempted to set primary schools within the wider context of society as a whole. We have seen that ours is an unequal society, that schooling is a political issue and that it has a role to play in wider social developments. From the point of view of teachers the interaction of the elementary and developmental traditions continues to produce dilemmas and sources of role conflict as goals such as teaching 'basic skills' vie with those such as developing individual growth and self-expression. The contrasting images of the child as inherently deficient and in need of instruction and of the child as inherently good and in need of experiences also survive intact.

We have also seen that control of the education system itself is tending to become more centralised and that many teachers have found the developments of the late 1970s and early 1980s difficult. On the one hand there have been pressures towards increasing accountability, towards opening schools up to the community, towards involving parents more and towards responding to local needs and conditions. On the other hand, government advocacy of a core curriculum and an emphasis on 'standards' in basic skills was felt in schools through the mediation of such agencies as HMI, local-authority advisers and the media. The period was thus one in which the expectations that people had of teachers developed rapidly despite the fact that the supply of resources declined. Thus children with special educational needs were to be integrated into all schools, computers were to be introduced, science and maths teaching were to be developed, health education and development education were identified, multicultural education was considered to be essential, language and literacy remained vital and an awareness of the need for quality in school-work increased. Meanwhile schools were closed, staff were redeployed, promotion became a rarity, books, paper and other resources became increasingly scarce, and schools went unpainted. Not surprisingly, teacher morale dropped (NUT 1982).

Better things may be around the corner, but in the mid-1980s it seems clear that the social context in which primary schools are located is one in which they are both under pressure *and* suffering from constraint. Furthermore, the pressure is likely to be inconsistent.

As we saw in Part 1 of this book, significant elements of the perspectives which both teachers and children develop in order to cope with classroom realities are, in a sense, pragmatic, with each seeking to maintain their self-respect through giving priority to particular interests in the immediate situation. In this chapter we have considered some of the macro factors which structure this micro situation of the classroom and the ways in which these have been developed recently. We might judge that in such difficult circumstances a degree of adaptive classroom pragmatism is inevitable. We have also seen, though, how the responses that teachers make to their situation both are influenced by and contribute to the dominant hegemony of our capitalist society. There is thus an ironic sense in which teacher and child adaptations may actually reinforce, in the long term, the structures to which they are responding. Such are some of the most important issues which link the social world of primary schools with society as a whole.

A second layer of social context, of course, is that of the school itself, and this is the subject of the next chapter.

6

Inside Primary Schools

INTRODUCTION

While the previous chapter attempted to locate primary schooling within the context of society as a whole, this chapter focuses on primary schools themselves. In particular it aims to investigate what has variously been called 'school ethos', 'climate' or 'institutional bias'—terms which have been used in attempts to encapsulate the rather intangible 'feel' of schools as organisations.

In this chapter I shall use the concept of institutional bias to refer to those understandings which grow up between teachers, pupils, parents and others about 'what a school is like' and 'what is done here'. In doing this I am consciously rejecting the notions of school ethos (Rutter et al. 1979) and school climate (Halpin 1966) because of the unquestionable impression of cohesion which they sometimes tend to convey and because of their weak treatment of the issues of power and influence in a school.

As with other parts of this book, the main parts of the chapter are intended to present concepts, ideas and forms of analysis which have been generated from the study of particular schools as cases rather than simply seeking to provide a more generalised review of types of primary-school organisation. I make no claims for the typicality of the cases and examples drawn on, but I would claim that the analysis raises some interesting and challenging issues.

Of course, the importance of this layer of contextualisation arises because the institutional bias of a school greatly influences the processes that take place within each classroom, for teachers and children cannot entirely detach or insulate themselves from the social conventions and assumptions which immediately surround them. To take an example, a student teacher about to begin a period of school experience will very often ask, 'But what is the school really like?'. This is not primarily a question about the school's formal structure, its lines of hierarchy and responsibility; rather it addresses the question, 'What will the school feel like to work in?'. Such a question is asked because when anyone visits a school they do not just enter a group of buildings representing a physical context. They also become participants in a social context in which cultural patterns and social understandings are highly significant. Any stranger is, as Schutz (1964) suggested, immediately exposed to the problem of how to conduct him or herself when social conventions and assumptions are unfamiliar, and it is to this problem that a student teacher or any other visitor must respond. Of course a school is not, in itself, anything more than a particular collection of resources and people. We must be careful, therefore, not to reify any such institution by implying that it has some intrinsic character or quality in itself. To avoid this a symbolic interactionist view of the formation of an institutional bias will be taken in this chapter. Such a view asserts that an institutional bias is the product of the creative activity and negotiation of people within a school, bearing in mind not only their degree of power, influence and interpersonal skills but also the effect of the various external constraints and pressures which bear on them.

In essence, then, an institutional bias is a type of generally shared knowledge, a diffuse and often tacit set of social understandings or cultural assumptions about a school and about practices in it. These conventions are developed over time and frequently reflect the perspectives of those with most power and influence in the school. In the long term they often become routine and taken for granted. They may thus be experienced by new teachers, pupils, parents or others almost as social facts about a school and thus as features to which they must adapt. In this way an institutional bias influences behaviour in the present and is passed on to influence the future. On the other hand, because of the nature of its social origin, an institutional bias can never become entirely 'set' or static. It will always be subject to a degree of challenge and negotiation from those involved in the school and will thus have its own developing history as shared meanings are reworked.

The chapter begins by setting the scene with a factual review of the most important characteristics of primary schools and their staffs and a consideration of some of the more formal organisational features which exist, including a discussion of the leadership styles of head teachers. It then moves on to the analysis of the influence of head teachers on institutional bias. This is then balanced by a section on class teachers, their possible sources of power in the school and their negotiating and adaptive strategies. The chapter concludes with a discussion of the influence of children, non-teaching staff, parents and governors on the institutional bias.

PRIMARY SCHOOLS AND THEIR STAFF

It is worth while to begin with a brief factual review of some of the most important characteristics and variations among primary schools and their staffs.

In 1981 there were 20 993 schools in the primary age range in England and Wales. This was the total of all types of school deemed 'primary' by the Department of Education and Science, i.e. infant, first, infant/junior, first/middle, junior and 8–12 middle schools. Table 6.1 provides detail on school size and also shows that about half of the schools were of the 'through-primary' type in being either infant/junior or first/middle. Over 60 per cent had between 100 and 300 children on their rolls, which implies a small teaching staff in those schools of between four and twelve teachers. Of course, there are many other full-time and part-time staff who contribute to life in a primary school: caretakers, cleaners, cooks, kitchen staff, the school

Table 6.1 *Numbers of schools deemed primary with the following numbers of full-time pupils on the registers.*[a]

	Up to 25	26 to 50	51 to 100	101 to 200	201 to 300	301 to 400	401 to 600	601 to 800	801 to 1000	Total
Infant	19	85	546	2510	554	29	1	—	—	3744
First	99	299	424	1139	717	188	52	—	—	2918
Infant/junior	258	1054	1779	2831	2475	902	347	23	—	9669
First/middle	2	2	12	65	163	83	57	4	—	388
Junior	—	6	42	661	1638	871	280	7	1	3506
Middle (deemed primary)	—	—	3	103	313	238	102	9	—	768
All schools deemed primary	378	1446	2806	7309	5860	2311	839	43	1	20993
Percentage of all schools deemed primary	1.8	6.9	13.4	34.8	27.9	11.0	4.0	0.2	—	100.0

[a]Calculated from DES *Statistics of Schools*, Jan. 1981, Table A3/81.

secretary, ancillary workers, etc. Even so, primary schools have always been relatively small institutions.

They have been becoming even smaller in recent years because the number of primary-school-aged children nationally has been falling since 1974, a decline which, as we have seen, has come at a time of financial cutbacks in education. These factors have had important consequences for teachers and schools. For instance, a problem has developed over long-term career structures so that in the early 1980s a relatively high proportion of primary-school teachers had achieved promotion to Scale 2 from the Scale 1 starting position, but were then finding it very hard to get further promotion. Job mobility has also been low, so that the average number of years spent by primary teachers in particular schools has been lengthening. Such stable staffs have also aged, and the age profile of the profession has thus changed shape. By 1990 three out of five teachers are expected to be over 40 years old. The point which has to be made clearly here, then, is that not only are most primary schools quite small institutions, but they have also been very stable, from the staffing point of view, in recent years.

As we have seen, these small and relatively stable institutions have been both criticised and financially squeezed in recent years so that, despite any philosophical rationale for school policies which may be articulated, head teachers and their staffs have undoubtedly felt under pressure. The result of these factors—small size, stable staff, and the necessity for a certain amount of defensiveness—has undoubtedly been to increase the significance of the institutional bias of schools for those learning, working and teaching in them.

It is worth noting, however, that the late 1980s and the 1990s are expected to produce a more changeable situation, since demographic trends indicate that the numbers of children of primary-school age will rise. Assuming that pupil–teacher ratios do not increase, the number of posts for primary teachers will also rise, with the result of greater staff mobility and increases in recruitment both from newly trained graduate teachers and from those returning to paid work having brought up their children. The patterns of job mobility, age and qualifications of primary-school staffs will thus take on new shapes, and this will undoubtedly influence the expectations which develop in schools.

One other set of basic factors which we should also note concerns the sex balance of school staffs. Teaching in primary schools is a predominantly female occupation, as Table 6.2 shows clearly, and this is particularly true for teachers of younger children. If the sex of non-teaching staff is also considered, the pattern is reinforced, for it

Table 6.2 *Full-time teachers in maintained primary schools.*[a]

	Men	Women	Total
Infant	216	26381	26597
First	2530	18493	21023
Junior/infant	18620	53143	71763
First/middle	1190	3425	4615
Junior	13353	25042	38395
Middle deemed primary	3591	6340	9931
Total	39500	132824	172324
Head teachers	11925	9068	20993

[a]Calculated from DES *Statistics of Schools*, Jan. 1981, Table A8/81.

is only among school caretakers that significant numbers of men are to be found. Of course the contradiction to this pattern is that a disproportionate number of head teachers and deputy head teachers are men. Indeed, it is not at all unusual to find schools where an all-female staff are 'led' by a male head teacher. Whatever the reasons for this (see Spender and Sarah 1980), it is bound to have consequences for the organisation and may introduce a further layer of demarcation between a headmaster and female members of his staff beyond that of their formal differences in status.

PRIMARY SCHOOLS AS ORGANISATIONS

Any approach to analysing the social context which school organisations represent has to take appropriate account of both formal and informal power and authority relationships. For this reason the nature of school leadership, which historically reflects the trends in such relationships, is of some relevance here.

There was a time in the last century when the ethos and practices in many schools were considered to be almost direct reflections of the perspectives and beliefs of their head teachers. Indeed Norwood and Hope (1909) suggested that headmasters were the 'autocrats of autocrats' and held positions of 'absolute power'. In his paper of 1956, Baron argued that although head teachers were no longer so universally authoritarian, they were still the 'pivot and focus' of any school and were still expected to 'lead if not to rule' by staff and pupils alike. Since Baron wrote this, the development of new management styles has continued at a rapid rate and these have become increasingly open, democratic and participatory, thus sometimes involving the whole staff in aspects of school decision-making (Gray 1982, Bone 1983). Despite this fact the formal and legal responsibility and power within a primary school still rest with the head teacher.

Since the vital structural fact of these legal responsibilities remains in their hierarchical cast, it is important to consider the more formal aspects of schools as organisations. A simple way to do this is to match primary schools against Weber's classic analysis of the characteristics of bureaucracies (Gerth and Mills 1948).

Among the key elements of a bureaucratic organisation which Weber identified are the following:

1. There is a hierarchy of positions and a structure of authority.
2. There is specialised training for the various functions carried out.
3. There is a clear career structure.
4. There are fixed rules and procedures.
5. People both within and outside the bureaucracy are dealt with impersonally.

Several aspects of this ideal type can be seen in primary schools. First, there is almost always a hierarchy of positions and a structure of formal authority. For instance, Fig. 6.1 shows the structure of Burns Road Infant School and the hierarchy which existed there regarding teaching staff. However, while the head teacher and deputy head teacher retained their formal authority position, it was cut across at other levels by the fact that the deputy head was also a class teacher and by the system commonly adopted in primary schools of allocating

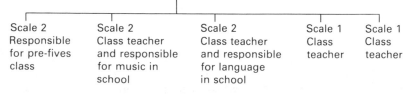

Burns Road Infant School

(140 children on roll: 4–7 years old)

Head Teacher

Deputy Head Teacher
(Class teacher and responsible
for science and maths)

Scale 2	Scale 2	Scale 2	Scale 1	Scale 1
Responsible for pre-fives class	Class teacher and responsible for music in school	Class teacher and responsible for language in school	Class teacher	Class teacher

Figure 6.1 *Structure of Burns Road Infant School.*

promoted or 'scale' posts of responsibility for particular curriculum areas throughout the school. In schools attempting 'team teaching' this spread of responsibility is often even a specific aim. The hierarchical idea also has to be modified when one distinguishes between the 'formal authority' which a teacher in a particular position may be entitled to and the 'functional authority' which a person in a low-status position may develop if they are able to create power and influence through their expertise.

Regarding Weber's point about specialisation, it would be fair to say that there is a degree of specialised training available for the various teaching positions held in primary schools, but it is most unusual for this to be systematically developed by local education authorities. It is far more common to learn 'on the job', and the extent of in-service courses, which varies in different parts of the country, is generally regarded as being small. Weber's third point is satisfied in that there is a clear career structure, but again there is a qualification in that it is *very* short. Because of the small average size of primary schools, it is not unusual for teachers to move from a Scale 1 probationary post to Scale 2, and thence to a deputy headship and headship. Another way of looking at this is to say that it is quite common for teachers to stay in the *same* position for many years and that the pyramid of posts in primary schools is very 'flat', with the important consequence that there are relatively few differences in the status of teaching staff compared with some other comparable spheres of professional activity. The career structure is thus clear but it is poorly developed.

Weber's fourth point, about the existence of fixed roles and procedures, also requires qualification when applied to primary schools. There are several problems here. First there is the tradition of granting teachers professional autonomy in their classrooms, which obviously works against standardisation. This tradition is partially derived from a second problem, which is that there are too many competing opinions about educational goals and policy to make it possible to 'fix' roles, rules or policies with any real long-term certainty. As we have seen, there are contradictions in what teachers expect and are expected to do, and they face daily dilemmas as they work (Berlak and Berlak 1981). In addition, and this also relates to Weber's final point, schools are directly concerned with personal change in people. In fact the 'developmental tradition' which has been explicitly taken up in the primary sector argues that children learn best when the teacher 'connects' with them personally as individuals. Thus, to be effective, primary schools cannot be impersonal in the sense in which Weber characterised bureaucracies, and schools are likely to remain relatively flexible and responsive with regard to rules and procedures. All this amounts to a significant degree of 'structural looseness' (Bidwell 1965) in primary schools and reflects the tension, at each level of the organisation, between the societal and individualised goals of education. Consideration of Weber's model thus usefully highlights certain aspects of primary schools even though it must be concluded that they do not match a formal bureaucratic model closely except perhaps in respect of the hierarchy of formal authority. Linking this with the concept of school ethos for a moment, it is undoubtedly the fact of the significance of the head teacher's dominant formal position which has led some researchers almost to equate the perspectives of head teachers with the school ethos itself (e.g. Sharp and Green 1975). I would suggest that this is an inadequate conceptualisation and that it is necessary to develop a form of analysis which, while capable of considering the critical influence of the head teacher, can also take into account the perspectives, influence and strategies of other major participants in the life of the school.

To do this I want to focus on the symbolic interactionist idea of negotiation (Strauss 1978) and, with it, to develop the concept of institutional bias (Bachrach and Baratz 1962). Together these ideas lend themselves not only to an analysis of the dynamic development of social understandings within a school but also to a consideration of the power relationships which are always involved. They thus provide a means of perceiving the processes by which taken-for-granted understandings about the values, aims, attitudes and procedures of a school are created by all the people who study, teach and work there.

We can note that the approach is grounded on three basic assumptions:

(a) that individuals in organisations play an active, self-conscious part in creating the sense of social order;
(b) that organisations are dynamic and constantly change as people interact together;
(c) that power is not absolute but changes in relation to conditions between people in different times and circumstances.

The emphasis here is thus on the fluid and developing nature of the social understandings which make up the social context of an organisation such as a school. The everyday realities and knowledge about a school are thus seen to be constantly defined and redefined by the people in it. In addition, the concept of institutional bias draws attention to the fact that any influential person or group within an institution may try to set up a 'mobilisation of bias' within the organisation so that particular social values and institutionalised practices are created. These limit the possibilities for action and change to issues which are believed by that person or group to be comparatively innocuous to them. In other words, power is used to influence assumptions, to set parameters and to protect interests.

The issue raised here thus concerns the processes by which taken-for-granted understandings and routine institutional practices can come to reflect the social values of those with most power and influence within a school. Of course, it remains likely that in most primary schools the person with most influence will be the head teacher, and in such a case it leaves teachers, parents, ancillary staff and others negotiating only *within* the framework created by the head teacher's influence and power.

An analysis of the institutional bias of any school using this approach raises a number of questions. What is the nature of the institutional bias and how is it formed? Is it the case that the head teacher has a particular degree of influence? How is the institutional bias maintained? Given that it will be experienced partially as a 'social fact' by teachers, parents and children, how do they negotiate within it and negotiate to change, develop or overturn it?

The sections which follow will address these issues. The first focuses on the influence of head teachers in the creation of an institutional bias.

HEAD TEACHERS AND INSTITUTIONAL BIAS

Perhaps the most detailed sociological study of the influence of a head teacher on a school is that of Burgess (1983) and, despite the fact that the school which he studied was a comprehensive secondary school, it is of interest here. Indeed, the head teacher, Mr Goddard, taught a significant amount each week and involved himself energetically in many school activities in a way which might even impress some of the many hard-pressed primary head teachers who teach a class full-time. According to Burgess, a head who participates in the school to this extent:

> . . . takes on the role of the educational supercook who blends together ideas that have been derived from teaching experience, discussion, conferences and reading.
>
> (Burgess 1983, p.48)

Burgess suggests that the result in Mr Goddard's case was that he was able to 'define the school' and 'create an identity' for it.

There are many primary-school head teachers who seek to do exactly the same thing. For instance, King (1978) describes the efforts of Miss Fox, head of Langley Infant School, to maintain an image of the 'high standards' which were both required and achieved in her school. He describes the view which Miss Fox had of parents— 'interested, informed and ambitious' and '75 per cent professional'— and the steps which she took to show parents that their children were 'successful', such as providing concerts by the hand-picked school choir and recorder consort and the country dancing display which was 'the result of months of practice and a masterpiece of social control'. The expectation which Miss Fox had, of high levels of success and high standards of behaviour, was felt as a direct pressure by the teachers. King describes how they were urged to 'stretch' the children, how levels of attainment were compared between classes to indicate teacher success and how they feared censure from Miss Fox. At another infant school studied by King, Burnley Road, the situation was significantly different. Many families in the catchment area of the school were considered to be deprived and teacher expectation of the children's behaviour and academic achievement was low. The head teacher, Mrs Brown, aimed to support the families and children. Thus she 'put on her smile' to greet parents at the start and end of school, dealt with problems, advised on health and financial matters and facilitated between parents and external agencies such as the school doctor, social workers, speech therapist, educational psychologist, social security officer, police and health visitors. Within the school she 'exercised only light control over the teaching methods of the teachers'. She required no weekly or termly records from them and, rather than pressurising them, she developed a skill at obtaining extra money from the local authority so that they had 'all the materials and facilities they wanted'. Regarding the children, she tried to overcome their lack of academic success by creating 'an alternative success system' of creative or craft work, with an annual public exhibition. While the teaching staff at Langley were described by King as being 'mildly anxious' as they pursued the cause of high standards, those at Burnley Road, with their 'professional equanimity, pleasantness and affection', were more inclined to ignore poor behaviour when it came their way and praised such 'improvements' as they could.

Clearly the institutional bias in these two infant schools was quite different, with very significant effects on the atmosphere and work context which they provided. Although the nature of the pupil intake of each school is important in King's analysis, it is through the perspectives and policies of the head teachers that he seeks to explain the major social assumptions and educational priorities which were predominantly maintained in each school.

Obtaining empirically based data about something as intangible as institutional bias is not easy, but one excellent opportunity to gain a concise impression of the ethos of a school is provided by the study of assemblies. There are several reasons for this, again some of which have been discussed by King (1973, 1984), and although he had secondary schools in mind his analysis is relevant here. King suggests that assemblies are forms of ritual symbolising three things: the modes of behaviour expected of pupils, the cultural values which the school attempts to transmit and, most importantly, the basic authority relationships within the school. They thus act as part of the system of social control in the school and are likely to reflect salient aspects of the institutional bias. Of course, looked at another way, assemblies may be seen as a means of expressing the sense of community which makes up the school, and this is perhaps a particularly common feeling in primary schools. In addition, assemblies are religious events because of the legal requirement of the Education Act 1944 and, even though in many schools this requirement is broadly interpreted, it is still generally observed. The result, as King (1984) puts it, is that:

> there is a fusion between the religious, communal and authority presentation purposes of the assembly. The school community is the body of worshippers, worship sanctifies the community and the idea of the school as community is legitimised by these connections. The authority of the head teacher is fused with the authority of religion.
>
> (King 1984, p.87)

School assemblies highlight an institutional bias not only because they provide an occasion for transmitting and maintaining the values and perceptions of the head teacher and senior staff, but also because, being regular activities involving large numbers of children, the social stability or control which the institutional bias provides is often called for to maintain order. This is seen in comments such as:

Head teacher   Come in more quietly please. We don't make a lot of noise like that in school, do we?

Let us look at some examples of the contribution of head teachers to an institutional bias in more detail.

We can begin with Summerlands Infant School, built in the late 1950s and serving a council estate on the edge of a northern industrial town. The school staff had been very stable, with several teachers, including the head teacher and her deputy, having taught at the school since it opened. Only two members of the nine teaching staff had taught there for less than five years. The institutional bias at the school was very strong and consistent in projecting a sound and traditional image; indeed advisers had recommended the school to me for study because it was a good, formal school which achieved sound results. I noted two substantive features of the institutional bias, the first of which was the role of religion. In assemblies there was no doubt that 'God' expected good behaviour and hard work and He was regularly called on to help achieve them. The second feature was the faith in formal pedagogy, in structured routines and an emphasis on basic skills. The head teacher's official position was that parents in the area wanted such methods and priorities, but her unofficial position, and that of her staff, was that children from the estate *needed* order and standards to compensate for their 'deprived' home backgrounds. It was felt that the school could provide a much-needed security through firm routines and organisation and could also make up for the 'lack of standards and values' at home by providing discipline and moral instruction.

The head teacher saw the school as a coherent community and as the means by which such goals were to be achieved. In fact, so strong was her concern to develop the identification of the children with the school that 'its birthday' was celebrated each year. I observed one of these celebrations.

Example: A school birthday party
Eight classes were drawn up in the school hall in the horseshoe shape which was normal for assemblies. The teachers sat behind them and 'settled down' those shuffling about or otherwise 'not helping'. Tension grew waiting for the entry of the head teacher and it was not until everyone was settled that a signal was given, the background music was turned off and the headmistress entered. She explained that this was a 'party' because of the school's birthday, and she produced matches and a taper with which to light 17 candles which were arranged with some attractively wrapped parcels in the centre of the horseshoe. To symbolise the school community, candles were then lit by the head, deputy head, a retired teacher, the caretaker, the school secretary, one of the kitchen staff, a past pupil, the oldest child, the youngest child and then one child from each class. Clapping broke out, and some talking which received a reprimand—'now don't spoil it, you want to give the school *your* present by sitting nicely and being good'.

Three children's songs were happily sung with full participation, and then excitement grew as the moment came when the school's presents were to be given out. First, the head teacher explained that she was giving these presents to the school, and that there would be some for each class, then, with much ooh-ing and aah-ing, the labels on the presents were read out. The presents were collected in turn by a selected child from each class and delivered to their teacher. There were two for each class, to be opened back in their classroom.

The head teacher then drew the celebration together: 'So let's sing 'Happy Birthday' to *us*, because *we* are the school; yes, we are the school.

> Happy Birthday to us,
> Happy Birthday to us,
> Happy Birthday dear School,
> Happy Birthday to us.
>
> Happy Birthday to us,
> From good friends and true,
> May God's love go with us,
> Happy Birthday to us.

Three cheers were given, and the head teacher dismissed each class in turn. Later, in the classrooms, the presents were opened; most classes got a jigsaw and some aprons. The teachers did not know what they were going to get, but every year they received a part of that year's school requisition in this way.

This is a particularly clear example of a strategy which is frequently adopted by head teachers to establish both their authority and a sense of order and commitment in their school. In the ceremony, the school and everyone involved with it is treated as a living family led by the head teacher. The school is seen as enduring—having connections into the past and into the future; it is benevolent—inviting the children to its party, caring for them, sharing its presents; it is personified—like children it has its birthday, and we must 'be kind' to it and not misbehave. In later discussion with teachers at the school it became clear that the head teacher had been both skilled and consistent in developing these themes over many years. She had the support of most of the staff and impressed them with her commitment. As one teacher put it, 'We know just where we are and what we are trying to do'.

Of course an institutional bias may not necessarily be so coherent, despite the efforts of a head teacher, and this can be illustrated by the example of Moorside Middle School. We can begin with an account of an assembly conducted by the head teacher, Mr Smith.

Example: An assembly
(In this example numerals will be used for further reference.)

Mr Smith stands at the front of the hall holding his books; he looks at the children hard, trying to convey messages about the manner of entering the hall. The children file in.

Mr Smith (1)   Who's talking now? . . . Shut up. Stop your din and shut up . . . I'm going to smack somebody in a minute . . . You didn't hear what I said . . . I said

that when you come in here you sit down and shut
up . . . now when I've taken a moment to stop being
cross . . . we'll start. Right.

A hymn is projected onto the wall using a slide projector, but it is
difficult to read because of the sunlight. The children sing 'Take it to
the Lord in Prayer' rather badly.

Mr Smith (2)   That was terrible. We'd better check these words; it's
not that you don't know the tune; it's that a lot of you
can't read well enough.

Mr Smith goes through the words. He appears to be unaware of the
quality of the projection, but no-one dares to tell him. The hymn is
sung again.

Mr Smith   Right, now who can tell me a story about friends?

Mr Smith introduces the theme for the assembly, but there is no
response to his question.

Mr Smith   What? Nobody out of 600? Come on, you all play with your
mates. Oh (a hand has gone up), OK John.

John tells the story of the Good Samaritan.

Mr Smith (3)   Yes, OK, you can have some house points then. What
house are you?

John   Johnson.

Mr Smith   What colour is that? I can't remember all these names.
Oh, it doesn't matter. Ask your teacher for some.

Mr Smith's tone of voice changes and this signals the explicitly religious
part of the assembly. There are prayers about helping each other,
about friends and about wars. The prayers finish with:

Mr Smith (4)   Oh Lord, help us to be kind and thoughtful towards
each other in the playground.

Mr Smith reads a grace and moves on to the administrative part of the
assembly:

Mr Smith (5)   [loudly] *Now*, there's too many fights going on. Even
fights being *arranged* by silly boys and girls. I know
there may be some justification for fighting like boxing
or wrestling but there is no reason for fighting just to
prove who's the best fighter in the school. Anyway
[grins] I think you'll find that I can beat you all when I
get my cane out. I'm not having you running about the
woods and showing the school up. I've also had a
complaint from a lady about running through gardens.
Don't do it. Do you understand? Don't say you haven't
been warned.

(6)   Where's Timothy Leach?

Timothy raises his hand looking extremely worried.

Mr Smith   Come on out here. [long pause] I've got your certificate for cello playing. [laughs] I bet you thought you'd had it!

There is relief and laughter all round. The certificate is presented and Timothy is clapped.

Mr Smith (7)   Have we played any netball or football games at all?

Children   Yes, netball.

Mr Smith   OK, who did we play . . . St John's? . . . Did we beat them?

Children   Yeah, yes. [numerous calls]

Mr Smith   OK, give them a clap.

(8)   Right, stand—no—sit down again. There are far too many children coming to school late. You must be here by nine o'clock. Right, stand.

The children leave noisily.

In this example at least four aspects are immediately apparent. First, there is the use of authoritarianism to preserve the order of the assembly (1, 2, 5, 8). There are several threats, which are used partly to counter the disturbance caused by discontinuities in the planning and sequencing of the assembly. For instance, there is the hymn-reading problem (2), the noisy entry (1), the muddled exit (8) and the several changes of mood between threat and appeal, instruction and prayer. The headmaster shows a casual approach to the house system (3) by not remembering the house colours, and at (7) he indicates his vagueness about inter-school sports activities. At (4) a link between religion and order in school is made. At (6) Mr Smith makes a joke at Timothy's expense. This joke was not untypical of Mr Smith's strategies in his dealings with the children and, while his authoritarian style was regularly used, he also obviously enjoyed joking and 'messing about' with the children. For instance at a jumble sale he acted the part of a market stallholder calling out the bargains; when a snatch of music was heard in the dining-hall he danced with his plate to his table; and when the Christmas pantomime was on he revelled in the role of an Ugly Sister and delighted in custard-pie routines. As we have seen, in assemblies a more direct use of his power as head teacher was usual, but this was sometimes combined with a degree of casualness which tended to puncture the atmosphere and undercut his authority in the eyes of the children.

In fact the children found him rather confusing. As one of the teachers commented:

> *Mr Matthews* The children don't quite know how to take him; it gives them a sense of being frightened of him because they don't know how to take him; it doesn't lead to a happy situation in his lessons or in a lesson he walks into . . . because one minute he can be fooling around with 'em and laughing and joking and the next he's come on so strong they just don't know where they are . . . there doesn't seem to be a gradual drift from one to the other; there's never any stereotyped situation; one day he'll react to a situation in one way and the children may expect that another day, but it doesn't always follow . . .

Unfortunately Mr Smith's enforcement of the rules and instructions which he gave was not always consistent either. His well-worn phrase 'and don't say you haven't been warned' had become a joke among some of the children, which illustrates the degree to which they knew that, despite forceful statements about such things as dropping litter, running in school, keeping off the grass bankings, fighting, lining up for dinner quietly, etc., they could expect a far less forceful follow-up. Thus, for many of the children, the obvious conclusion was simply not to get caught.

> *Robert C.* Well, like, if he's in one of his moods then you'd better watch out, but normally it doesn't matter much.

Such an analysis shows the extent to which the inconsistencies between Mr Smith's casual, genial entertainer and his authoritarian strategies were understood, and of course many of the children had developed their own strategies to fit in with them.

The teaching staff at Moorside held rather mixed views about Mr Smith. On the one hand he was greatly liked, particularly by the male members of staff, for his openness, for his professional support and for his sense of humour. On the other hand, the staff sometimes found him as confusing as the children did. Mr Taylor, for instance, commented about the staffroom:

> *Mr Taylor* It's a very happy, relaxed staffroom. It's very nice, and it's one of the reasons why I don't want to move, 'cos it's very good . . . and this atmosphere I think is fostered by the Head; Neil [Mr Smith] is very relaxed, he couldn't stay out of the staffroom and shut himself in his office like many headmasters do . . . he comes in the staffroom . . . and seeing him relax I think has an effect on us as well. The only thing is I don't think the teachers have as much respect for him as they should have. People can like him though; he's more of a friend; he's more like a teacher colleague than a headmaster.

This last point particularly worried some of the senior staff:

Mr Matthews	One minute he's in there laughing and joking and the next minute he's trying to assert his authority.
Mrs Goode	That's the thing about Neil [Mr Smith]; he's far too open in the staffroom for his own good. He tells people things that he has no need to and all this playing about doesn't set much of an example either.

The events which prompted the latter comment followed a particularly 'heavy' assembly on the subject of litter, keeping the school tidy and 'being sensible'. However, at playtime in the staffroom that day Mr Smith entertained the staff by sliding full ashtrays, in the manner of shove-halfpenny, down the central table and aiming at the salt and pepper near the table edge. In ways such as this he stimulated relaxed comment and humour and he involved himself with his colleagues in a way which certainly diverted attention or compensated for frustrations.

Mr Rowe	He makes for a lot of difficulties but he's a great laugh sometimes.

If this style did not always stimulate great respect, it did have the effect of developing a local reputation for the school as being a very happy place to work.

A more serious strategy which Mr Smith adopted with staff was the use of pragmatism, and on this issue it is worth recalling that the school was large, with over 600 children on the roll, and was organised into year-based 'units', each with a leader. These units were physically separated as part of the school's design and over time they had become relatively autonomous and different in pedagogic style. Because it was sometimes difficult to avoid conflicts in approaches between these units from becoming apparent, Mr Smith would often make decisions on a unit-by-unit basis. This was a perfectly conscious policy decision on his part to avoid disturbances:

Mr Smith	I'm a great believer in give and take . . . it has to be . . . otherwise you get so many of these conflicts . . . It's not necessarily good or necessarily moral or ethical, but it's pragmatic . . .

However, part of the rationale for this policy was also more personal:

Mr Smith	You can break an icicle but you can't break a piece of wire . . . and whatever happens I'm going to survive, as far as I can, myself.

Mr Smith's pragmatism was interpreted by some staff as a desire for a 'quiet life'.

Mr Matthews   What he's actually decided on will depend on what
group of staff he's been with; he'll say one thing to one
and another thing to another group to try and please
both ways . . . but if they have to get together then
obviously there's a conflict . . . so trying to please
everybody doesn't always work.

I tend to find his attitude is rather 'anything for a
quiet life' as opposed to sometimes asserting his
authority on a certain issue . . . and I personally
would find it far more acceptable if he took more of a
lead . . . it's very difficult, I think, when he has this
approach of being quite jovial etc. and never really
wanting to commit himself one way or the other; I'd
far rather a clear lead be set—by all means consult
with other people, for the smooth running of the place
that's got to be done—but the ultimate decision is his
and sometimes he just leaves things in the air.

Mr Taylor   All the units do things differently. That's the one major
complaint I have about the system . . . nobody knows
what anybody else is doing . . . he doesn't ask the
people in charge of, say, science or environmental
studies to order the systems throughout the school, so
the kids might do things more than once in different
units, simply because we don't know. It's muddled.

The institutional bias at Moorside thus reflected the perspective,
personality and strategies of the head teacher. It sustained diversity
in attitudes, values and procedures among a large staff and among
units, but bound them together in what was generally regarded as a
happy and relaxed staffroom. The head teacher confused both the
children and the staff with regard to 'school rules' and other social
expectations because of his inconsistency. On some occasions each
felt anxiety, with most of the children aiming to keep out of Mr
Smith's way and most of the staff aiming to 'keep quiet'. For all this
there was a partial acceptance of the relative incoherence that
characterised the institutional bias of the school among the staff and
also an appreciation of some of Mr Smith's difficulties. As Miss
Newsome put it, with regard to the children:

Miss Newsome   I think deep down he really wants to be a 'nice'
person that they can relate to and have a bit of fun
with . . . and then he turns round and he sees
himself as the headmaster of a big school who really
is the king-pin and therefore must act, and people
must know how to speak to him . . . he's pulled two
ways.

Like most head teachers, Mr Smith was in fact pulled in far more than
two ways. However, to understand this we would have to attempt to

locate the school and his period of headship in its wider social context and also to show how his values, beliefs and biographical background influenced his decisions (see Pollard 1981). Although this is an interesting topic, the issue of the contribution to an institutional bias of other people in a school is more important to our present concerns.

CLASS TEACHERS AND INSTITUTIONAL BIAS

As we have seen, the influence of head teachers on an institutional bias is bound to be great because their status and position normally legitimise any initiative which they may take and because of their power to counter other proposals. They are thus well placed to set and maintain the parameters of routine action and conventional practices in a school within the range of their own interests. However, they do not have a completely free hand, since everyone in a school is, by sociological definition at least, a participant and will make a contribution of some sort to the sense of social order which develops. While this contribution may simply be to accept or reinforce an existing institutional bias, it could also be to bypass, subvert or challenge it. Having looked at various sources of class-teacher power, I will therefore focus this section on examples of teachers adopting such strategies.

I have argued that an institutional bias is the product of negotiation between participants in an organisation, but of course the whole concept of negotiation hinges on the proposition that each party has a degree of power which must be taken into account by the other. We must therefore pay some attention to the sources of the power of class teachers, such as it is. At the most fundamental level their power derives from the fact that they work at what used to be called 'the chalk-face'. They teach and have contact with children far more than any head teacher can manage (excluding the teaching heads of very small schools). Head teachers are thus in a position of being largely dependent on their class teachers for the quality of the education provided in the school, and this can give class teachers a significant degree of power, particularly if a head teacher is vulnerable or is anxious to establish a reputation. To obtain graphic evidence of this fact one has only to talk to a new head teacher. Almost always one hears an account of staff resistance to new ideas and of the new head's attempts to counter 'inertia'. An investigation of such a situation is likely to reveal a process of negotiated transition between one institutional bias and another, with the new heads using their power to initiate and the existing staff—if adjusted and adapted to the routines and conventions of the previous bias—seeking to parry, evade, delay and otherwise defend their interests, attitudes and established practices.

A second, but related, source of class-teacher power is the tradition of teacher autonomy, a tradition which still remains strong in primary schools despite open-plan design and collaborative teaching approaches. As King (1984, p.91) put it, 'teachers' autonomy in the classroom is often used to tell other people to mind their own business'. Of course the feeling that teachers should be relatively autonomous is a central part of the idea of teaching as a 'professional activity', and any serious encroachment on the autonomy of a teacher is quite likely to be seen as a threat to the profession generally. It may thus receive opposition not only from other staff but also from the teacher unions. Head teachers' power is thus circumscribed by this convention of classroom autonomy in a significant way.

Alliances between staff form a third source of class-teacher power, particularly in larger schools. The bases of such alliances can obviously vary from those which focus on specific issues to those which reflect more wide-ranging departmental or ideological interests. This topic has not received detailed study in primary schools, but the work of Ball and Lacey (1980), who compared the influence of the English departments in four comprehensive schools, is interesting. They suggested that the institutional 'strength' of these departments, as indicated by their influence on policy and their levels of resource allocation, was related to the degree of coherence and consensus within each department. It is not at all uncommon to find the same phenomenon in primary schools, where staff in a particular area of 'strength'—be it junior department, nursery unit, year group, curriculum area or simply a group of staff with strong beliefs—are able to exert an influence on the school which is quite disproportionate to their number.

The final source of class-teacher power which I will identify here is also significant; I refer simply to the knowledge, competence and skill of being a very good teacher. There is no doubt that power can be, to an extent, 'created'. It is thus possible for teachers to earn the respect of colleagues, including head teachers, through the quality of the work they do, and they are thus able to influence the school as a whole. This development of functional authority may be supported by in-service study, and even by qualifications such as advanced certificates, diplomas or degrees. However, the crucial factor is always likely to be proof of an exceptional classroom competence against which other teachers can match their experience. The four sources of teacher power which I have discussed—the fact that class teachers do most actual teaching, the tradition of classroom autonomy, the possibility of alliances and the opportunity to influence others through exceptional competence—appear to amount to a considerable resource. However, a major qualification must be made, for, while it is possible for class teachers to use their influence to promote change, it is far more common for their power to be used to resist or qualify the initiatives of a head teacher or senior staff. The point here, of course, is that the activity of junior members of staff is circumscribed by their status and position. While it is normally regarded as being perfectly legitimate for them to comment on and influence school policy or procedures when they are directly affected, it is usually considered less appropriate for them to propose, suggest or initiate anything on issues which might affect other people. This means that the power of class teachers to influence an institutional bias tends to be used defensively, and is sometimes not deployed at all.

In the second half of this section I shall discuss and illustrate four ways in which the power of class teachers may be employed with regard to an institutional bias. I have called these ways acceptance, bypassing, subversion and challenge.

Acceptance

Acceptance is the base-line position. It may indicate agreement with the attitudes, values and policies which are projected by the institutional bias in the school, but it could also indicate a decision to take the line of least resistance and 'live with' things as they are. This distinction is well illustrated by the teachers at Mapledene Lane Infant School, the school studied by Sharp and Green (1975).

Sharp and Green used interviews with the head teacher to describe what they called the 'school ethos'. In the first place the head teacher distinguished his school from more formal and traditional schools because of the 'care and concern shown for individual children', and he explained the school's aim as:

> . . . trying to develop a child and help him to mature and become a person rather than that he should be a good user of adjectives or doer of multiplication sums.

However, the working-class pupil intake of the school was regarded as being difficult and highly significant. As the head put it, 'the educational attainments of children are determined entirely by their backgrounds' and:

> much of what we do here in a school like this is compensatory education, we are trying to make up for, and compensate for, this kind of deprivation.
>
> (Sharp and Green 1975, pp.49–56)

Sharp and Green thus argued that the Mapledene ethos involved 'a fusion of . . . a child centred perspective towards education . . . [with] a social pathology view of the community from which [the] pupils were drawn' (Sharp and Green 1975, p.62).

Sharp and Green studied several of the teachers at the school in detail and thus provided examples of their perspectives and classroom policies in relation to the institutional bias. I will consider two of them briefly here: Mrs Carpenter, who accepted and agreed with the favoured school practices and the head's views, and Mrs Lyons, who accepted them but had serious misgivings.

Mrs Carpenter regarded the children's homes as being generally deprived and she was very ambivalent about the involvement of parents in the school. However, she 'was regarded as the ideal child-centred teacher within the school' (Sharp and Green 1975, p.76), aiming to provide children with wide experiences unhampered by a formal curriculum. Sharp and Green's data clearly show that she was very supportive of the institutional bias which the head teacher sought to project; she accepted and agreed with it.

Mrs Lyons, who was the deputy head, held similar views about the children and the deficiencies of their home backgrounds, but she took a rather different view on the type of pedagogy which was thus called for. Although respectful of each child she rejected 'complete informality and permissiveness' and affirmed 'the need for discipline' and structure. As Sharp and Green put it:

> She acknowledges the need for firm control from the top and [is] in favour of facilitating controlled participation from the pupils rather than leaving them very much to their own devices.
>
> (Sharp and Green 1975, p.89)

Now the important point for the present analysis is that these differences in attitudes and pedagogy were not publicly articulated by Mrs Lyons, nor were they a source of conflict. She was respected in the school and had the full confidence of the head teacher. Clearly she accepted the institutional bias of the school despite the fact that as deputy head she held a position from which initiatives for change might have been made. She decided to 'let things lie'. Mrs Carpenter and Mrs Lyons thus illustrate two alternative types of 'acceptance'.

Bypassing

The second, and more active, way in which class teachers may employ their power is through a strategy which I have called 'bypassing'. This involves a withdrawal from the institutional bias behind the defence of either autonomy of expertise, or both. At Burns Road Infant School one teacher consistently set herself apart from the others despite the open-plan design and collaborative philosophy of the school. This teacher was greatly admired for her enormous commitment to teaching, for her energy and for her skill and enthusiasm with music. However, the flamboyant pedagogy which she so much enjoyed was felt to be 'disturbing' in other parts of the school so that, rather than compromise on her principles and beliefs, she adopted the policy of 'just getting on with it' in her own classroom. She was thus effectively able to bypass the conventions, attitudes and routine practices of the school because of her personal qualities. However, bypassing is not dependent on being exceptional, and there are undoubtedly some long-serving teachers in primary schools who, because experience is often seen to strengthen autonomy, are routinely able to bypass new developments as they occur. For converse reasons, bypassing is not a strategy which is easily open to probationers.

Bypassing can also be adopted by whole groups of staff on occasion, and some of the year-group units at Moorside Middle School provided examples of this. It may be recalled that the institutional bias at Moorside was rather incoherent—a fact which the staff attributed to the lack of 'clear guidance' and to the pragmatism of the head teacher. However, within the parameters which the head teacher did set, some teachers found a collective way of producing a partial coherence. For instance, Mrs Jones, the leader of the fourth-year unit, commented to me that, despite the:

> . . . lack of consistency in the school . . . all three teachers working with me have the same standards . . . and whenever you have that, you've got an unwritten rule and you don't have to write down any rules, it's *there* and the children respond automatically.

This group of staff had indeed created a high degree of routine in their unit. Attempts were made to enforce rules consistently and there was an air of ordered purposefulness. The children generally complied with the expectations of the unit and it was regarded as being 'fair, if a bit strict'.

To a lesser extent, the staff in other units had also acted to create teaching climates in which they could feel comfortable. However, the result was that because each unit's response was independent, each being an attempt to bypass vagueness perceived elsewhere, they tended to reinforce the inconsistency within the institution as a whole. Too much bypassing clearly made matters worse in this case.

Subversion

A third way in which classroom teachers may use their power is that of subversion. This may sound rather colourful and, while conscious attempts to subvert some established school practices undoubtedly occur, a common type of subversion comes from those who, while not accepting the institutional bias, have neither the sense of resignation required for bypassing nor the self-confidence or motivation to make a challenge to the status quo. Subversion has even been recommended as a progressive educational strategy (Postman and Weingartner 1969).

Unfortunately, documented examples of subversion are rare in sociological literature, although a vivid sense of it is conveyed in the 'social dramas' at Bishop McGregor Comprehensive School which are described by Burgess (1983) and the attempt of a liberal teacher to 'work within the system' to 'get into a position of power' has been described by Grace (1978, p.138).

I shall illustrate subversion here with the case of Mr Harman, a teacher at Ashton First School. Ashton First School served a council estate and had a staff of fourteen teachers. Two basic groupings of staff were discernible. The larger group of teachers in their forties and fifties was well established. A key member of this group was the deputy head teacher. She had worked at the school for many years, had strong views on the need to provide 'skills and discipline' for the children from the estate, and had developed a highly routinised form of pedagogy. The attitudes and practices of this group can be taken as representing the institutional bias of the school. The second group consisted of four young teachers in their first school. They did not accept the values and priorities of the institutional bias and gradually sought to influence and change it. The chief instigator of such initiatives was a young man called Mr Harman, a somewhat unusual teacher of six-year-olds who had a social science degree as well as his teaching certificate.

Mr Harman derived many important elements of his views on teaching from reference groups outside the school. He had been influenced by his study of sociology and had incorporated it into a developed child-centred perspective. In particular, Mr Harman stressed the relativism of his own perspectives and the personal validity of the perspectives of other people. This was particularly so for groups to which he felt a commitment, and most importantly for the children in his class. For instance, he explained that 'the estate environment, which I find boring, they find endless delight in', and he applied this type of argument to a range of situations, including acknowledging the legitimacy of a child's feeling bored in class and finding something 'better' to do, because, as he put it, 'if they don't attend to what I'm saying then it may not have any relevance to them'. This theme recurred again and again in Mr Harman's attitude to the children, education and practical teaching, and it engendered a wide range of issues on which he disagreed with the older group of staff. For instance, Mr Harman felt that the priority of the school should not be on teaching skills or knowledge, but on 'learning how to think and how to learn'.

Mr Harman did not openly oppose the institutional bias but he did so implicitly through his work. In this he had the support of the group of junior staff. They were a close group who met socially out of school, played badminton together regularly, and spent a good deal of time discussing the children, the school and educational issues. Together with these 'allies' Mr Harman used his classroom autonomy to develop what he called an 'inspirational' way of teaching. Thus, while most teachers in the school held to their established routines and their focus on skills, Mr Harman was extremely flexible and focused on children's experience. The work of his class was always very immediate and direct while the work of other classes reflected much more teacher direction, 'polish' and concern for appearances. While the majority of classes 'practised' in a variety of workbooks, Mr Harman's children could be found immersing themselves in a range of activities—clay, sand, water, play, etc.—which, while not exceptional for many infant classes, were nevertheless not very common activities at Ashton. Although what went on was different in style and content, Mr Harman's classroom was not disorganised and the strength of his personality and projection meant that discipline problems were rare.

Such a style and such activities were understandably seen as a threat to established norms by many of the staff, and the deputy head actively opposed them in the staffroom. However, Mr Harman was more than able to express his educational philosophy not only with coherence but also with references to other authorities. In addition he was very active in the school as a whole. He started a variety of 'clubs' for children—chess, table-tennis, badminton, recorder; he coached the football team; he organised youth-hostel weekends for the older children; and he worked on a new maths scheme. The children liked his enthusiasm and his humour, and his concern for them was apparent to parents and other staff.

The eventual result of all this activity, in analytical terms, was that Mr Harman created a degree of personal power and influence. With the guidance of advisers, the head teacher, who for a time had distanced herself from events, came to recognise that many of the most worthwhile developments at the school were the result of Mr Harman's commitment and his skills. Although not overtly supporting him against the established staff, she began to take up some of his ideas and eventually she even promoted him.

Here, then, is an example of a type of successful subversion. With the support of his friends, Mr Harman used his autonomy, his competence and his energy to create an influence in the school. Through the quality of what he was doing, which was much favoured by local advisers at the time, he managed to undermine the sense of what was possible and what should be done at Ashton so that in the end even the head teacher began to be influenced by him.

Challenge

A challenge to an institutional bias is the final possible use of class-teacher power that I shall discuss here. Perhaps open challenges are not commonplace in primary schools, but they do emerge on occasions when teachers feel, as did several secondary teachers studied by Grace (1978), that they have 'a real sense of having to "fight" against the school as constituted, in order to achieve their pedagogic ends' (Grace 1978, p.184). An example of this occurred at Moorside and was reported to me by Mr Matthews:

> Mr Matthews   I aired my views in a staff meeting and I said that I thought some of the children were getting a bit too cheeky . . . you know that we should have a bit more of a lead on discipline and that lead should come from the top . . . and . . . I'd got backing from lots of people previously but come the staff meeting it was yours truly who spoke up; Mrs Graves backed me up a bit but . . . nobody else would actually say anything . . . and sort of . . . I was then in a situation where I was in direct confrontation with the headmaster . . .

A.P.	What did Mr Smith say about it?
Mr Matthews	Well, he asked if everybody was happy or if they weren't to say so . . . well, nobody said a word, so he took it that everybody was happy with the situation . . . and . . . er . . . he said, 'Well, I'm happy with the running of the school and everybody else seems to be, so . . .' I was sort of pushed out on a limb.

This teacher got nowhere having confronted the power of the head teacher directly. Probably the limits to the scope for negotiation were understood by his silent colleagues, and of course Mr Smith handled the situation skilfully by directly challenging other staff to join Mr Matthews.

Hargreaves (1981) provides what can be taken as another example of challenge in his development of the concept of 'extremist talk' in staffrooms. At Riverdale Middle School a young teacher called Mr Button expounded arguments containing elements of deschooling, Marxism and phenomenology, and directly confronted established educational views in the school. For instance, he described education as 'just an assault upon a child to make him conform with set aims' and argued that 'whether we like it or not, the purpose of education in society is to provide workers'. However, 'extremist talk' is not just a left-wing phenomenon, and at the same school Mrs Speaker also set herself apart from her colleagues by arguing that children should both be taught to conform to dominant values and be made 'as socially acceptable as possible'—a view which did not accord with the institutional bias of this new open-plan and participatory school. Data on the responses to these challenges by staff at Riverdale are not directly supplied by Hargreaves, but his discussion of another form of staffroom talk, 'contrastive rhetoric', supplies some clues. Rather than take an authoritarian, confrontational line to maintain the institutional bias, as did the head at Moorside, it appears that the senior staff at Riverdale set the boundaries of normal and acceptable practice by the ways in which they introduced talk of alternative educational practices into staffroom discussion. This they did in 'stylised, trivialised and generally pejorative terms' (Hargreaves 1981, p.309), thus connoting their unacceptability. For instance, the example of contrastive rhetoric given by Hargreaves is that of senior staff distorting and ridiculing various supposed practices at the highly innovatory Countesthorpe College. Hargreaves suggested that such staff used not only the *de jure* power which their position legitimated, but also an element of '*de facto* interactional power'. This was derived from their wide experience and knowledge, which was a crucial resource when employing contrastive rhetoric. However, we should not forget the influence of gender here either. Interactional power has been clearly shown to be skewed in favour of men in most situations (Spender 1980), and with the disproportionate number of men in senior positions in schools (see Table 6.2) this is likely to put more junior, female staff at a serious disadvantage in influencing events.

Perhaps too we have examples here of the strength of the influence of head teachers and senior staff whatever the leadership style. At the hierarchical Moorside the institutional bias was maintained, despite challenge, through the use of confrontational power. At Riverdale, a school which was committed to the principle of democratic decision-making, the same effect was achieved through the use of contrastive rhetoric. Attempting to directly challenge an institutional bias is obviously not easy.

OTHER INFLUENCES AND INSTITUTIONAL BIAS

Having considered the possible influence of teachers on an institutional bias in some detail, I aim now to review briefly the scope of various other participants in the life of a primary school.

The Children

The children in a primary school are in one sense relatively powerless. It is certainly only rarely that they are able to take an initiative regarding the establishment of social expectations and conventions. However, there are two ways in which they have a considerable effect. In the first place they bring social expectations to the school, and the institutional bias of the school will have to be developed to take these into account. An institutional bias will thus tend to be related to cultural forms within the school's catchment area, a fact which contributes to our understanding of the infant schools studied by King (1978) and referred to earlier in this chapter. In the case of Moorside the northern, predominantly working-class nature of the intake undoubtedly influenced the way in which 'rules' were projected and enforced, and this explains much of Mr Smith's forcefulness.

In a second respect, children can influence the form and nature of an institutional bias by their *response* to it and by what they learn about it. As we saw in the case of Moorside, the children lacked a clear indication of what was expected of them, and they were also very interested in what they could get away with. The result of this child awareness was that staff felt that it was essential to articulate certain basic rules regularly and forcefully. The children saw this in terms of 'things they're always going on about' and in a sense it defined an agenda, a terrain across which behaviour was constantly negotiated.

Dinner Ladies and Kitchen and Cleaning Staff

These important groups of support staff also respond and contribute to an institutional bias, though their influence is likely to vary. Dinner ladies, being non-professional, generally non-unionised and on relatively short-term contracts, are often of low status despite the fact that they often have children who attend the school. However, they may still have a considerable influence on playground activities during dinner-time. At Moorside they experienced many difficulties, since they were often attempting to control large numbers of children with no clearly accepted rules, few management skills and from their low-status position, which was always a structural weakness. The result was that they tended to be 'baited' by the children, to find control hard to gain, to lose their tempers and to become, in the children's eyes, 'right mad'. When they occur, such difficulties are likely to undercut the ability of dinner ladies to influence even dinner-time policies.

Kitchen and cleaning staff have a more secure role in a school. Their contracts are generally longer term, they are unionised, they are regarded as being more skilled and they have clear and differentiated jobs which are generally insulated from the children and yet which are essential to the smooth running of the school.

At Moorside, for instance, the caretaker and the cook were able to use the degree of power that their positions gave them to negotiate directly with the head teacher. Thus attempts to establish rules about such things as clearing away plates at dinner, how much 'had to be eaten', putting chairs up in the classrooms at the end of the day, not dropping litter in the playground, what to do with wet shoes indoors, etc., derived much of their impetus from the non-teaching staff who were directly affected by the consequences. The same influence was apparent at Burns Road Infants School, where the head teacher and teaching staff constantly felt it necessary to maintain rules which derived primarily from the concerns of non-teaching staff.

The contribution of other internal and external support staff, such as health visitors, welfare officers and particularly school secretaries, could be documented in a similar way.

Parents and Governors

Parents are, in analytical terms, in a very similar position to children in respect of influence on the institutional bias of a primary school. They have an influence by their very presence and social composition and because of the accountability which they can increasingly demand of a school. They are also able to respond to school events and school policies, and to negotiate and influence future policies. Thus parents can seek to have an effect on the institutional bias of a school through PTAs, through representation on boards of governors or through individual discussions with staff. Clearly they do so from a relatively powerless position, and they lack information about the internal workings of the school. It is therefore often the case that their influence can be exercised only within the parameters defined by the head teacher. At Moorside, for instance, parents were welcomed at parents' evenings to receive a report on their child, but otherwise played very little role in the life of the school. In an increasing number of primary schools, parental involvement has been developing rapidly in recent years, and obviously this will influence the institutional bias significantly. It is now common to find a head teacher leading 'parental partnership' innovations, with many other staff feeling vulnerable and defensive.

Governors occupy a more formal position than parents, but one which is variously interpreted. As Kogan et al (1984) found, in many cases their influence on the internal workings of a school is minimal, except where they are involved in staff appointments.

I have thus drawn attention to a number of groups of people who are able to exert some influence on the social expectations and institutional bias of a school through their actions. Of course, this influence is likely to be proportionate to their power in relation to that of other parties.

CONCLUSION

In this chapter I have focused on the concept of institutional bias and on the influences which contribute to the institutional bias of primary schools. I have argued that an institutional bias is likely to reflect the relative power of the participants in a school.

Despite the fact that senior teaching staff are likely to be particularly significant and that factors outside the school also apply constraints, we should not forget the images of contest, struggle or resistance which were introduced in the previous chapter. As I argued there, no hegemony is ever total or all-embracing; nor is any institutional bias. Subversion and challenge are teacher strategies which constantly push the development of the institutional bias onwards and press for further adaptations and negotiations. We should not forget either that such pressure can come from many directions. However, the most common cases are probably those of a new head trying to influence an established staff and a class teacher trying to influence an established head.

In any event, the institutional bias in a school represents a layer of social context, a 'negotiated order' which, although not immune to influence and action, has to be recognised as a present social reality by any participant in school life. It thus significantly influences and mediates the classroom action of both teachers and children.

We are now in a position to begin to pull together the various strands of the argument which have been presented in Parts 1 and 2 of the book. This is attempted in Part 3, which focuses on the ways in which teachers and children interact together as they respond to their situation.

PART THREE

INTERACTION

7

Coping with Classroom Life

This chapter is central to the analysis presented in this book in that it attempts both to relate many of the factors which have been considered so far and to provide a platform for further developments. The specific focus of the chapter on processes of teacher–pupil interaction derives explicitly from a symbolic interactionist theoretical framework. In other words, the chapter begins to identify how shared meanings and understandings develop from interaction in classrooms. Several of the concepts which are introduced will be important in following chapters, particularly those of coping strategy, working consensus and rule frame.

COPING: ROLE FACTORS AND MATERIAL CONSTRAINT

In Part 1 of this book an analysis of teacher and child perspectives was presented which included two important themes: role expectations and culture.

Beginning, then, with role expectations, there was a consideration of the ways in which the behaviour of teachers and children was socially ascribed and influenced. We looked at the way in which teachers in the late 1960s were encouraged to adopt the child-centred philosophy stemming from the Plowden Report, but later, in the 1970s, were urged to attune their teaching methods and the curriculum more to newly defined social and economic needs. We also looked at the ways in which childhood is perceived and the child role defined. We saw that there is a good deal of inconsistency in the social expectations of children stemming from adults' hopes and fears and their images of children as having elements of 'good' and 'evil'.

Of course, identifying such generalised features of socially ascribed roles does not help us in establishing how teachers and children actually do act. It simply supplies a layer of social context at the widest macro-societal level. The fact that they each face a range of pressures, expectations and exhortations stemming from various interest groups—parents, the government, the media, industrialists, educationists, etc.—simply identifies a layer of social context to which they must respond.

A second theme of the analysis which was contained in Part 1 concerned culture. Some aspects of the staffroom culture of teachers were described which, although very different in subject from the culture of children, showed many similarities. In each case shared understandings had grown up as a collective and subjective response to the situation in which the teachers and children found themselves. Each provided group support, a forum for interpreting events and a means, in some cases, of defusing and re-interpreting the pressure of social expectations so that they could be related to true 'reality' as known to 'members'. Each also provided, as a set of cultural expectations, a degree of social pressure on members themselves. Culture can thus be seen as mediating wider social expectations for both teachers and children.

In Part 2 we considered the social context of the classroom, first at a 'macro' societal level and then at an institutional or organisational level. At the societal level we saw how primary schooling has been influenced in its structures, its assumptions and its resourcing by its history, by the nature of the British system of national and local government and by the hegemonic climate of the times. At the organisational level we saw how those with most formal authority in a school could attempt to set up an 'institutional bias' and how this could be accepted, bypassed, subverted or challenged by others. Within this institutional bias, specific features of teacher and child culture would of course be developed.

Having reviewed these elements, it is now possible to relate them together diagrammatically (see Fig. 7.1). In this diagram we see the two main layers of social context which surround the classroom: that of society, its social hegemony and its history, and that of the school and the institutional bias. This is the overall context within which teachers and children act when in the classroom. Any action that they take must be specifically responsive to their role, for all its dilemmas, as socially ascribed by various interest groups in society at large and as mediated by cultural forms within the school. If we relate this

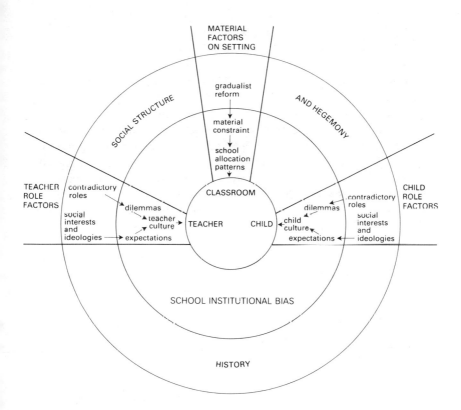

Figure 7.1 *Role factors and material constraints in a model of coping strategies.*

directly to the concept of coping strategy, what we have considered so far covers those factors which essentially 'have to be coped with'. They largely provide the constraint and the pressure (Hargreaves, A. 1978). However, any individual's action is far more than just a response to pressure and constraint.

COPING: BIOGRAPHICAL FACTORS

'Coping' is essentially subjective. Thus individuals can judge if they are or are not 'coping' only by reference to criteria which are part of their own perspective regarding their situation.

Of course people's perceptions of any situation will be patterned by various aspects of the culture around them, but for any individual there will be unique features depending on his or her biography, socialisation and previous experiences. We saw this in Chapter 2 when the self-images of Mrs Jones, Mr Matthews, Miss Newsome and other teachers were discussed. In each case a view of their own personality, character or 'type of person' existed which they related to their biography and to their discussion of favoured teaching methods and strategies. Similar examples could be drawn on for individual children.

The point, then, is that ultimately coping can be defined only personally, bearing in mind the background biography of each individual. This issue has been considered by Woods (1977) in terms of teacher 'survival'. He contends that teachers are often greatly challenged by their classroom work and that:

> . . . what is at risk is not only [the teacher's] physical, mental and nervous safety and well-being, but also his continuance in professional life, his future prospects, his professional identity, his way of life, his status, his self-esteem.
>
> (Woods 1977, p.275)

Woods' definition is wide, but at the heart of it lies the symbolic interactionist concept of 'self' deriving from the work of Mead (1934).

The crucial point in Mead's account of self is that its origin is social. Thus an individual's conception of 'self' is a product of interaction between his or her subjective experience and reflection on other people's responses—interaction between the 'I' and the 'me', as Mead put it. Individuals are thus active in childhood socialisation processes. These involve play, games and interaction and result in the

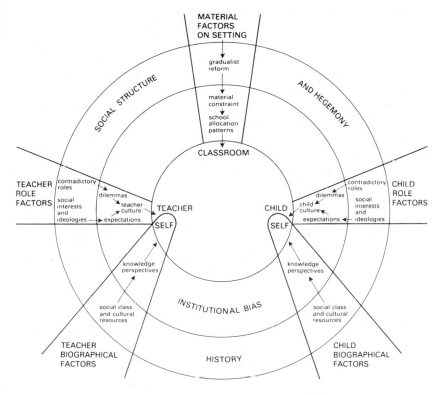

Figure 7.2 *Biographical, role and material factors in a model of coping strategies.*

creation of a sense of identity and of 'self'. Although the development of this sense of self is never entirely static, childhood experiences are formative. As Mead notes:

> We are individuals born into a certain nationality, located at a certain spot geographically, with such and such family relations, and such and such political relations. All of these represent a certain situation which constitutes the 'me'.

(Mead 1934, p.182)

Factors such as social class and cultural background are thus likely to be particularly influential in the development of the image of self which teachers or children hold as they enter the school and as they manage their 'presentation of self' (Goffman 1959) in the classroom. The concern to protect 'self' which Woods identified is of paramount importance in the potentially threatening context of the classroom. It is thus by the degree of success in defending self that classroom coping can be defined.

Lest this discussion seem rather abstract, we should recall that we already have some more detailed purchase on the issue, having identified in earlier chapters various facets of self which constituted interests-at-hand for teachers and pupils in the classroom.

The outcome of this analysis, then, is that Fig. 7.1 can be augmented by the addition of a biographical dimension leading from the structural and cultural position which influenced each individual's early socialisation, through the specific perspectives which they will develop regarding school, and to the particular sense of self which they will hold and present in the classroom.

In Fig. 7.2 we see an almost complete representation of a teacher and a child in a classroom. They face each other as unique individuals with a particular self-image. However, they are each subject to role expectations and dilemmas and they each act in the particular material context of their classroom.

COPING: STRATEGIES AND ACTION

Any analysis seeking to use the concept of coping strategy requires the two initial inputs which we have discussed. These are, first, regarding the context and situation which has to be coped with, and second, regarding the meanings and perceptions of those individuals who seek to cope. We have considered each of these aspects in the case of teachers and children, and this section therefore moves on to focus on strategic *action*—the creative response of an individual to his or her situation.

It is a central tenet of symbolic interactionism that action is based on meaning. W.I. Thomas expressed this as long ago as 1928 in his famous statement that 'if men define situations as real, then they are real in their consequences'. The point, then, is that any individual's action will be based on his or her 'definition of the situation'. Of course it is unlikely that a particular definition will actually *determine* a course of action; rather, as Harré (1974) has argued, it will legitimate a *range* of possibilities to be considered before a final decision to act is taken. This calculus is essentially a strategic one in which the actor considers his or her subjectively defined perceptions and his or her interests together with the likely impact and effects of alternative courses of action. As Blumer put it:

> In order to act the individual has to identify what he wants, establish an objective or goal, map out a prospective line of behaviour, note and interpret the actions of others, size up his situation, check himself at this or that point, figure out what to do at other points and frequently spur himself on in the face of dragging dispositions or discouraging settings.
>
> (Blumer 1971, p.12)

Of course, such strategic decisions are not taken afresh in each and every situation which arises. Indeed, many of them will be routinised by longer-term 'policy' decisions which teachers or children might make about how they will manage or 'front' their presentation of self in the classroom. These characteristic patterns of decision then become associated with identity. Strategies will also, of course, be influenced by the cultural context which surrounds each individual. Teacher or child culture of various types may well offer and legitimate particular types of strategy in preference to others. Indeed, in the case of teachers, Hammersley (1980) has even suggested that a 'technology' of teacher practices may be inherited in a school; this would be 'tailored to circumstances' and provide 'a repertoire of accounting procedures, typifications of situations and lines of action' (Hammersley 1980, p.58).

A coping strategy, then, is a type of patterned and active adaptation to a situation by which an individual copes. It is a creative but semi-routinised and situational means of protecting the individual's self.

One of the objectives in the chapters which follow is to demonstrate how each individual strategically 'juggles' his or her interests-at-hand in the ebb and flow of classroom processes to seek an overall level of satisfaction of self. However, this juggling occurs within the micro social context of the classroom which the participants themselves create as they strive to cope with each other. This brings us squarely to the issue of *inter*action.

CLASSROOM INTERACTION: THE POTENTIAL CONFLICT

Despite the diversity at detailed levels, there is a high degree of similarity in the fundamental structural features of primary classrooms. Thus most actual class sizes remain at between 25 and 35, most school days last about six or seven hours, most activities take place in classrooms, a relatively uniform curriculum is accepted as being appropriate, children are generally obliged to attend school, and the resources available in schools are relatively few. Within this context the participants must create their strategies and must seek to cope. As we saw in earlier chapters, in making their attempt, the teachers have the benefit of their socially sanctioned power while the children derive strength from their numbers. Thus teacher and pupil meet in the classroom with their roles partially defined but with emergent perspectives and interests which may not concur. In fact, as I have suggested before, there are good reasons for suggesting that, because of the basic differences in the structural positions of the two parties, there is always an inherent degree of conflict. Indeed, as we saw in Chapter 2, Willard Waller (1932) saw the fundamental teacher–pupil relationship as one of 'institutionalised dominance and subordination'.

We can get a sense of Waller's meaning by relating the classroom interests-at-hand of teachers and children together (see Fig. 7.3).

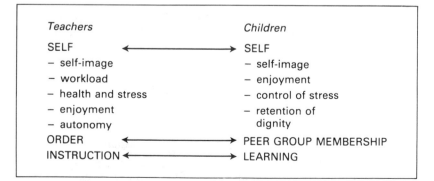

Figure 7.3 *Primary and enabling interests of teachers and children.*

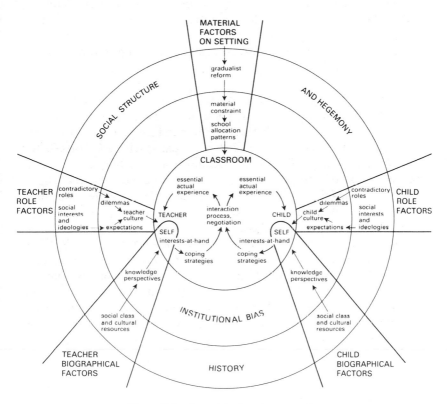

Figure 7.4   *A model of coping strategies.*

Clearly the potential for conflict is great. Each party has essential experiential concerns which may well threaten the interests of the other. Children may want to push 'a laugh' too far for the teacher. In turn, a teacher may want to reduce his or her workload, resulting in boredom or repetitiveness for the children. Children may want to talk with friends and make more noise in class than the teacher will permit. A teacher may feel harassed and 'bawl out' a child to get order, thus attacking the child's dignity and self-image. The number of issues in which such conflict of interests arises is very great indeed. Conflict is, in that sense, an ever-present reality in classrooms—and yet it does not often take the acrimonious form which Waller so vividly described.

It is now almost possible to complete the model of coping strategies which has been constructed in this chapter. Biographical, role and material factors affect both teachers and children as they face each other in a classroom. They each have a particular sense of self by which their coping will be defined, and from this they each derive particular sets of interest priorities in the immediate situation. These interests are juggled to form the coping strategies which teachers and pupils use in their interaction and in their negotiation with each other. Fig. 7.4 shows this classroom interactive process and the way in which the interaction also influences the teacher's or pupil's sense of self because of their 'essential actual experiences' in the situation.

Perhaps the most important concept in this model is that of negotiation, for it is through negotiation that the teachers and pupils develop ways of coping which are not based on overt conflict. This specific point can be developed much further using the concept of working consensus.

THE WORKING CONSENSUS

As we have seen, the interests of teachers and children are different in many ways and yet, in a sense, teachers and children face an identical and fundamental problem: they both have to cope if they are to accomplish their daily classroom lives satisfactorily. I contend that this is possible only with some degree of accommodation of each other's interests. This is the essence of the interaction concept of working consensus, which encapsulates the idea of teacher and children mutually negotiating interdependent ways of coping in classrooms. This working consensus is created through a process of establishment (Ball 1980) at the start of the school year. For instance one experienced teacher at Moorside commented:

> I always start off the year carefully, trying to be well organised and fairly strict so that the children get into a routine, and then we get to know each other gradually. Usually by the summer term I can relax the routine, do more interesting topics, have a few more jokes and discussions. By then everyone knows what sort of things are allowed, and I know the children well enough to do that kind of thing without them trying things on.

In this 'getting to know each other' period the teacher usually attempts to set up routines, procedures and standards which are offered as 'the way to do things'. This attempt to impose routines is not surprising, since the most salient threat to a teacher's interests is that of the large numbers of children, and routines will to some extent absorb some of the pressure. Meanwhile the teacher watches the children, interpreting their actions from the point of view of her perspective and evaluating the effect of them on her interests.

The teacher often holds the initial advantage and may think that everything is going well. However, from the point of view of the children, the salient threat to their interests is that of teacher power, the particular use of which is initially unknown. Thus the children have good reason to watch and evaluate, gradually accumulating a stock of knowledge and experience of the teacher and of situations, most of which is defensively organised around the threat of teacher power. For instance:

> *John*   Last year was great; Mrs Biggs, she was very strict to start with, but then she used to sit at her desk and mark books a lot, so we could talk and send notes. I used to play noughts and crosses with Nigel and draw pictures. If she got up we'd just slide the papers under our books. When she was explaining things to people—that was good, but we had to hand our work in or if we didn't we'd get lines, and it had to be reasonable or we'd get into bother. It wasn't too bad really.

Gradually, as incidents occur and as sparring goes on, classes are seen to settle down and children feel they have got to know their teacher better.

This more settled accord is often described by teachers and other educationists as a 'good relationship'. It is rightly regarded as being extremely important and a teacher may well be judged by colleagues partly by his or her ability to foster such a relationship with pupils. However, as I suggested in Chapter 1, the concept of a good relationship has always been a rather vague one, only accessible in some accounts to those with particular levels of sensitivity and intuition.

In fact it is possible to be more analytical. In my view the process of establishment normally and naturally leads to a stabilisation of relationships because of mutuality of the coping needs of the teacher and pupils. What emerges is essentially a negotiated system of behavioural understandings for the various types of situations which routinely occur in the classroom. Through interaction, incidents and events, a type of case law of inter-subjectively understood rule systems, expectations and understandings emerges and begins to become an assumed, taken-for-granted reality which socially frames each situation. These socially understood, but tacit, conventions and rules constrain the behaviour of the children to varying degrees, depending on the quality and definition of the working consensus, but it is not unusual to find classes in some primary schools which a teacher can confidently leave for a time in the secure expectation that productive activities will continue just as they would have done had the teacher been present.

It is significant that these rules and understandings constrain not only the children, but also the teacher. This point follows from the fact that the rules are interactively constructed through negotiating processes to which teachers are party. Thus, from the child perspective, teachers can be seen as morally bound, and indeed the working consensus can be seen as providing a type of moral order in the classroom.

If the teacher breaks the understood rules then the action is considered unfair:

Child   Well, I just dropped this marble in class and usually she just tells us off, but she took it and wouldn't give it back. It wasn't hers to take just because I dropped it.

Child   I answered the register in a funny voice and he went right mad. Yesterday he was cracking jokes himself. He's probably had a row with his wife.

These examples are instances of the most common teacher infringement of the working consensus—that of reaction to a routine deviant act which is seen as being too harsh. Such a reaction tends to produce bad feeling and often provokes more deviance.

It is thus the case that if the working consensus and the good relationship are to be maintained, both teacher and pupil strategies are partially circumscribed by them.

Of course it has to be recognised that a teacher's absolute power resources are greater than those of pupils. However, it can be argued that to an extent the working consensus incorporates and accepts differentiated status and behaviours, that it takes into account material realities and differences in socially sanctioned authority, differences in knowledge and differences in experience, and that these become accommodated into the relationships and understandings which are established between teachers and children.

The working consensus is thus an interactive product; indeed it can be seen as a collective, interdependent adaptation by the teacher and children to survival problems which are, in different ways, imposed on them both.

RULES AND RULE FRAME

As we have seen, a crucial feature of classroom life which derives directly from the working consensus is the system of intersubjectively understood rules. These are tacit and taken-for-granted conventions which are created through the dynamics of interaction and through negotiation. They develop through incident and case law as the teacher and children come to understand each other and to define the parameters of acceptable behaviour in particular situations. The result is that such tacit understandings influence and 'frame' the actions of both teacher and pupils.

Two further points have to be made. In the first place such rules are not static; they change depending on the situation, which, as I shall suggest below, can be analysed in terms of the time, place, activity and people involved. In the second place they vary in strength. On some occasions the rule frame may be high and the expected behaviour is very clearly defined, while on other occasions, when the rule frame is weak, action is less circumscribed.

We can look at this in more detail by relating it to other studies and by illustration.

Rule Frame Relating to Time

This type of rule frame has been identified very clearly by Hargreaves, Hestor and Mellor (1975), who analysed lessons in terms of phases. They suggested that there is often an entry phase, a settling-down phase, a lesson-proper phase, a clearing-up phase and an exit phase, each of which is socially structured by expectations in slightly different ways. In terms of the strength of rule frame, entry and exit phases are often only moderately framed, with the introduction and feedback phases being most highly framed.

This could be seen at Moorside, where some of the teachers were very conscious of the problems of the entry and settling-down phases when children were arriving for sessions over an extended period of time. In Mrs Jones's case she had made a series of 'little cards' which the children could 'get on with'.

> Mrs Jones   They're easy, small and they can get on with them on their
>   own, and they enjoy doing them. When they're all in we
>   put them away and start properly.

In this case the rule frame for the entry phase was raised because of teacher provision. On the other hand, Mr Taylor recognised that he often had trouble in these phases:

> Mr Taylor   They'd come in too noisy and I'd try saying 'shut up' and I
>   might bang the ruler on the desk but sometimes it would
>   take rather a while to get them quiet.

Clearly the rule frame here was low and was a considerable strain on Mr Taylor.

Rule Frame Relating to Place

The relationships between particular places and behaviour have been noted by ecological psychologists such as Barker and Gump (1964), and in primary-school classes there are observable differences in rule frame between settings such as a library and a painting area, a maths area and a children's toilet—that traditional child retreat. For instance, here is a child from Moorside:

> Matthew   I was supposed to be taking a message so I went to the toilet
>   for a bit 'cos the lesson was boring. But people kept coming
>   in and Miss heard us talking so I got done. We like doing
>   things in the toilet.

Another ecological factor of some importance is the siting of the teacher and his or her desk. A higher rule frame tends to exist near a teacher, while 'messing about' is much more likely in peripheral positions. This aspect of rule frame thus changes all the time as a teacher moves about.

Rule Frame Relating to Activity

This type of curricular rule framing brings us close to the use of the concept of framing originally used by Bernstein (1971). The point is that some lessons may be highly structured and directive while others may leave more room for individual responses. This depends partly on teacher strategies of lesson introduction and planning, but it is also the case that subjects such as maths lend themselves to higher degrees of explicit behavioural framing than do others, such as art or craft. Children are conscious of this:

> *Child*   I like art lessons 'cos we can do what we want and mess about n' that, but maths is awful 'cos we have to do sums off the board.

The phase, the setting and the subject are thus critical factors in rule framing. A particularly low-frame situation which I have regularly observed is tidying up after a craft lesson in an art and craft area. As one teacher commented:

> *Teacher*   God, it's awful. I stomp about trying to get 'em to pick things up but half of 'em just carry on talking. They don't seem to care.

This teacher ended up sweeping-up by himself when the children had gone home. In contrast, the same teacher in the lesson-proper phase of a classroom-based maths lesson commented:

> *Teacher*   I like this sort of lesson; when they've got their heads down I can really get round to help people.

Temporal, ecological and curricular factors are significant, then, in rule framing, but by far the most important is the personal rule constellation associated with each teacher.

Rule Frame Related to People

Children's classification of teachers by type—good/bad, strict/soft—is the simplest and most superficial index of their knowledge. I believe it can also be shown that children accumulate considerable knowledge of the likely responses of particular teachers in particular situations, and that they have a developed ability to interpret warning signs. This is not surprising, since, as I have suggested, pupil knowledge is likely to be organised defensively about their greatest threat: the power of the teacher. One of the most salient pupil categories of teachers in different situations is that of mood. They may be in a 'right bad mood', in which case the rule frame is high, or they may be in a 'good mood', in which case the rule frame is generally low. Projection of mood can be genuine or it can be artificial. It is this aspect of rule framing which teachers are manipulating by the quality of their 'front' performances. It is also interesting to note that the teachers' reputations which are constructed by children are often passed on to other children. In this way they can contribute to pre-structuring situations even before they arise.

This is not intended as an exhaustive list of rule-framing categories, but it does suggest something of the complex intersecting and dynamic constraints on behaviour which are evolved in classrooms as products of negotiations and the working consensus.

A final point which has to be made is that, since interaction is a continuing process, the understandings of the working consensus will be continually developing. Each action in a classroom both is responsive to the micro social context and contributes in a dynamic way to the interactive process which recreates and develops that social context; such is the dialectical nature of experience.

It may be useful to illustrate the existence and dynamic nature of rule-frame configurations in school, and an example is provided below from Mr Harman's class. (Mr Harman was the 'subversive' teacher at Ashton First School.) In the example it can clearly be seen how taken-for-granted rules accumulate to constitute a part of the hidden curriculum (Snyder 1971) to which the children relate. The example shows how the teacher's and children's behaviour changes. 'Switch signals' between phases are shown in capitals.

Time (a.m.)	Events	Commentary
8.55	CHILDREN IN PLAYGROUND Parents and prams around, children playing, some skip, some play marbles, some stand with parents.	*Pre-9.00 phase* Playground-setting rules for legitimate play areas, toys and behaviour. Slightly confused by absence of teacher (symbol of school rule system) and presence
8.58	Children begin to assemble in lining-up areas.	of parents (symbols of home rule systems).
9.00	BELL Children form approximate class lines.	*School-entry phase* Arrival of teacher brings phase rules and expectations into full
9.01	Duty teacher enters playground. Lines straighten up, children still playing run to lines, children watch teacher for permission for their line to go.	operation. Children adopt lining-up procedures (no pushing, stand still, don't mess about, wrap up your skipping rope, etc.). They monitor the teacher to assess mood and the strength of personal rule frame.
9.02	'OK. LEAD ON CLASS A.' The line is led towards the school; at the front the children walk; the line elongates and straggles; at the end it breaks down and the children run.	

Time (a.m.)	Events	Commentary
9.03	ENTER SCHOOL CORRIDOR First children in cast an eye up corridor. Their walk stiffens as they see a 'strict' teacher. The line contracts again but it is irrecoverable, and they walk in groups towards coat-hanging area.	School rules are stronger inside the building. The corridor setting requires no running, no pushing, don't shout, walk 'nicely'.
9.04	ENTER COAT-HANGING AREA Children take coats off at varying speeds, some very fast, others sit on benches, chat, show new toys.	This is entry to Mr Harman's jurisdiction and therefore the personal rules associated with their negotiated definition of the situation apply.
9.05	CHILDREN ENTER CLASS	Within Mr Harman's classroom
9.08	Mr Harman greets children, they chat, show him comics, toys, T-shirts, tell news.	many of the rules which have been identified were open to some negotiation, particularly in
9.09	TEACHER SITS AT DESK Children with dinner, crisp or biscuit money form a line around desk. Mr Harman collects and records money, balances books and cash, sends dinner register, crisp and biscuit requirements and cash to secretary.	circumstances where it was defined as reasonable or in keeping with the teacher's aims to modify them. There was thus some flexibility within the working consensus. The degree of flexibility varied with Mr Harman's mood and immediate aims, and the children seemed able to sense and detect when rules were non-negotiable from cues provided by Mr Harman, such as tone of voice, 'front' and other presentational acts. Mr Harman expects children to come in when their coats are off, but does not mind delay provided children are in for register and don't hold up administration. A warm, low rule frame greeting.
9.11	'RIGHT-O'. Look at the ceiling, look at the floor, look at your nose, look at me.' Register is called.	*Administrative phase* During this phase the official rule is that children should sit at their places with a library book. The negotiated rule is that children can talk to friends and move about *provided* the teacher is not disturbed. *Register* *No* talking or movement allowed; audible response required. Mr Harman skilfully gets the attention of the whole class and thus asserts the frame of the register sub-phase.

Time (a.m.)	Events	Commentary
9.14	'RIGHT. LINE UP PLEASE.' The line forms; some children are slow to find a partner. Mr Harman helps them, and quietens the tail-end of the line. 'Are we ready then?' The line quietens.	*Exit phase* The rules of the exit phase require that children stop whatever else they are doing and quietly, without pushing, choose a partner, get in the line, and wait for the next instruction. There is often competition to 'lead the line' and to be last. Mr Harman's question 'Are we ready then?' re-asserts these understandings.
9.16	'LEAD ON TO ASSEMBLY.' The line walks down the corridor. Mr Harman is in the middle of the line; those in front of him walk carefully, those behind him less so.	Travel through corridor setting means re-entry to public areas in which institutional rules apply. At this time of day the corridor often has the head teacher watching and asserting 'corridor rules'.
9.17	ENTRY TO HALL SETTING Children file carefully between other classes to their seating rows; the right-hand side of the column forms the front row, the left-hand side the back row; they stand in position until Mr Harman checks them and indicates that they can sit. Headmistress moves to front of hall.	*Assembly phase* The rule frame of this phase is very high and is routinised and maintained by the head teacher. She is thought of by the children as being 'strict' and her personal rule frame is strong. When entering the hall there is an emphasis on order, quiet and discipline.
9.20	'GOOD MORNING CHILDREN.' (chanted response) 'Good morning, Mrs Woods. Good morning, staff. Hello God, here we are again.' A hymn is announced and sung, Bible story plus moral related to children. Hymn. Prayer. Recorder players play.	*The rules during the assembly* emphasise relevant participation and total attentiveness, and tolerate *no* deviation.
9.35	'RIGHT, MR HARMAN'S CLASS.' Children stand, turn to face exit, wait for Mr Harman's signal to leave. ENTER CORRIDOR Relief shows in some chattering.	*Assembly exit*, again much emphasis on order and discipline, but not as powerfully felt as on entry, since children are going out of presence of head teacher. Corridor-setting rules often not salient at this time.
9.37	ENTER THE CLASSROOM Children arrive first, mill about. Mr Harman follows and says . . .	The classroom rules define basic parameters of behaviour but the children wait for the teacher to define this particular situation and phase.
9.38	'OK. COME AND SIT HERE.'	Children interpret that 'sitting together' conventions apply, i.e. sit on floor, cross-legged, be visible to teacher, face him, wait.

Time (a.m.)	Events	Commentary
	'Now, today I want to work with the maths group so, when I say, will they come and sit on these two tables with Fletcher books and a pencil. That's Carol, Dick, Jill, Keith, Martin and Philip. Kathleen, Jo, Gareth, Stuart, Stephen, Sandra and Linda, I want you to do a story. When that's done you can choose. The rest of you can do the cards I put on your tables, then you can choose, and later on I'll hear some of you read.'	On this occasion the setting is used for an *organisation phase*. Mr Harman gives clear instructions and conveys a sense of purpose and constancy in his mood. The activities are not unusual and the children thus have relatively clear expectations about time, place and purpose. The rule frame is at a routine level and reflects the working consensus which has been negotiated. The children will work and then 'choose'.
9.42	'RIGHT. OFF YOU GO.' The class dispenses. The maths group goes to get equipment, sits at tables, waits for teacher.	This signal switches on the major *work phase*. The maths group knows it is about to experience a series of teacher-directed phases in a situation defined as 'work'. These phases are normally sequential:
		1. *Check* everyone present with equipment.
		2. *Introduction* of task and method (attentiveness required).
		3. *Task to do.* (Effort, speed, neatness and correctness are the ideals. Children know they can get sympathetic help from teacher at early stages of this sub-phase, and that at later stages they will have to prove that they have tried.)
		4. *Marking* of work (work has to be shown to teacher).
		5. *Tidying up* (each child responsible for equipment he or she used).
	The story-writing group gradually collects story-books, word-books and pencils. Some discuss what to write about, others go to a drawer containing stimulus pictures and start looking through them.	The story-writing group know that they have been directed to their work and that the teacher considers them to be able to work alone. They know that certain results and standards will be expected and checked on before they will be allowed to choose. (Expected standards depend upon personal child–teacher negotiations.) The children also know that the definition of this unsupervised work situation requires that they concentrate to produce an interesting story and,

Time (a.m.)	Events	Commentary

		unless absolutely necessary, they do not interrupt the teacher.
	Children doing cards get books and pencils and copy the date from the blackboard. Mr Harman selects cards and delivers them to their tables. Children inspect them, discuss them and, at varying rates, begin them. During the work phase children constantly scan teacher activity, since they know that at any point they may have to account for their use of time.	The children doing cards know that they are expected to work. They expect the normal quota – one maths card and one literacy card – and know that within the terms of the working consensus they can switch by right to a situation defined as 'choosing' as soon as their quota is finished. Since the cards are given without explanations, the children know that they are expected to be able to do them without help.
10.03	Mr Harman finishes work with the maths group, leaves them to complete their tasks, and is available for the evaluation phase.	
10.05	'WHEN YOU FINISH, BRING IT UP PLEASE.' The quick workers finish and show Mr Harman. Some are sent back; some are allowed to begin choosing.	*Evaluation phase* This is a negotiating phase between teacher and individual children. The critical indicator in this classroom is *effort* because the teacher has negotiated an individual contract of satisfactory work with each child. A child may thus present a front to convey 'I tried hard but with little success', which the teacher judges, or a child may fulfil his or her work contract and go straight to choosing. Various negotiating strategies are possible; for instance early finishers often get sent back because Mr Harman looks at the work carefully and may raise his requirements. At peak stages Mr Harman is under pressure from a lot of children wanting work checked and may check less thoroughly, or not have time to explain errors. At very late stages Mr Harman tends to soften and let children off. Institutional rules prevent children being kept in at playtime, and teacher plans for the next lesson may prevent insistence on work completion. Interested children know these factors influencing the teacher during the evaluation phase.
	Gradually most of the class finish work and pass through the evaluation phase. Each thus has a personal signal to legitimate choosing.	

Time (a.m.)	Events	Commentary
	Children who are choosing move away to many activities such as Lego, plasticine, bricks, jigsaws, Wendy House, sand, shop.	Behaviour when choosing is defined by general classroom rules plus derivative rules for particular settings and apparatus. *General rules* cover:

(a) care of equipment and tidying up when finished;
(b) classroom noise level and movement;
(c) interpersonal rules such as sharing equipment, taking turns, not fighting;
(d) 'busyness' and being 'involved' in something.

These general rules produced *derivative rules* and conventions for particular settings and activities. For instance, when painting:

1. Wear an apron.
2. Use a different brush for each colour.
3. Wipe up spills.
4. Wash hands after use.
5. Hang picture in drying-place when finished.
6. Replace paper-holding clip on easel when finished.
7. Extra care in moving in painting corner, because of danger of spills, smudges, paint on clothes.
8. Don't move out of painting corner with anything that drips.
9. One child per easel, others to wait, no pushing in.
10. Paint with care and thought.

Time (a.m.)	Events	Commentary
10.15	Most of the children are now choosing. Mr Harman briefly circulates to talk to them, and perhaps to structure and extend their activities. Sometimes the children look bemused and torn between getting on with their play and 'pleasing teacher'.	Mr Harman values this circulating opportunity, being a believer in guided discovery learning. He attempts to extend the activity *within* the children's definition of that situation, but towards his definition of educational experiences. Mr Harman's personal circulation at this time also serves to strengthen the rule frame as increasing numbers of children start to choose – in itself a generally low-frame activity. This circulation is particularly necessary since he intends to hear a reader and is thus forced to

Time (a.m.)	Events	Commentary
		disengage from other activities to an extent.
10.20	'OK. WILL KATHLEEN BRING HER READING BOOK.' Kathleen gets it, goes to Mr Harman's desk and waits. Mr Harman arrives, they find the place, and Kathleen starts to read.	This is an individual phase and an activity of great importance. The child is very vulnerable because very few strategies are available for 'accomplishing' the situation other than by reading the book. It is a situation with considerable pressure on both participants from parents, the head teacher and each other. For the child, reading ability may also be an important factor in the negotiation of identity and social status among her peers.
10.34	'RIGHT. TIDY UP NOW.' Some children stop what they are doing and begin to tidy up. Other children, fully involved, carry on, but begin to scan the teacher constantly. They wait for the teacher's escalating signals and judge his tone of voice before deciding to begin tidying up.	This *tidy phase* has rules such as 'everyone should stop what they are doing and put away what they have used in accordance with the conventions for that apparatus or setting'. In the class, conformity with these phase rules is not popular with all children, especially since full involvement has previously been required.
10.38	'OK. EVERYBODY COME AND SIT DOWN HERE.' 'We have just got time to see some paintings and for Adam to read you the story he's done.'	The 'sitting together' setting is here used to round off the lesson, to reinforce 'good work' and to share ideas with the whole class.
10.40	BELL Children fidget as 'showing' finishes.	The official school signal for the end of the session.
10.41	'ALL THOSE WEARING BLUE CAN GO OUT TO PLAY.' Those children wearing blue are the first to depart; they go through the corridor and out into the playground. The duty teacher is there. A group of children go to a far corner to play marbles, others play tig, some skip, some hold the teacher's hand.	This dismissal technique staggers the *exit phase*. In the playground setting only school rules constrain the child's full use of own definition of situation. Proximity of duty teacher is important to conformity to these at any time.
10.44	Mr Harman walks to the staffroom and his coffee.	Teacher is 'backstage'.

This example shows in use expectations and conventions which derive from an established working consensus. The rule frame varied as the situation changed depending on the time, purpose, place and people involved. Mr Harman and the children showed both their knowledge of the taken-for-granted rules and their skill in using them.

CONCLUSION

In this chapter I have attempted to bring the previous parts of the book together and to provide a means of analysing the social context *within* classrooms using the concepts of working consensus and rule frame. These concepts have, in my view, considerable analytical power, as I hope to demonstrate in the chapters which follow.

We have particularly seen here how they relate to self, interests-at-hand and coping as the product of processes of classroom interaction in which the coping necessities and interests of each party are likely to have played a major part.

The working consensus represents a mutual agreement to respect the dignity and fundamental interests of the other party. As such it is produced by creative and interactive responses to the structural position which teachers and pupils face in their classrooms. The point, though, is that these responses themselves create a micro social structure and context—analysable in terms of rule frame—to which individuals have to relate as they act.

8

Classroom Strategies

This chapter begins by attempting to analyse the dynamics of strategic interaction between teachers and children in classrooms. It does this by relating decisions about strategies to the ways in which teacher and child interests are affected by changes in the rule frames of different situations.

A means of classifying types of strategy is then introduced and, following interactionist principles, various common and related teacher and pupil strategies are discussed and illustrated.

STRATEGIES AND THE JUGGLING OF INTERESTS

We can begin with an example drawn from field notes and recordings made when observing a class of eleven-year-olds and their teacher in an English lesson. When the lesson was finished it was discussed with the teacher and several of the children, and the comments they provided are the primary basis for the analysis which is given for each part.

Registration

> The bell for 9 a.m. goes; about half the class are in, mostly reading books. The teacher enters breezily: 'Morning. Ah, that's good, getting those books out'. The teacher sits at his desk, tidies up, and gets the register out. Meanwhile most of the other children have come into the classroom. The later arrivals talk, some children swop football cards, and they occasionally glance at the teacher.

Teacher	Right. Let's do the register then. Hurry up and sit down, you football maniacs—I see that Manchester United lost again.(1)
Manchester United suppor- ters	Oh yeah, well they're still better than Liverpool.
Teacher	[joky sarcasm in voice] Really? It must be all the spinach they don't eat.(2) Now then . . . Martin . . . Darren . . . Alan . . . Mark. [Calls register and children answer.]

A child comes in late, looking sheepish, and walks to his seat. Other children point and laugh.

Child	Hey, Duncan. What are you doing?(3)
Teacher	Duncan, come here. You're late *again*; three minutes late to be exact. Why? (4)
Duncan	Sorry, Sir.
Teacher	I said, 'Why?'.
Duncan	I slept in, Sir.
Teacher	Well, are you awake now? (5)

The other children laugh.

Duncan	Yes, Sir.
Teacher	Well, you'd better stay behind for three minutes at 4 o'clock and don't go to sleep again until after that. (6)

There is more laughter, and Duncan sits down. The teacher finishes the register.

Registration is the first phase of the day and thus an important occasion in which the children interpret the mood of the teacher and the teacher interprets the mood of the children. In this phase the basic underpinnings of order are a strategy of routine and the constraints of a workplace setting and of a discrete task. The children are expected to enter, sit in work places, take out their reading books, and answer their name when it is called. Given a basic level of compliance with this explicitly ordered and structured routine, the teacher is able to indulge his own interest of self-enjoyment by joking and teasing (1 and 2). This is probably partly a front performance, a strategic decision, to set the tone for the day within the parameters of 'appeal' strategies such as fraternisation, culture identification and entertainment, since the teacher believed that his academic interests would be easier to satisfy in an overall atmosphere of co-operation. The difficulty is that the children interpret the teacher projection as a type of playing about mood, with a low personal rule frame. One child thus feels secure enough to initiate teasing of Duncan when he arrives late (3). The teacher immediately recognises the situation: the Duncan issue has become the first test case of the day, which, if left, would communicate to the children that anything goes. In that situation the children's interest-at-hand of self-enjoyment would probably be satisfied; on the other hand, the teacher's interests of order, instruction and, ultimately, self would suffer. The teacher adaptation is to assert his authority firmly and seriously (4), a mood change for the incident, and to show Duncan up. This is done in a manner which, by playing to the audience and by not being vindictive (5 and 6), re-establishes the tone of appeal but with a clearer back-up of firmness. This teacher response is accepted by the children; it is within the parameters of teacher responses for that type of situation as legitimated by the working consensus. To have sent Duncan to the headmaster would have been unfair, too harsh for that type of offence and situation. Such a misjudgement would probably have made 'appeal' strategies non-viable and might have necessitated teacher use of more dominative strategies such as threat and punishment.

Story Writing

Teacher	OK, now we're going to do some creative English work before playtime.
Children	Ohhhgg, again?
Teacher	Now, don't be silly; anyway, last time most of you did very well.(7) I found lots of good describing words in those stories about the Martian landing. I'll read you one . . . Karen, let's have yours.

The teacher reads Karen's story.

Teacher	There, now, that was good, wasn't it? (8) I liked the bit about everybody getting 'splodstuck in the Marsbar glue'; perhaps that's what happened to Manchester United last night! (9)
Children	Oh. [laughter]
Teacher	Anyway, the full stops and capital letters were OK. Watch your spellings, though, Karen.
	Thank you. [He returns Karen's book.]
	Now, today I want you to think really hard and use your imaginations. Imagine you had some special way of becoming invisible so that no-one knew you were there . . .

The teacher exposition continues; some child responses are made and are extended by the teacher. He continues:

Teacher	. . . I also want you to imagine some of the things people would *say* when you surprised or shocked them, and for that you must use speech marks like I showed you last week. OK?

The teacher finally completes the lesson launch with an enthusiastic:

Teacher   Right then, let's see if we can do really well today. (10)

This English lesson, which followed the calling of the register, took place in a seat-work classroom setting, it occurred at a time when everyone expected work (despite the routine protests), it involved relatively discrete curricular tasks, and a preliminary assessment of teacher mood had been established during registration. The lesson was thus quite strongly framed by knowledge of appropriate situational behaviour.

The lesson introduction is a careful mixture. It consists primarily of instructional structuring of the task, but this is spiced with a certain amount of entertaining rapport (9), morale boosting (7 and 10) and illustration of good work (8). This is the way in which the teacher attempts to use his appeal strategies to get an instructional pay-off in an ordered work-phase. If all goes well his primary interests will be rewarded by a well balanced and structured lesson with supportive rule frames of phase, setting and subject, together with understanding of the teacher's friendly but firm mood projection.

Crisis

Time passes as the children work. The teacher circulates briefly, then sits at his desk to hear slow readers. A child, Mark, drops a marble. (11)

Teacher	Mark, what are you doing?
Mark	Nothing, Sir.
Teacher	What's that on the floor then?
Mark	A marble, Sir.
Teacher	Well, pick it up and bring your book over here. (12) [Mark brings it.]
Teacher	Ye Gods, you've only done three lines in 35 minutes. Three lines!

[Mark looks; doesn't reply.] (13)

Teacher	Why?
Mark	I couldn't think of nothing, Sir.
Teacher	Well, everyone else has, so why can't you?
Mark	Dunno, Sir.
Teacher	Well . . . come on; (14) you could pretend you were at home and went round moving things and frightening your Mum . . . or what about pretending you are invisible and playing football? Could you do that?
Mark	Yes, Sir.

| *Teacher* | OK, then, you do that and show me later.
Now everybody, (15) I hope you are remembering speech marks, and do look words up if you aren't sure how to spell them. |

The teacher continues to hear readers. Later Mark is spotted being inactive.

| *Teacher* | Mark, come on! (16) You can do it; you did a good one last week. |

Later, the teacher stops hearing readers, (17) leaves his desk and goes from table to table, his annoyance visibly and audibly growing: (18)

| *Teacher* | But look at it, Timothy; yours is as bad as Beverley's; you've got hardly any describing words in . . . 'a frightened boy' . . . well, I suppose that's something, but you haven't *thought*, have you? And your speech marks are *all* in the wrong places—you should put them round what's actually spoken, not the 'he said' bit. |

Many children exchange anxious glances (19) and compare work. The teacher is still uncovering errors, especially in the use of speech marks. He halts:

| *Teacher* | Now look, (20) everybody; put your hand up if you don't *really* understand how to use speech marks. |

Slowly, tentatively, hands go up until all but two are raised.

| Teacher | Oh. (21)
Well. |

The teacher looks at his watch; it's eleven minutes to playtime.

| *Teacher* | Well, (22) I don't think I've time to explain it again now, so . . . so you'd better do the best you can, that's all we can do now, I think. I'll show you again tomorrow, OK? |

Relief shows on the children's faces. The teacher, returning to his desk, inspects Mark's book.

| *Teacher* | Mark, (23) you've done nothing. It's hopeless. It's not that you don't understand; you've just not tried. If you can't get on you'll have to stay in at playtime and do it then . . . now *get on*! (24) [Shouts.]
The rest of you, don't forget to read it through and look for mistakes. |

The room is very quiet.

Initially, having set the lesson on course, the teacher judges it appropriate to rely on its degree of frame for maintenance of order. He can then attempt to satisfy an important aspect of his instructional interest and educational concern by hearing slow readers.

As time passes, the lesson, to the desk-bound, reader-hearing teacher, seems to be progressing satisfactorily in that he is getting through the readers and the children appear to be busy. There is no threat to order, there is very little stress, he isn't having to walk around, children are learning: the situation appears to be entirely supportive of his professional and personal self-esteem and of his other interests.

The dropping of the marble (11) is the first noticeable incident which indicates that the situation is not entirely as it appears. When the marble falls the teacher's experience 'tells' him that an increase in child deviance usually means a decrease in compliance with the teacher's instructional objectives; he therefore asks to see Mark's book (12). His initial anger at Mark's three lines elicits highly defensive responses from Mark which contain a mixture of hurt and refusal (13). The teacher decides not to take this on by confrontation and domination: to do so would change the negotiated definition and overall tone of the lesson, because it would involve discarding the appeal strategies on which the existing balance of interests was based. He therefore offers Mark some ideas and encouragement (14)— more strategies of appeal. To make it clear to the class that the marble incident has not altered the type of situation, he again offers encouragement and some reminders of the instructional structuring (15).

This policy is maintained as the teacher continues to work at his desk, although he is more careful to watch and encourage Mark (16).

The problems start when the teacher begins to move round the class, his initial intention being to encourage (17). In fact he discovers more errors than he had expected. It becomes clear to him that his instructional aims, and therefore interest, have not in fact been satisfied and he is frustrated (18). The fact that this has been realised also becomes clear to the children (19).

The teacher decides to find out the extent of the problem (20), with the intention of teaching it immediately to a small group, but is surprised to find that almost the whole class profess not to understand what to do.

This presents a crisis. The children know by their anxious exchanges and tentative responses that the teacher response could go badly: he could get 'right mad' and 'go off the deep end'. However, the teacher knows that he is running out of time (21); retrospectively he knows that the problem over speech marks is one which he has partly caused himself by over-complicating the task initially and by having misjudged the children's understanding. The balance of interests which he thought his appeal strategies had created had been revealed as deficient and in reality as having been in imbalance all the time, an imbalance which the children had not chosen to reveal, it not being in their immediately perceived interests to do so, since it would have involved potentially threatening evaluations and potentially boring explanations, and would have left them with no excuses for their end product. Waiting for the bell is obviously a better strategic alternative for the children. Finally, the lesson had run out of the time necessary for major restructuring (22).

The teacher's overall judgement in this crisis was to cut his instructional losses for the lesson and to re-assert the appeal tone in the hope of getting more from its strategies in the other lessons of the day. But Mark becomes the scapegoat (23) as the teacher vents some of his frustration. As Mark 'gets done' the children know that they must proceed very carefully henceforth because the manner of Mark's lecture and the teacher's shout (24) indicate that the teacher's mood has changed for the worse. He is now 'a bit mad'. The rule frame has therefore tightened and the situation is a new one in which the risks of deviance are a good deal higher.

This new situation and the new teacher mood are clearly dominative, a situation which is inconsistent with the strategic decision made at (22). However, the act of getting angry serves the teacher's self-interests primarily by giving vent to frustration and also by replacing the stress and confusion of the crisis with a clear assertion of his power. In fact, the teacher confided in interview that he 'didn't mean to blow up, but sometimes it just gets too much'.

Tidying

Later:

Teacher   OK, there's only two minutes left, so will you finish off the bit you are doing (25) and put your books on the pile. Hurry up now. Mark, you'll stay in.

Children comply; talking increases (26) as they pack up, stack their books and put pens, etc. in their drawers.

In this tidying-up phase the teacher attempts to continue the existing rule frame by careful timing and explicit behavioural structuring. This is only partly successful (26), since the amount of necessary movement provides cover for all kinds of other activities and conversations: tidying up after a lesson often merges into getting ready before a playtime. Nevertheless, the carry-over of mood which was conveyed in the teacher's switch signal and instructions is enough to minimise such activity and to maintain his interest of order for the phase. Order is clearly the priority here, since the intrinsic value of the instructional task is demeaned by acceptance of only partly completed work (25).

Exit

> *Teacher* Right, you should be sitting at your places.
> Come on.
> The bell goes.
>
> *Teacher* OK, stand behind your chairs then.
>
> Some children push their chairs under the table and start to leave.
>
> *Teacher* I didn't tell you to go! Did I? Well, stand by your place, then. Right—girls you may go, quietly. Now—boys, and don't run in the corridor. Mark, I'll see your work when I get back.
>
> As the children get through the door and out of the teacher's sight, they charge for the playground.

In the exit phase the teacher again tries to structure and control the situation so that order is maintained, being particularly aware of the impression given to colleagues by the behaviour of his class outside his room. His strategy is a routine procedure of sitting, standing and walking out which is to be carried out on explicit commands. Such a strategy works perfectly within the setting, within sight of the teacher and within the phase—before the switch signal which ends it is given. It then collapses completely as the children enter their playtime and respond to entirely different sets of social forces.

This account of a lesson illustrates the ways in which teachers and children juggle with their interests-at-hand in the ebb and flow of classroom life. This juggling is part of the strategic decision-making process which is employed when situations change. Such strategic adaptations are necessary because, as we saw in earlier chapters, interests-at-hand are strongly linked to self. Thus the achievement of an overall satisfaction of interests is the way in which each participant seeks to cope in the classroom; if their interests are regularly left unsatisfied or are continually threatened then they are likely to feel a great sense of personal vulnerability.

An additional point is that the nature of the rule frame in a particular classroom situation will affect teacher and child interests very directly. In particular, when the rule frame changes during processes of interaction, so too will the degree of interest satisfaction which the teacher and children can achieve. Changes in rule frame thus represent changes in the level of threat of different situations for particular individuals—a point which derives from the prior role of rule frame in providing social structuring and from the necessity of coping for each individual.

Of course changes in rule frame will not affect all individuals in the same ways. In the simplest case it is obvious, because of the inherent conflict built into the structure of classroom life, that teacher and pupil interests could often be opposed. For instance, a threat to the teacher could well be a source of great enjoyment to children. Similarly, a tight rule frame which is established by a teacher to ensure the satisfaction of particular interests may leave some children relatively unsatisfied. At another level, the type of teacher, their biography, their perception of the teaching role and their sense of self will obviously produce variation. A similar range of factors will influence children, for clearly goody, joker and gang members have quite different perceptions of schooling and of the ways in which they might seek to cope with it.

In addition it is necessary to note that the levels of satisfaction of different interests are unlikely to vary together. Thus different situations will produce imbalances. For instance, in the case of teachers, a teacher-induced laugh may be personally satisfying but makes a poor contribution to order. A strategy of showing up a deviant may be good for short-term order, but creates ill-feeling and may be bad for instruction. A well-established routine may be good for order but poor for the teacher's self-satisfaction in that it may be boring, and poor for instructional objectives in that the children may tend to work to a tried and tested formula.

It is possible to think of many more examples of imbalance. However, the three teacher interests of self, order and instruction are mutually interrelated in the way in which they affect survival, since order and instruction are enabling interests for the various facets of self-interest. Survival, in the long run, depends on achieving a satisfactory degree of *balance* of interest satisfaction.

This has implications for the short-term immediacy of every lesson because, as classroom situations and their structuring change, the particular configurations of degrees of interest satisfaction will continually be thrown into imbalance.

As we saw in the example above, when these imbalances occur teachers will sense and assess the survival threat created and attempt to restore the situation by switching to new strategies to achieve a new balance. They will juggle with their interests, changing priorities as classroom processes evolve.

Of course this is an analytical description of what most experienced teachers take for granted as essential skills and knowledge. As one put it:

> *Teacher* You can sense how a lesson is going. You learn to do that after a while, and then you can switch what you are doing to suit the circumstances. Sometimes that's essential to avoid chaos.

Another teacher commented:

> *Teacher* Sometimes I feel as if I'm teaching—sort of—by the seat of my pants.

A similar process of juggling with interest priorities to secure an overall balance of satisfaction can be seen with children. For instance, in Mr Harman's class of six-year-olds, I once had an opportunity to study the work-evasion skills of a boy called Matthew as he negotiated with his teacher. He was a popular member of a large friendship group of boys of diverse ability. He was considered by Mr Harman to perform about average at reading and writing, but to be a bit lazy about them. He was interested in maths and was among the best children at it. Regarding his behaviour in class Mr Harman commented:

> He is often on the fringe of trouble and is clever enough to get away with it . . . if I catch him doing anything against the class rules he'll quite honestly acknowledge what he's been doing and stop doing it . . . he's got a nice way of doing things so I don't get mad . . .

Matthew could also get a joke, and Mr Harman stated that Matthew 'didn't work as hard as he could but he's quite creative'; he was, in other words, a type of evasive joker, and was particularly skilful at negotiating to take advantage of his teacher's sense of humour. The following illustration is drawn from field notes of classroom observation focused on Matthew.

Field notes	*Comments*
The children enter the classroom from a movement lesson and enter a 'getting dressed' phase, to be followed by 'working from cards'.	Each phase is rule-framed by behavioural expectations.
Matthew dresses fast; he is the second child to be dressed. He goes directly to Mr Harman and asks what to do.	Matthew projects eagerness to work and earns praise for getting ready quickly.
Matthew gets his writing-book and pencil from his drawer; he is first to do this. He sits at his table, opens his book, holds his pencil, scans the teacher and talks to Joe, who is finishing dressing.	Matthew produces an overt working impression. Mr Harman is busy helping children dress and his scanning from across the room probably registers Matthew as working.

Field notes	*Comments*
Matthew browses through the work cards which Mr Harman has distributed to each table. He chats to other children about them and looks about. Almost all the children are now dressed, and many have started writing.	To study the work cards is legitimate in the teacher's definition of the situation; this provides cover for extensive discussion within the children's definition.
Matthew has a card, his book is open, his pencil poised, but he has not yet written anything; he continues to talk and scans the teacher.	Again an overt performance and covert inactivity.
Matthew leaves his seat, puts his pencil in his drawer, looks around, hovers by his drawer and exchanges comments with Keith and Adam. Then he takes his pencil out and returns to his seat.	Going to his drawer gives Matthew's movement around the class legitimacy if the teacher questions it; thus talking to Keith and Adam can be accomplished safely.
Matthew leaves his seat to visit Len, who has a pencil sharpener, borrows it, goes to the dustbin and sharpens his pencil.	He tries the same tactic as above, but with a new legitimating cover.
Mr Harman looks up and spots Matthew and Len conversing around the dustbin. Mr Harman: 'Come on, you two; you'll be able to sew with that pencil soon!'	Mr Harman interprets the situation as probably unnecessary timewasting. A mild desist and the rule frame is re-asserted.
Matthew and Len look at each other and grin.	The children accept it, and comply behaviourally with a post-desist performance of conformity to the teacher's definition of situation. Peer group solidarity is drawn on.
Matthew: 'It'd be better as a rocket . . . brrrm' and he 'flies' it back to his seat, sits, turns to face Mr Harman seriously, studies his work card and begins to write.	
Mr Harman continues to go around the tables helping children and marking work.	The desist sequence is over.
Matthew holds his pencil but begins to talk with Joe. They both begin 'flying' their pencils. Joe falls off his chair. Mr Harman looks across but at once Matthew has taken up a working position. Joe is reseated and Mr Harman makes no comment.	A serious mistake which both children know will draw attention. Matthew coped with the situation by the quality of his 'front' performance.
Mr Harman is working round the tables and is not far away. Matthew and Joe 'set to', write fast and manage to produce a reasonable five lines and to project an air of studiousness when Mr Harman reaches them.	The children know they have to show evidence of trying, particularly after the falling-off-the-chair incident, and because of the proximity of Mr Harman. The rule frame has tightened.

Field notes	Comments
Matthew indicates difficulties and the teacher explains. Matthew listens. Mr Harman moves on; Matthew continues to hold his pencil but does not write.	Matthew projects the degree of his effort by indicating the degree of his difficulties. Once the evaluation phase has been accomplished Matthew retains his working front, but does not perform, relying on the bell, time running out, and Mr Harman's need to see many other children.
The bell goes, and Mr Harman gives permission for exit to playground.	

Matthew coped with this work period by the quality of his 'front' performance and by strategically judged tactics. This could not have been done without a high degree of social competence. Matthew knew the rules and appropriate behaviour for that phase and setting: he knew Mr Harman's mood at the time and the consequent degree of likelihood of rule enforcement, and he knew how to recover a situation where his evasion may have been exposed. This is a clear case of the juggling of interest priorities. Having minimised work and maximised enjoyment with a range of tactics which enabled him to interact with his peer group, he then found the rule frame tightening as Mr Harman worked round the class. Had he continued with his evasion strategy he would undoubtedly have been told off for not doing any work and for wasting time. This might have threatened his dignity and caused some stress. He thus switched to make the enabling interest of learning a priority for a while: he wrote fast and projected effort. Having satisfied Mr Harman in the highly framed evaluation phase, he reverted to earlier strategies and interest priorities.

This was a highly skilled performance. Matthew knew how to time and measure a satisfactory amount of work production and how to negotiate an evaluation phase; he knew the pattern of demands on the teacher and the likely frame which would be projected. He paced the flow of the lesson so that he ran out of time. He worked as much as he had to, with a realistic assessment of his structural position, but he maintained his own perspective and by his activity constructed aspects of the process of which the teacher was unaware. Throughout Matthew skilfully used those tactical opportunities open to him, for instance by leaving his seat to go to a drawer or to sharpen a pencil.

The form of the analysis as it relates to teacher and child strategies is now complete. In essence it suggests that, as the participants in classrooms experience interaction, they juggle their interests-at-hand to maximise an overall level of satisfaction for self. As situations change they act strategically to cope, thus creating further situations to be experienced sequentially. Such is the dialectical nature of action and experience.

This section has focused on the *process* of strategic action; in the next section we shall review some of the common *types* of strategy used by teachers and children in primary schools.

TYPES OF CLASSROOM STRATEGY

Strategies, as we have seen, are essentially ways of accomplishing interaction in particular situations so that self-interests are protected or enhanced. Strategies thus have a great deal to do with power and control. Each participant in interaction will adopt strategies which best serve their interests in the context of the situation and will actively seek to define or influence that situation.

Teachers, with their socially ascribed role position, have more power of a significant type and are generally able to initiate, propose and pre-structure situations. Thus children's strategies are often essentially reactive. In most cases the strategies of teacher and pupils develop together and become legitimated as the working consensus is negotiated during the process of establishment. However, some children who feel less bound by the working consensus may well act in ways which are better described by the term 'counter-strategies' (Denscombe 1980b). Again, though, particular teacher strategies will tend to produce characteristic types of counter-strategy.

There are thus several reasons for expecting teacher and pupil strategies to be linked, and this tendency will be illustrated below in a consideration of four basic types of teacher strategy and their related pupil strategies. The four types of teacher strategy are open negotiation, routinisation, manipulation and domination. They have been analytically separated for clarity, but it must be remembered that although different teachers will tend to use particular ranges of strategies, depending on such factors as their biography and training and the staff culture and institutional bias in the school, it is also the case that there are likely to be changes between strategies over very short periods of time in response to changing situations or to particular pupils. Thus, for teachers, the use of one strategy often slides into another.

In contrast, the range of child strategies used is likely to be far more restricted than those of teachers, since each child will tend to settle on those strategies which best serve their interests depending on their particular sense of identity, their particular structural position in the class, their particular peer group, etc. Unlike a teacher, who must relate to, control and 'educate' the whole class, each child arguably has need of a more limited range of strategic action. Of course, having said that, it must be recognised that pupil–pupil strategies are also of consequence, although I have not attempted to deal with them in any detail here. We shall return to the point about the range of pupil strategies used towards the end of the chapter.

Open Negotiation

Processes of negotiation have been discussed in the previous chapter with regard to the process of establishment and the production of a working consensus. Because of the power of each party to threaten the interests of the other, it was argued that some form of negotiation is a fundamental teacher/child necessity in all classrooms.

However, a particular type of negotiation takes place when each party seeks to recognise and respect the interests and concerns of the other in addition to their own, and this can be termed 'open negotiation'. As Woods (1983) puts it:

> Open negotiation is where parties are aware of the contract, move some way to meet each other of their own volition, and subsequently arrive at a consensus.
>
> (Woods 1983, p.133)

From the children's side, open negotiation implies that they trust and respect their teachers and the reasonableness of their initiatives, and that they also know that their own initiatives and feelings will be respected. Open negotiation is thus possible where there is an extremely 'good relationship', where the parameters of the working consensus are well defined and where its legitimacy is accepted.

We saw in Chapter 4 how much children vary in their views on school, and clearly open negotiation is unlikely to be a strategy which is often favoured by children with feelings such as those of gang members. However, for goodies, open negotiation is a serious and potentially rewarding possibility, and for jokers it is the main strategy. It is thus a very common child strategy when interacting with a teacher who is judged to be suitably appreciative and fair. Similarly, teachers will attempt this form of strategic negotiation when interacting with children with whom they feel it to be appropriate and whom they know to have sufficient social competence to make it possible. With other children the feeling that 'you just can't trust them' is likely to proscribe its use.

Some of the key features of this strategy which I would identify are explaining and reasoning, having a laugh and maintaining interest, avoidance of confrontation, and friendliness and respect. These features are all linked by the idea of respect for the dignity and experience of the other party. Thus teachers both give explanations and actively listen to the reasons which children give for their views and actions. They discuss and reason when there are disagreements. Laughs, red-herrings and diversions can be shared without the teacher feeling that the social order of the classroom is being subverted or the children sensing that one of their number is being humiliated as the butt of a joke. Both the teacher and the children show interest in the activities of the other. Teachers seek to stimulate and genuinely connect with the children, while the children similarly bring things into school and contribute actively to the momentum of the class activities. This momentum is interactively constructed, the teacher being willing to negotiate the curriculum to build on the children's interests. In primary classrooms where open negotiation takes place, a type of warmth becomes apparent in the way that the teacher and children relate to each other, and a type of respectful friendliness exists. Thus social distance can be reduced or extended by the teacher when appropriate without misunderstandings resulting. Children do not take advantage or feel a sense of being slighted on these occasions. Both the teacher and the children try to avoid confrontation and prefer to try to find ways around difficulties by reflection and discussion. The awareness and social competence of both the teacher and the children are relatively high.

We should remember that open negotiation is described here as a situational strategy, not as a longer-term teaching style. In the longer term teaching styles are made up by organisational and pedagogic policy decisions and by tendencies to use a particular range of situational strategies. Open negotiation, for all its attraction and the associated rhetoric and advocacy which it has enjoyed from Rousseau onwards, remains a difficult strategy for either party to sustain in the context of the structural and material realities of classroom life. Nevertheless, there are classrooms where open negotiation is a predominant strategy and, of course, with its basis in trust, a long-term continuity in the use of the strategy is essential.

From Routinisation to Drifting

Routinisation is a very common teacher strategy, not only because it provides a straightforward way of giving children practice at learning activities but also because it provides a highly dependable way of coping with the complexity of classroom life. Indeed it could be argued that some of the emphasis which is often put on the importance of classroom organisation in fact reflects a recognition of the need for routines to take the stress out of the tasks of managing the children and structuring classroom activities. Routinisation thus reduces the need to initiate and converts complexity into predictability.

Some of the key features of the strategy which I would identify are regularity in the organisation of work tasks and activities, the setting of occupational work rather than work which is more challenging, the appeal to tradition and precedent when controlling children, and a degree of distancing in relationships. Clearly a greater degree of adult control is employed here than in the case of open negotiation.

However, from the point of view of the children, the predictability of the routinisation strategy is a great asset. In a variety of ways it becomes possible to 'drift' through classroom sessions without being exposed to any significant degree of threat. This is possible primarily because 'pleasing teacher' has been made relatively easy. Not only is it clearly defined behaviourally by the routine, but the level of work set is generally attainable: the child simply has to produce it. This strategy is similar to the 'docility' described by Henry (1955) and to the 'colonization' described by Woods (1979). As Woods points out, there is an indifference to both ends and means; the point is simply to get the task finished.

Of course the adoption of the drifting strategy implies an acceptance of the working consensus and of the normality of teacher expectations; indeed, there could even be an element of ritual built into some of the routines. However, there is likely to be an element of divergence when children seek to 'have a laugh' or to get the teacher 'off on a red-herring'. In addition the existence of routinised work tasks makes it much more likely that children will develop collective means of satisfying them.

From Manipulation to Evasion

Manipulation is a strategy with which teachers seek to motivate children to act in ways which will satisfy teacher goals. Teacher coping is thus not achieved through open negotiation or through a reliance on routines, but by an attempt to get children to want what the teacher wants them to want. This is, of course, a particularly sophisticated use of power (Lukes 1974). It must be said that this manipulative use of power may be employed entirely in what is thought to be the children's best educational interests and, if it is successful, the children may well be willing participants. In fact a great deal of what is recognised as 'good teaching' is achieved by this means, and a considerable amount of teacher effort goes into issues such as how to motivate the children, how to present work in an attractive way, how to create a positive classroom climate, etc. The point, of course, is that the gap between what a child is interested in and what a child is deemed to need has to be bridged. However laudable the intention may be, the strategy remains, in analytical terms, manipulative.

We saw an example of this strategy in use earlier in this chapter where a teacher attempted to generate interest and enthusiasm for a creative writing task. He presented himself very positively, attempted to develop a rapport with the children, particularly using humour, praised examples of previous good work and tried to convey the enjoyment which could come from engagement in the task. This teacher was skilled in the use of manipulative strategies despite his problem in matching this particular task to the children's existing level of understanding. Typically control was obtained through 'appeal' both to children's better instincts and to personal loyalty. Interestingly, the decision, part way through that lesson, to cut some educational losses was made in order to maintain the credibility of the manipulative strategy for the future, the essence of it being that teacher goals and pupil compliance should be achieved by high levels of teaching skill rather than by the naked use of power.

Teachers' acting ability, their skill in communicating and the way they are able to use praise, example, flattery and appeal are all factors which will influence their degree of success in using this type of strategy. Where the teacher is skilled and sensitive the response of most children is likely to be to comply with the goals set and to begin to accept the value of the tasks and activities presented. At the extreme, however, or where teacher skills are poorly developed, children will see through the 'facade' presented and, having interpreted the work more negatively, will seek to evade it.

Evasion is a very interesting child strategy which is made possible, to children with a high level of social competence, by teacher manipulation strategies. This is so because, if manipulation is to be successful with the class as a whole, a teacher must temporarily forsake the type of overt use of power which is used in domination strategies. This withdrawal provides a degree of credit or slack at the interface of the two strategies which can be exploited by those who are aware of it and who are suitably motivated and skilled. In the infant-class example cited earlier this was clearly Matthew's initial intention, though it soon became apparent that he had misjudged the teacher's response.

From Domination to Rebellion

In its most literal form domination is a strategy which explicitly attempts to use the expected power differential between teacher and pupils. It is thus qualitatively different from open negotiation, routinisation and manipulation, since it is overtly confrontational— the strategy of last resort. It is unusual to find this strategy in routine use in primary schools, but that does not mean that it is not often used in specific situations where teachers feel under a particular degree of threat.

Examples of this type of domination are thus not hard to find. It occurs in the form of threats and commands in many classrooms. For instance:

> If you don't finish that work you can't go out to play.

It occurs, as Hargreaves (1979) noted, when teachers police the classroom insisting primarily on conformity to behavioural rules, and particularly on 'getting on with work', when children are 'shown up' or when sarcasm is used by teachers in attempts to maintain control.

Such domination is clearly against children's interests, but their strategic responses will vary. A type of conformist withdrawal is common. In this withdrawal strategy children appear to conform but they do so by going through the motions rather than with any engagement. They thus distance themselves from the teacher but protect themselves by overt compliance. Another strategy is refusal or an attempt to minimise work and involvement. This is not uncommon when children feel misunderstood or devalued. Then they turn to the protection of their peer group as an alternative value system and source of dignity.

Pupil strategies such as withdrawal and refusal are essentially defensive and are most often called upon in teaching sessions when the class is dispersed and each child is comparatively isolated. In situations where the class is being taught together, for instance in class discussion sessions, the fact of high pupil numbers can begin to tilt the balance of power so that 'rebellion' becomes a viable strategy. This is particularly likely if the children judge that the teacher is essentially 'soft' or unskilled. Rebellion is not uncommon, for instance, on student teaching practices when a negative cycle of teacher–child relationships has been established. On these occasions children's skills are highlighted and the variety of deviant acts in which they engage can be very wide.

CLASSIFYING STRATEGIES

I have reviewed various types of teacher and child strategy which, I would argue, are commonly associated with one another. In this section an attempt is made to analyse them further.

All strategies have a great deal to do with power and control, and it is possible to use that fact to distinguish between them. For instance, we can immediately make a distinction between those strategies in which the power resources of teachers or children are used unilaterally and those in which the use of power is circumscribed by the interactively constructed understandings of the working consensus. If it is accepted that this is a matter of degree then strategies can immediately be categorised on a circumscribed–unilateral dimension. Having said that, it remains possible in my view to make relatively clear distinctions between three different types of strategy. First, there are the unilateral strategies, such as domination and rebellion, in which teachers and children confront each other directly. The use of unilateral strategies is not circumscribed by the working consensus. Second, there is the theoretically consensual strategy of open negotiation in which teacher and child interests are mutually accepted and accommodated. Third, and most significant, there are the range of routine negotiative strategies, such as routinisation–drifting and manipulation–evasion, which are the product of a continuing struggle between the interests of the children and those of the teacher, but which still remain within the bounds of the working consensus. Such strategies are thus accepted as part of the taken-for-granted character of classroom life; they are not directly consensual but neither are they overtly confrontational.

Table 8.1 attempts to represent this classification of strategies concisely. This model can be illustrated further in relation to types of pupil deviance and teacher censure. In this respect it can be seen that, while open negotiation is likely to produce activity which is conformist in terms of the working consensus, the cases of drifting and evasion represent deviant but non-subversive child strategies. Such 'routine deviance' also lies within the bounds of the working consensus and is almost expected and taken for granted, although it

Table 8.1 *Classifying strategies.*

Teacher acts				Pupil acts
	Working consensus			
Unilateral strategies	*Routine negotiative strategies*	*Consensual strategies*	*Routine negotiative strategies*	*Unilateral strategies*

	open negotiation
	routinisation ◄————————► drifting
	manipulation ◄————————► evasion
domination ◄————————————————————► rebellion

will call forth a similarly routine type of teacher censure. Routine deviance thus conceptualises the fact that both teachers and children expect certain forms of child deviance to occur and to be treated in a matter-of-fact way. For instance:

Teacher   You can never get kids to be good all the time; it wouldn't be natural anyway.

Child   If we did just what we're meant to we'd get bored stiff; most of the teachers will have a bit of a laugh with us.

Teacher   It doesn't seem reasonable to expect children to work hard all the time; besides, messing about is part of life for these lads.

Teacher   You always get a bit of mischief in every class, but we generally rub along together.

These expectations may rest on understandings such as 'boys will be boys' or 'you get this with all children', but they can also be traced very directly to the teacher's obligations under the working consensus to leave the children scope for viable adaptive strategies for their own predicament. 'Having a laugh', which relates to children's interest in enjoyment, is the prime example of this, and teachers are often evaluated by children on the basis of their skill at having, and willingness to have, a laugh.

Thus the working consensus, with its roots in the necessity of interdependent survival, defines not only the parameters of conformist actions but also the parameters of certain forms of legitimate deviance.

Such understandings cover not only various aspects of drifting, such as staring out of the window, not listening to the teacher and working very slowly, but also aspects of evasion, such as standing in queues, 'losing' pencils, going to the toilet, 'not understanding', working 'even more slowly', not handing in work, and talking a lot to friends.

Over time, rules and definitions of contextually 'acceptable' and routinised deviance accumulate to form histories of 'case law' which are secured in the tacit knowledge of the participants. This knowledge also includes understandings of legitimate teacher reactions and legitimate penalties, and it is these which constitute routine censures. For instance:

Child   When we got done after she got my note, well, I thought that was fair 'cos we all knew we might, but it was good fun and we only got lines.

Child   It's OK if you get done for something like talking because you usually get a telling-off, but if you swear at a teacher or something you might get sent to the head for the slipper.

Child   Whispering's best because you don't get found out much and even then it doesn't matter much; we'd only get lines if we kept on doing it.

In my view the teacher–child strategies of routinisation–drifting come squarely within the bounds of these understandings, as, in most cases, do forms of manipulation–evasion strategies.

Of course teachers may break the accepted rules of reaction in some cases, and they will then be seen as being 'too strict' or 'unfair'. In analytical terms they will have begun to act unilaterally and to have adopted a form of domination strategy. Children usually feel very negative about such domination, for instance when they think they are being shown up, picked on or got at. The point here is that such teacher actions are regarded as being illegitimate reactions to the child's act; they are outside the parameters of teacher reaction which the working consensus legitimates, since they attack that very dignity which the pupils' contribution to the working consensus is made to protect. The outcome of this is that rebellion in one form or another becomes much more likely.

On the other hand, the actions and strategies of some children may also break the rules of routine rule-breaking and acceptable strategies. In such cases the actions are no longer framed by the understandings of the working consensus. They are the product of either social incompetence or a more direct and conscious rejection of, or opposition to, the working consensus.

Child   If we get done it's not fair because the smelly gits never listen to what we have to say; they just play bloody hell. So we don't bother with 'em now; we just get on and mess about as much as we can.

Such strategies of rebellion are thus of a type in which the particular child's perceived interests are implemented without the influence of interactive understandings with the teacher. In this sense they are directly comparable to unilateral teacher strategies of domination. Such child strategies are likely to be framed by 'rules of disorder' (Marsh, Rosser and Harré 1978) emerging from a particular peer-group culture. Interestingly, both teachers and children see each other's unilateral acts as semi-mindless or uncontrolled—the teacher goes 'mad', the children 'act daft' or 'get silly'—yet they each see their own unilateral acts in terms of recouping dignity—the teacher 'shows who's boss' while the child 'proves he's tough'.

PARAMETERS OF CHILDREN'S ACTION

Having identified and then classified various types of strategy—essentially on the basis of the type of power employed and the degree of restraint which is generated through negotiation—the question then arises of whether particular types of teacher or types of children characteristically use particular ranges of strategies.

This issue takes us almost immediately into the area of teacher and pupil 'styles', on which a considerable amount of research has been carried out (e.g. Galton, Simon and Croll 1980). Unfortunately, however, it is difficult to relate studies of behavioural style to studies of strategy because of the difference in emphasis between the quantification of observed behaviour in the case of studies of style and the qualitative appreciation of the meaning of actions in the case of studies of strategies. There is considerable scope for collaborative research here in the future.

However, in respect of pupils, the Moorside study did produce some interesting differences between types of group, and these can be related to the strategies and types of pupil action which have been discussed. In Chapter 4 the perspectives of three types of friendship group—goodies, jokers and gangs—were described. These types of group can be seen as empirically grounded ideal types. Thus, while we might not expect to find exactly the same pattern repeated elsewhere or with a different age group, the three types of group can be used as an analytical device for comparative purposes. Indeed, in that compliance, negotiation and opposition are strategies of a very fundamental kind with which the types of group articulate, then there is a certain logic to them which makes it likely that the model will be transferable. There is also evidence to support this view with regard to both older and younger children. Thus, while early secondary-school studies identified opposed cultural pupil groupings (Hargreaves 1967, Lacey 1970, Willis 1977), more recent work has begun to identify a wider variety of strategic adaptations between such poles (Woods 1979, Ball 1981, Turner 1983). Studies of younger children are far less common, but again, as we saw in Chapter 4, those that do exist are broadly supportive.

It will perhaps be recalled from earlier chapters that the types of group at Moorside were distinguishable not only by their attitudes to each other but also, and particularly, with regard to the issue of teacher 'fairness'. This is highly significant, since it is directly related to the children's perceptions of their teacher's appreciation of child interests and to their view of the way their teacher uses power. As we saw, the members of good groups tended to accept the goodwill of teachers and the legitimacy of their strategies with little question. In contrast, members of gang groups often felt that teacher actions were unjustified and unfair attempts to pick on them and to attack their interests. However, this rather polarised view is critically trans-formed when the perspective of the jokers is introduced, for it can be argued that they play the crucial negotiating role. In fact, in my view the working consensus—that body of tacit understandings by which the social order of the classroom is defined—is largely the product of negotiations between joker groups and the teacher. These children neither conform nor actively rebel: they negotiate for a viable *modus vivendi*. They accept teacher authority when it is within the bounds of the negotiated working consensus but regard it as unfair when a teacher act is unilateral. They also act, in most situations, within the bounds of the working consensus. Thus the parameters of their strategies are those of drifting, evasion and routine deviance, for these provide laughs and a release from boredom, but they generally do not participate in unilateral acts of disorder or rebellion. Gangs, on the other hand, have no such inhibitions and make situational choices of action from a less fettered range of possibilities. While in some contexts gang members may conform or be content with interest derived from routine strategies, they tend to feel few inhibitions about 'mucking about' and obtaining the excitement which committing unilateral acts of disorder often brings.

Such, then, are the *parameters* of children's actions, the normal extremes of their strategies. Of course on most occasions it is likely that strategic choices will be made which are well within these parameters.

GENDER DIFFERENCES

It has often been suggested that the behaviour of girls in school is qualitatively different from that of boys because of differences in early socialisation experiences. For instance, Clarricoates (1978) suggested that:

> Through their conditioning girls are more amenable to school and create fewer problems for the teachers. By being conscientious, neat and tidy, and able to 'get on' with their work without constant directives . . . they are viewed as less problematic.
>
> (Clarricoates 1978, p.361)

It is also certainly the case that most studies of deviance in school have been focused on boys, with the tacit assumption being made that girls' deviance is of far less significance.

On the other hand, the empirical studies of girls' perspectives which are available have consistently shown that not all girls are conformist in their view of school. For instance, Lambart's study of the 'sisterhood' (Lambart 1976) and Meyenn's report on the 'PE girls' (Meyenn 1980) both provide examples of deviant female peer groups and, going back to the last century, using oral history, Humphries (1981) claims that:

> there is evidence to suggest that inside schools girls were as disobedient as, or even more disobedient than, boys . . . but because girls often employed more subtle and devious techniques of resistance than boys, much of their misbehaviour has remained hidden and unrecorded in school log and punishment books.
>
> (Humphries 1981, p.76)

The perspectives of the girls in friendship groups at Moorside reported in Chapter 4 also show the existence of deviant girls' peer groups such as Janine's Terrors and Samantha's gang. Indeed it was the close similarity in the perspectives of boys' *and* girls' friendship groups regarding school which led me to focus primarily on the goody, joker and gang distinction as having more analytical power than that of gender. Nevertheless, gender differences in the strategies adopted by children in primary schools undoubtedly do exist and I shall attempt to relate them to the open negotiation, drifting, evasion and rebellion strategies which have been discussed above.

Of course our society is essentially patriarchal, and while boys may act by drawing on the relatively simple and masculine cultural forms which predominate, girls in school undoubtedly have to adapt to the further relative weakness of their position: they are not only pupils but are also female. As the quote from Humphries suggests, the basic outcome seems to lie not so much in differences in the perception of situations regarding teachers and school, but in the range and level of sophistication of the girls' actions which result.

Boys and girls have different cultural resources open to them and thus develop related variations in their strategies. In particular it seems that girls are likely to develop negotiative strategies much further than boys. This may be so because of the 'Catch 22' which Clarricoates (1978) identified in the hidden curriculum. Clarricoates argues that if a girl conforms she is likely to be taken for granted, since conformity is consistent with the passive female stereotype. To engage in some sorts of open negotiation with teachers may run this risk. If she is unilaterally deviant and adopts strategies of rebellion then she violates two sets of values—those of behaviour and those of gender—even though for boys aggressive behaviour is regarded as being acceptable and almost natural. The result of this is that a girl who is unilaterally deviant is likely to run much higher risks than a boy. As Clarricoates put it:

> Girls' misbehaviour is looked upon as a character defect, whilst boys' misbehaviour is viewed as a desire to assert themselves.
>
> (Clarricoates 1978, p.363)

The calculus of a girl seeking to establish her identity and defend her interests is thus likely to result in a focus on negotiative strategies such as drifting and evasion. Success here requires a high level of social competence, which girls often do develop. However, the relative efficiency of these strategies for girls does not entirely preclude an involvement in more rebellious events. Indeed a study by Jones (1984) suggests that some primary-school-aged girls are covert, complex and subversive in their deviance in contrast to the overt and relatively crude 'mucking about' of boys. For instance, she reports that girls 'schemed' to set up the boys to cause trouble. Girls thus have a laugh but do not incur risks. This is a very similar argument to that developed by Davies (1983). In a secondary-school context she highlighted certain aspects of what she called the 'feminine wiles' which are used as 'short term strategies to cope with immediate status threats' (Davies 1983, p.50) and thus to generate a degree of situational power.

The point, then, is that the classroom strategies of girls and boys will vary in emphasis because of wider cultural influences despite what, in my view, is a close similarity in their basic perspectives regarding classroom life. This is so because what people say can be relatively more independent of social context than what they do, and what they do *has* to work in practice. The classroom strategies of girls and boys will thus be adapted by their relative efficiency in enabling the children to cope with the classroom context, and this judgement will include factors relating to gender.

CONCLUSION

This chapter has considered teacher and pupil strategies in the ebb and flow of classroom situations and the ways in which their interests-at-hand are affected by changes in rule frame. Some common strategies were then discussed and were classified essentially on the basis of the degree to which they were circumscribed by the understandings of the working consensus. We then looked at differences in the range of strategies adopted by goodies, jokers and gangs and at variations based on gender differences.

This type of analysis constitutes one way of looking at classroom processes and is the product of an attempt to generate grounded theory from observation, discussion and participation in classroom life. There are many possible applications for such an analysis in the reflection by teachers and others on their practice. However, one area which I am particularly interested in developing concerns the identification of possible social consequences of common classroom processes, and this is the subject of the next chapter.

9

Classroom Processes and Social Consequences

INTRODUCTION

In the book so far I have considered the perspectives of teachers and children in primary schools, the structural, historical and institutional contexts to which they must relate, and the ways in which teachers and pupils strategically interact in order to cope. This chapter is intended to take the argument a stage further by focusing on some aspects of classroom processes which may have significant social consequences.

Of course, we have already established that we live in a society in which power and wealth are unequally distributed. As we saw in Chapter 5, some people argue that this distribution of resources is justified because opportunities are open to all, and in particular because the education system provides a meritocratic route to qualifications and jobs. Others argue that existing levels of inequality advantage some groups and disadvantage other groups from the start. Furthermore, they argue that schools often amplify differences and are not meritocratic.

Now, very few teachers like to think of themselves as being involved in producing *or* reproducing social differentiation in society: it is hardly an educational aim. However, in that teachers are concerned with the growth and development of children, it is inevitable that they will be engaged in this differentiation process to some extent, whatever the age of the children they teach. While it is only at the secondary stage of schooling that the process is made overt by examinations and by the struggle for certificates, it can be argued that processes in primary schools are more subtle but no less effective in contributing to the growth of each child's sense of identity, the quality of learning and thus to his or her ultimate life-chances.

We have to be careful here, though, because the identity and self-image of children will develop through interaction with others whether they are at school or not. The teacher's position is in that respect no different from that of any other adult. However, the point becomes a serious one if it can be shown that particular processes in classrooms systematically *distort* such developments in particular ways to the advantage of one type or class of child over another.

Researchers have often claimed to have found exactly this type of distortion, particularly with regard to social class. For instance, in a classic study by Rosenthal and Jacobson (1968) teachers were systematically *misled* about the supposed potential of their pupils. Pupil achievement was tested later and was found to have changed in the directions which had been indicated to the teachers. This gave rise to the theory that a 'self-fulfilling prophecy' was at work in many classrooms and that the under-achievements of working-class children could be accounted for partly by low teacher expectations. In another study Rist (1970) suggested that the kindergarten teacher whom he studied used a 'roughly constructed ideal-type' based on social-class criteria with which to classify children into a hierarchical grouping system within her classroom—a 'caste system', as he put it. Consequent variation in teacher behaviour resulted in differences in child performance and the caste system began to be institutionalised throughout the school. In another important study Sharp and Green's (1975) analysis of teacher ideologies and social control in the progressive Mapledene Infant School concerned itself with the formation of child identities through the teacher-structured processes of the classroom, in particular as an implication of the teachers' 'busyness ideology'. They concluded that:

> Whilst the teachers display a moral concern that every child matters, in practice there is a subtle process of sponsorship . . . where opportunity is . . . offered to some and closed off to others.
>
> (Sharp and Green 1975, p.218)

Similar claims have been made with regard to gender. For instance, Clarricoates (1981) suggests that:

> Despite the evidence that girls are 'brighter' than boys, in general teachers find the boys more creative and more interesting to teach . . .
>   In schools, girls' creativity is negated in favour of the creativity of the boys which is seen as the only real and imaginative force within our male dominated culture.
>
> (Clarricoates 1981, p.202)

If these studies are looked at collectively, together with other available reports, then there seems to be a very good case for thinking that teachers' knowledge, expectations and behaviour do have an influence on children in particular and patterned ways so that some are advantaged more than others. However, in my view this case is not *fully* substantiated by empirical research, either in terms of the link between particular teacher expectations and behaviour and levels of pupil achievement or in terms of the intervening classroom processes which logically would have to exist.

As I suggested in the introduction to this book, ethnographic methods lend themselves most readily to the *generation* of theory about social relationships rather than to their *verification* across a wider range of situations. If this limitation is accepted, then the model of teacher-pupil relationships which has been constructed up to this point can make some contribution to the issue of social differentiation in classrooms which has fascinated sociologists and worried teachers for so long.

In this chapter, then, I shall consider two aspects of classroom life which seem to me to have considerable social significance. The first concerns the classroom basis of teacher knowledge about children, and the second concerns the ways in which teacher and child strategies 'mesh' together to reinforce and 'multiply' social consequences.

TEACHER KNOWLEDGE ABOUT PUPILS

The work of Hargreaves, Hestor and Mellor (1975) is probably the best account available at present of how teachers develop typifications of the children they teach and, although it was based on studies in secondary schools, it is of considerable relevance here. Their starting point was:

> one of the most basic ideas of the symbolic-interactionist perspective—
> that man understands things by naming them, [and that] to type other
> people—to name them, categorise them, label them—is an inherent
> part of understanding them.
>   (Hargreaves, Hestor and Mellor 1975, p.143)

Teachers, in other words, understand pupils by categorising them.

Hargreaves, Hestor and Mellor postulate three stages in the process through which 'types of pupil' are produced: speculation, elaboration and stabilisation. In the speculative stage the teacher uses her knowledge of the 'typical history' of the children in terms of their age, social background and previous experiences and this sensitises her to particular hypotheses about them. Elaboration takes place if initial hypotheses are confirmed. During this elaborative stage typing becomes extended and more specific as the teacher comes to know the child better. In the final stage of stabilisation, the teacher's knowledge of the pupil is 'woven into a relatively coherent whole' (Hargreaves, Hestor and Mellor 1975, p.88) and becomes 'an integral part of the teacher's common sense knowledge of the classroom and the pupils' (Hargreaves, Hestor and Mellor 1975, p.216).

In my view, Hargreaves, Hestor and Mellor have provided a very plausible description of the stages which are passed through as teachers come to 'know' their pupils. Indeed, their account resonates with teachers' own descriptions of the process in primary schools just as much as in secondary schools. However, it is arguably far less satisfactory in analysing *why* such typings are generated and in documenting their content and implications, and for this reason the analysis offers us few insights into the ways in which the typification of children by teachers might be linked to classroom differentiation.

The question of why teachers should want to type pupils is a crucial one in any explanation of this process. In addressing this issue it must first be recognised that the use of typifications is a normal part of interaction in many social situations. However, the classroom context is a particularly significant one in which the teacher has to face and cope with relatively large numbers of children. This, in phenomenological terms, is a critical element in the 'essential actual experience' of the teacher's classroom life. Given this experiential reality, typing is a means of reducing the complexity or, as Schutz (1970) put it, of making the world of everyday life 'cognitively manageable'. Thus the teacher simplifies by categorising.

Of course, as we have seen, the problem for teachers is not just to cognitively manage their experiences but also to cope with them satisfactorily in terms of their interests-at-hand in the particular situation in which they find themselves. When this is considered it seems clear that one major factor related to the typing of children is the fact that, because the procedure projects from the past into the future, it enables a teacher to anticipate and thus to cope with perceived problems before they arise. Typing children serves teacher interests in prediction and control in the classroom.

This may be seen as regrettable because it is obviously at odds with the educationist concern which requires a teacher to develop detailed and appreciative knowledge of individual children. In fact I think it can be argued that the *extent* of typing will vary and will depend substantially on the quality of the teaching itself. If teachers are highly skilled, develop a positive working consensus and cope very successfully, then they are likely to create the space and time in which to think about and relate to each child as an individual. However, the structural features of the classroom do not make this quality of teaching easy to sustain, and where teachers are less successful, suffer from the stress of confrontation with the children, or even just feel insecure, then they will tend to employ a greater degree of typing. This is exactly the situation which children report when they protest at being picked on unfairly. Unfortunately, it tends to lead into a negative cycle of mutual recrimination and towards the increasing use of domination–rebellion strategies.

The second question which I think has to be addressed concerns the *content* of typifications. In my view there are three analytically discrete factors which require consideration. The first is the influence of the particular biography and teaching style of the teacher. This will undoubtedly influence the way she perceives children in relatively unique ways. The second factor is that of wider social and cultural ideas and conventions which in a sense supply ready-made typifications about children, for instance expectations of girls or of boys, of working-class or of black children. Being cultural, this second factor will tend to produce similarities in the typifications which teachers develop.

Despite the importance of these two factors, the third factor, which relates to teacher knowledge developed *in the situation*, is the one which I want to develop most extensively. My argument is that the content of teacher typifications relates directly to their interests as they seek to 'cope' in the circumstances in which they find themselves. As Leiter (1974) put it in a study of teachers working with kindergarten children, typings are part of an interpretive strategy which is:

> 'invented' by [teachers] to recognise features of the students' behaviour which if not recognised would result in the disintegration of the classroom structure. Thus social types are not theoretical abstractions, they are grounded in the practical circumstances and interests of the user.
>
> (Leiter 1974, p.72)

This argument has its precursor in Becker's (1952) analysis of social-class variation in the teacher–pupil relationship, which has been called an 'ideal-matching model'. Becker wrote:

> The major problems of workers in the service occupations are likely to be a function of their relationship to their clients or customers, those for whom or on whom the occupational service is performed. Members

of such occupations typically have some image of the 'ideal' client, and they use this fiction to fashion their conceptions of how their work ought to be performed, and their actual work techniques. To the degree that actual clients approximate this ideal the worker has no 'client problem'. In a highly differentiated urban society, however, clients vary greatly, and ordinarily only some fraction of the total of potential clients will be 'good' ones. Workers tend to classify clients by the way they vary from this ideal.

(Becker 1952, p.451)

Clearly the 'ideal pupil' for teachers is likely to be a child who acts in ways which are supportive of teacher interests-at-hand, who rewards their sense of self and who enables them to cope. If Becker was right, then other children would tend to be classified and typed by the ways in which they vary from this ideal.

I was able to investigate this proposition in my study at Moorside Middle School, the school from which the model of goody, joker and gang types of group was initially generated. The methodological procedure used was that each of the four teachers working with the year group was asked to record a verbal portrait of selected children onto cassettes, the selection being made to ensure data on children from each type of friendship group. These tapes provided data which could be analysed to see the influence of each of the three factors discussed above: biography and teaching style, culture and classroom necessity.

The data were analysed first by comparing the comments of each of the teachers about the same children. This was done in order to investigate the degree to which comments about the children reflected variations in aspects about each teacher which were unique: biography, teaching style, and also experiences during the year in question.

Despite many similarities, interesting differences of emphasis were found between the teachers, and these can be illustrated by considering their comments about a child called Carl. Mrs Jones, the experienced, respected and highly organised unit leader, tended to emphasise academic factors and to play down personal attributes and discipline concerns:

Mrs Jones commenting on Carl	Reasonable ability I think, but his work didn't always reflect much effort. No matter what he tried to do he made a mess of it. He wasn't at the bottom of the class but not far up it either. He was easily led by whoever happened to be around and you had to keep an eye on him, but not much trouble really.

On the other hand, Mr Matthews, the Scale 2 science specialist who preferred to 'have a bit of fun as well as work', tended to note the degree of children's confidence, their ability to 'get a joke', their capacity to be disruptive and their friendships. On Carl he commented:

Mr Matthews *commenting* *on Carl*	Reasonably intelligent but when it actually came to being in class he's never let on to being so 'cos he was a lazy little so-and-so . . . but if ever there was a class comedian it had to be him . . . he was really quick witted . . . he'd seize on the slightest opportunity and have the whole place in uproar. He loved people to be watching him, to be looking at him whilst he was fooling about . . . while he was doing something . . . um . . . a bit of a shame really because he was quite a bright lad but unfortunately when it came to actually working he didn't want to know . . . but . . . er . . . he was a real character. He never did anything that was so bad it'd get him into serious trouble. He was 'silly', but 'likeable silly' if you know what I mean . . . and all the others in the class . . . he'd more or less get on with 'em all OK really.

These comments can, I think, be taken to reflect the different strategies and personalities of two experienced teachers. Mrs Jones established a low-key, highly routinised, ordered and quiet atmosphere in her classes which most of the children complied with. Her main concerns thus became academic. Interestingly, she found a disproportionately high number of children to be quiet or withdrawn, indicating one aspect of the distancing and drifting strategy that some children adopted as a response. Mr Matthews preferred to mix periods of 'getting on' with 'having a few laughs'. This formed an appeal strategy which he called 'kidology', by which he aimed to get the best from the children and have some light relief himself. The rule frame in his classroom could thus vary considerably depending on phase, in contrast to the relative constancy of Mrs Jones's classroom, and it can be argued that his comments on the children reflected both knowledge gained during low-frame episodes ('has sense of humour', 'a real live wire', 'lots of friends', 'great personality') and the knowledge which it was necessary to have in order to 'manage' such events successfully (e.g. 'disruptive', 'knew the limits', 'silly').

The two other teachers, who were in their first year of teaching, also provided particular emphases in their comments which seemed to reflect their immediate concerns at the time. Both commented frequently on how well or otherwise they understood or got on with children, or on how well children fitted in or settled down. Arguably the salience of this issue can be attributed to the problems which they had in negotiating a working consensus during their probationary year. During this period their teaching techniques and strategies were being adapted relatively rapidly in order to accommodate both their own interests and the circumstances which developed around them. Neither was fully confident about discipline and control. Miss Newsome, who had finally attempted to develop closer personal relationships with the children, commented on Carl:

Miss Newsome *commenting* *on Carl*	I didn't understand Carl from the day I met him till the day he left the fourth year. Occasionally he would work very hard and really take a pride in what he was doing but most of the time he'd . . . he thought he was *above* the work he was set . . . he'd enjoy doing things the others weren't doing and finding different ways of doing things, for example if there was a simple way of finding out he'd have to find something more difficult—something he could say was his conception of how it should be done. He was a bit difficult to handle because of that; sometimes he'd be really awkward. I never felt I really got to know him.

Mr Taylor had adopted a more formal, authoritarian approach and appeared to find difficulty not only in getting to know many of the children, but also in obtaining 'adequate effort'. About Carl he said:

Mr Taylor *commenting* *on Carl*	I found him very strange 'cos he was very unpredictable. Sometimes he could be very nice whilst at other times he didn't want anything to do with you. His work was rather erratic as well. It could be good but more often than not he was quite content to mess about and do nothing. He wasn't any good at games and he didn't seem to want to join in with things really.

In my opinion the variations in the prominence of these factors within each teacher's recollection reflect the instrumental nature of the knowledge they held: it reflected a primary concern with prediction and control, within their circumstances and with the strategies with which they felt most comfortable personally. However, such variations are ultimately of far less consequence than the similarities which existed in the teachers' comments.

This brings us to the 'ideal-matching model'. The first task, of course, is to attempt to delineate the nature of the 'ideal pupil'.

The 'Ideal Pupil'

The essential characteristic of the 'ideal pupil', as perceived by the teachers, appeared to be that his or her actions were, in most instances, favourable towards, or supportive of, the teachers' own perceived coping requirements. These conditions were most routinely and consistently met by members of joker groups because it was primarily with the members of joker groups that teachers negotiated the understandings of the working consensus. This itself, it will be recalled, encapsulates the notion of the mutual accommodation of teachers and children to each other for the purposes of classroom survival and accomplishment. I have reported that the members of good groups tended to accept whatever understandings were reached relatively passively and tended to be conformist, while the members of gangs tended to feel less constrained behaviourally and tended to be likely to identify more exclusively with peer-group values and understandings. It is thus mainly with those children in the joker groups—which at Moorside formed a majority of the pupils—that the teachers reached their accommodation and indeed it was towards these children that the teachers studied appeared to have the most favourable attitudes. We can consider some of their comments, first on some joker-group boys:

Mr Matthews commenting on Stephen	He was a very intelligent lad who was in the top English and maths set, a member of the football team; he'd take part in this, that and the other activity . . . even very bright, very quick-witted, he'd seize on any opportunity to try and make it into a joke . . . er . . . he could get people laughing at him and so on . . . but he was so intelligent that he knew where to draw the line and he wouldn't end up in bother . . . although really I don't mean to say that he was disruptive anyway but he was so sharp, as it were, so quick to seize on anything and turn it into a funny situation . . . again a likeable lad definitely, he was liked by members of staff and by the children in the unit; he was one who seemed to get on with anybody and to be . . . able to cope with any children.
Mr Matthews commenting on Shane	Full of confidence and quite intelligent, he was part of the 'in' crowd of the fourth year. A comedian, liked a laugh . . . could be slightly disruptive but knew when to pick his moments and when to stop . . . a very likeable lad, very friendly and he had a lot of friends.
Mrs Jones commenting on Peter	He was a very bright lad . . . full of self-confidence . . . but controlled self-confidence . . . he knew when and where joking should end and the serious bits should start. He was very good in discussion . . . very good indeed.

Mrs Jones *commenting* *on Jim*	He was definitely in the top five of my class without any trouble at all. His academic work was very good. His behaviour was very good certainly within the classroom.
Miss Newsome *commenting* *on Stephen*	He was a very down-to-earth, happy boy. A very mature, likeable . . . I would say somebody who was easy to teach, did what he was told but at the same time had a sense of humour and enjoyed school. Very, very popular with both the boys and the girls.
Mrs Jones *commenting* *on Stuart*	He was another trier, always tried very, very hard to please . . . me or anybody else . . . and he certainly reacted well to encouragement. He'd like a joke but he was no trouble at all really.

These boys were first perceived as intelligent, as receptive and as easy to teach. This, of course, can be seen as a confirmation that they posed very few problems to the teachers' instructional interests. In the case of some of the less gifted joker children, e.g. Stuart, it was their willingness to try hard that satisfied this interest: they would 'get on' when necessary. At the same time these children were considered to be very active and outgoing. They were considered to be confident, quick-witted, bright and good in discussion. Just as joker-group children participated disproportionately in school clubs and activities, so these favourable teacher comments indicate them as contributing more than members of other types of group to positively regarded aspects of classroom life. The teachers could normally expect appreciative feedback to their lessons from these children, they could expect a little light relief from their sense of fun, but they could also expect this to be kept within bounds and to be appropriate because of the children's interpretive competence and their ultimate respect for the teachers: they 'know when to stop', they 'would not go too far', they 'knew when the serious bits should start'. These children did not therefore pose a problem for the teachers' interest in maintaining order. Certainly they could be slightly disruptive, but such high spirits could usually be brought under control without difficulty. In addition the joking was partly regarded as enabling the teachers to relax in the momentary dropping of their roles just as it served similar purposes for the children. Such deviance was thus regarded as a routine event and one which, particularly for the boys, was sponsored when the teachers were in a good mood by the subterranean value of the teachers, who expected 'boys to show a bit of spunk' (Mrs Jones) and 'the lads to have a laugh' (Mr Matthews).

The teachers' comments on the girls in joker groups show very similar concerns, but with some significant differences which appear to be associated with gender:

Mr Taylor commenting on Jayne

She was one of the best girls in the class as regards academically . . . a very quiet girl . . . a girl who entered into everything . . . she was very sporty; she used to be in the rounders team, the netball team . . . and always pleasant, her manners were exceptionally good. She used to go about with the better members of the unit and I think her attitudes stem from her mother . . . her mother seems to be one of those 'ladies' if you like, with this ladylike appearance and personality which was passed on to Jayne. She was always well dressed and took a great deal of pride in her appearance.

Mrs Jones commenting on Julie

Quite a bit of a live wire, but a pleasant live wire; she knew exactly what the limits were as far as behaviour was concerned; she certainly didn't cause any trouble at all. Good ability.

Mrs Jones commenting on Joanne

. . . was very, very good at sport, full of fun, full of life . . . always wearing trousers . . . definitely clever . . . she knew when to behave but she was a bundle of fun . . . always there if there was anything to be entered into . . . she'd put her heart and soul into everything.

Miss Newsome commenting on Paula

Absolutely full of fun . . . very, very conscientious . . . worked extremely hard and very well . . . very independent as well—if she knew what she was about then she'd go ahead and do it . . . none of this fussing about with 'do I do this or do I do that' . . . erm . . . not too popular though because of her independence. Very firm ideas of what she wanted from life.

Mr Taylor commenting on Heather

A super girl, a super personality; she'd do anything to help teachers and one of the best academically.

Mr Taylor commenting on Tessa

She was a *very* nice girl, very bright and *always* a pleasure to teach. She'd try her best at all times and she was always well mannered and well dressed.

Mr Matthews commenting on Tessa

Another of the high-flying, jet-set members . . . erm . . . very attractive, with-it type of girl who was full of confidence, quite intelligent, she'd got a lot of friends, a lot of people seemed to like her . . . er . . . I suppose she was very similar to Simon and Paul that I've mentioned . . . certainly keen to do anything . . . have a laugh . . . very confident and sure of herself . . . y'know quite a

> likeable young lady. Very, very popular and she was
> the sort of child who always worked well, she liked
> to do well and she was very conscientious, very neat
> and tidy . . . erm . . . at the same time she was
> almost a pupil's pupil in that she could hold her own
> both in the eyes of the teacher and in those of her
> peers . . . very popular indeed.

Again, these children were generally regarded as being intelligent and their conscientiousness was noted. They posed few instructional problems for the teachers. They were participatory, they would 'join in', were 'with-it' and 'full of fun', and had 'a bit about them', but again they could interpret the contextual appropriateness of their actions, were respectful and 'knew when to stop'. Thus they did not pose a disciplinary problem. In fact, the teachers tended to note a different quality of respect from that identified for the boys. While the boys might be 'a bit cheeky, but not rude' (Mr Matthews), the girls were more often noted for their 'pleasantness' or their 'good manners'. Thus the teacher–child interaction is still in the direction of consociate status (Schutz 1970) but is perceived as taking a slightly different form for the girls from that for the boys. The girls' dress and appearance were also noted far more than the dress or appearance of the boys. Clearly what we have here is an instance of the 'fostering of femininity' which Jones (1980) has reported. This gender-based variation in the way joker-group children are perceived is an example of the way in which wider cultural values and ideas influence the school situation.

Irrespective of gender differences, I would suggest that joker-group children can be regarded as 'ideal pupils'. They satisfied basic teacher interests in instruction and order and they also rewarded facets of teacher self-interests by providing moments of uninhibited enjoyment, of relaxation from stress and of positive regard. They were also of crucial structural significance for the teachers as mediators between each teacher and their class, since they were competent in the official social system of the school and dominant in the unofficial social system of the children (see Chapter 4). Perhaps a hint of awareness of this significance comes over in the frequent teacher comments about the degree of popularity of joker-group members. I do not think, therefore, that it is an exaggeration to say that the teachers' personal coping can be seen as being largely dependent on such joker-group children. They were the type of group providing the greatest potential source of personal reward and they were also the type of group which acted as the major medium in negotiation to mitigate the potentially more 'stultifying' (Mr

Matthews) effects of good groups or the potentially more stressful and unilateral actions of gang groups. As such they were seen by these teachers as not only 'ideal' but also as a great asset.

The members of good groups were not regarded quite so positively. Generally the teachers appeared to find such children no problem to their instructional interests or to their interest in order, but they often seemed to consider them to be lacking in imagination, to be too quiet and to be lacking in confidence. For instance:

Mrs Jones commenting on Una	She was so quiet, so painfully quiet but yet would look carefully and take everything in. She wouldn't miss anything at all but she would never ever have anything to say for herself . . . you hardly ever saw her smile . . . if you spoke to her you very rarely got a reaction from her . . . and this wasn't bad manners on her part; it was just the way she is . . . very, very quiet, my goodness . . .
Mr Taylor commenting on Adam	He was very intelligent, but he was very, very slow in coming forward; he'd never take part in discussion work or anything.
Mrs Jones commenting on Caroline	Well developed and a bit self-conscious but very, very quiet. She never had anything to say unless I asked her something. She'd never ever volunteer any information either about something that she'd done at home, at the weekend or what had happened in the playground, absolutely nothing. I had to ask everything I wanted to know from her. In oral work she'd never join in the discussion but obviously understood everything that had been said, otherwise her work would have suffered . . . and it certainly didn't.
Miss Newsome commenting on Caroline	Very quiet but quite mature with it . . . erm . . . didn't always have a lot to say for herself but the sort of child who'd always get her work done and perhaps not be noticed within the class.
Mr Taylor commenting on Kirsty	A very pleasant personality, very much like her mother's, very quiet but at the same time very nice. Her work was good. She always tried very hard. She was never very forward in discussion work, always left it up to everybody else to do the talking, but she obviously listened very carefully in class and did reasonably good work.

These examples show fairly neutral teacher responses to the children. Their unwillingness to participate openly in class work and contribute to the lessons is noted, but this is balanced with their willingness to 'get on', their politeness, their pleasantness and their hard-working conscientiousness. However, for a few of the good-group children, and particularly for the girls, their unwillingness to communicate openly with the teachers did produce unfavourable typings if evidence of underlying respect and pleasantness was not seen:

Miss Newsome commenting on Alison	Very quiet, an almost mean expression; she never appeared to trust what you said . . . very difficult to get to know . . . somebody who was a bit of a loner perhaps . . . Very nervous and shy, she always gave the impression that she was producing substandard work through lack of effort. She could do it really. She never seemed to trust anybody but she never did anything wrong for all that . . .

Unfavourable typings also seemed to follow if a child's desire to 'get the work right' resulted in their being 'too fussy':

Mr Taylor commenting on Linda	A very fussy and lonely child. She always had to gain your attention by asking you to check her work. She'd never step out of line but she'd go on and on.
Mrs Jones commenting on Linda	She was a bit of a one for seeking attention. I wouldn't have thought she lacked attention at home; perhaps she had a feeling of inferiority compared with her twin brother, but she'd always be talking or wanting something from one of the teachers.

For some girls of the good groups their reticence was interpreted as insecurity and produced a concerned response from the teacher:

Miss Newsome commenting on Lorrain	Very, very, very quiet . . . always a little bit wary of you . . . if you told her off you always nearly got tears . . . had to be handled carefully.
Miss Newsome commenting on Una	Una was perhaps a problem in that she was so very, very quiet, very, very sensitive to the extent that she was loath to speak to me as the teacher and I get the feeling that she was very lonely . . . she was so quiet that she couldn't even make contact with other children in the class.
Mr Matthews commenting on Una	Very, very quiet; she didn't seem to have enough life in her to cause any problems or to be memorable.

Goodness and conformity were thus seen by the teachers as normal and acceptable behaviour for the girls. However, this was not so for the boys.

One of the more retiring boys who was clearly 'good' both in his behaviour and in his academic performance was typed as being 'soft', 'lacking in spunk' and 'hiding behind his mother's apron', rather than regarded with concern as were the girls above. Such typings were particularly applied to one boy called Martin:

Mr Matthews commenting on Martin	He was very, very unsure of himself and he could never fight his own battles as it were. The slightest thing that went wrong then he'd run home and have his mum running up to school and causing all sorts of havoc. He was certainly pampered too much at home . . . not allowed to stand on his own feet enough, which is a shame really . . . very, very soft . . . the slightest thing would seem to upset him and that would be it . . . he could be a right pain at times.
Mrs Jones commenting on Martin	Unfortunately, I think the product of an overbearing mother who didn't allow him to live his life as he ought to have been able to do. He hid very much behind his mother's apron front and wouldn't make any decisions for himself . . . cried to mum if anything went wrong . . . unfortunate . . . something I don't particularly like, particularly in a boy . . . I think a boy of his age should have a bit more spunk about him . . . he was quite bright but he'd never stand on his own two feet.
Miss Newsome commenting on Martin	He was a very fussy boy; he wouldn't join in PE or games; given a chance to skip out he would do.

I have suggested that the members of good groups adopted a basic strategy of conformity to the teachers' wishes. They were generally unwilling to take risks by incautiously 'having a laugh' or by skimping their work. The teachers tended to take them for granted and to feel able to rely on them, but in many cases the teachers felt they knew 'little about them', that such good-group children contributed little to the flow of classroom activities and that they tended to be 'rather dull'. As Mr Matthews put it:

Mr Matthews	Well, these sort of kids . . . you know you can always count on them, they're totally reliable but when you've said that you've said it all. If you had a class full of children like them you'd get bored out of your head . . . they don't join in, that's the main thing, they're so quiet and shy.

Many members of good groups thus seemed to be conformist to the letter, to be sensible, serious and conscientious. By so doing they seemed to miss the more subtle point that, when contextually appropriate, the teachers were prepared to accept, and indeed thrived on, more active and positive contributions to lessons and even, when 'in the mood', to collaborate with forms of routine deviance. In their strict avoidance of such activities the members of good groups in fact deviated from the teachers' ideal pupil: the boys 'lacked spunk' and the girls were considered 'painfully quiet'.

The members of gang groups also deviated from the teachers' conception of the 'ideal pupil', generally because their actions tended to be seen as being potentially more threatening to teacher interests. However, a distinction was apparent here between those gang-member children for whose perceived attributes the teachers had developed a form of rationale and those whose behaviour and attitudes were perceived more exclusively, without mitigation, as a threat to teacher interests. In the case of the first type the teachers' reflection on the child and his or her problems and their generation of forms of sociological or psychological explanation indicate a 'professional' assessment of the child, reflecting their concern to understand the child as such. In the case of the second type fewer allowances were made and the teacher typings appeared generally to reflect a more primary concern with the coping problems which these children caused rather than with the children themselves. Some examples are given below.

In the cases of Lucy and Barbara their home background is used to explain the difficulties they caused at school. This constitutes a form of sociological explanation which mitigates the teacher's interpretation of their actions.

Mrs Jones commenting on Lucy	A seeker of attention, she came from a split family who lived together and I think she was perhaps lacking in attention at home and she used to try and make up for it at school. She would perhaps fake an illness, perhaps have hurt her leg, something like that, just to get a bit of attention. She was in the lower ability range but not much trouble apart from this constant attention-seeking.
Mr Taylor commenting on Barbara	She didn't have a very wealthy home background. She always used to look dirty and her clothes in need of repair. I can't remember a great deal about Barbara except that she was one of the less able members of the class and somewhat immature in her approach to anything. I recollect that she had this special friendship with Karen, who was very similar in both maturity and intelligence, but they never did anything really serious, just basically very talkative and giggly or silly far too much. Just very annoying, the pair of them.

David, on the other hand, was regarded as being 'a bit strange', as if there was something wrong with him physically or psychologically.

Miss Newsome commenting on David	I can't remember much about him apart from the fact that he was very difficult for people, not because he was so badly behaved but because he seemed to go off in his dream world fantasy-type things and it was difficult to bring him back to reality. A strange boy.
Mr Taylor commenting on David	Well, he was a little bit of a drip . . . he had very little concentration—couldn't concentrate on anything for any length of time. He was obviously of poor ability. He was a frail-looking sort of boy who didn't take part in anything. I don't think he liked coming to school and I think he was sort of looking forward to the bell every night; he was that sort of a boy . . . never seemed to have any life in him at all. He seemed to remind me very much of a sloth or something like that . . . he was not a very memorable or lively character. He didn't seem to do a great deal and he was never keen to take part in anything; he just seemed to wander around all playtime and play marbles or sit about. Yet if he did start acting about in a lesson he could be really quiet disruptive. He seemed to lose control of himself then . . . though most of the time he just mooned about. I don't know why he should have been like that . . .

However, the majority of gang-member children were described more directly in terms of their effect on the teachers, with fewer allowances being made for their circumstances or natures. In the descriptions which follow the behaviour or attributes of the children can be seen as being matched by the teachers against their conception of the 'ideal pupil' and the perception of their interests-at-hand in their daily classroom life.

Miss Newsome commenting on Jonathan	I never got on with him. I never could understand him. I never could get him round to my way of thinking . . . he was always absolutely harebrained as far as I was concerned . . . he wouldn't concentrate on his work . . . what he did was untidy . . . I didn't seem to be able to get any sense out of him either in English or maths . . . very, very difficult to get on with.
Mr Taylor commenting on Malcolm	I didn't get on very well with this lad. When I spoke to him he seemed very blunt and very supercilious, as if he had a high opinion of himself. Consequently I didn't really get to know him; in fact I avoided him where I could.

Mr Matthews commenting on Samantha	She sticks out with most of the staff because of the fact that she was such a nasty piece of work; she was *very* vulgar . . . erm . . . all the staff had great problems getting on with her . . . she seemed to resent anything and everything to do with authority or being told what to do and so on . . . she was a real little madam who would like to do things of her own without being told and she could turn round and be really nasty . . . bad language . . . not a very nice young lady at all, I'm afraid to say. I do remember she certainly resented being told off and when it happened she'd show her bad temper or burst into tears or go racing off and lock herself in the toilets . . . say she wouldn't come out, say 'that's it this time; I'm going to fetch my mum up to school' and this, that and the other . . . yes, certainly the type of young lady you can do without in your class.
Mr Matthews commenting on Mark	The point that sticks out about him is the fact that he was never keen to do a great deal of work . . . and he often tried to be as disruptive as possible . . . also remember that he'd be one who'd take offence when told off. He'd get insolent then and get in even more trouble . . . in fact he could be a bloody nuisance.
Mr Taylor commenting on Malcolm	He could be really awkward and disruptive. If he wanted to he'd cause a lot of bother and ignore anything the teacher said . . . he really didn't seem to care. He wasn't very good academically but the main thing was that he didn't bother about the teachers—once he even told Mr Smith to 'sod off' and really when he was around you had to keep him under careful control—try to get him interested 'cos if he thought you were watching out for him especially then he'd start something up to spite you.
Mrs Jones commenting on Carly	A bit of a stirrer . . . you could never prove anything but you always had the feeling that she might be behind it . . . and by trouble I don't mean anything more serious than somebody falling out with someone else . . . it was not desperate trouble but little things that went wrong. Carly would tend to be behind it.

In my opinion, the teachers' interests here are prominent in their descriptions of the children. They regret being unable to get on with or understand the children: in interactionist terms they felt unable to negotiate with them. They deplore the lack of effort which the children put into their academic work and the degree of disruption which they cause, whether directly in the form of creating a scene or indirectly in the form of 'stirring'. Both the teachers' instructional interest and their interest in order were thus seen as being threatened by these children. They also felt personally threatened by insolence, superciliousness and vulgarity and by the resentment of teacher authority and the 'taking of offence' which the children sometimes displayed.

Some children, of course, were not perceived in the same way by all the teachers. Kevin is one example of this. He was seen as being disruptive, work-shy, dim and insolent by Mr Matthews and Mr Taylor:

Mr Matthews commenting on Kevin	He stands out due to the fact that he was extremely disruptive, especially I remember to Mr Taylor with him only just having come to the place. Kevin would be able to pick this out and he'd seize on any opportunity he could to be disruptive. I remember the nasty side of him. He disliked being told off; it was all right if things were going his way and he could mess about and fool about and get people to think he was funny—although I don't think they really did. I think most of the children in the class thought he was an idiot—and if he was told off he'd simply race out of the classroom and generally create havoc and say he was never coming back. There was once or twice when I could have absolutely flattened him. If you told him off he'd sulk for a time.
Mr Taylor commenting on Kevin	He was in the bottom end of the class academically. He had a strange attitude to work . . . well, he didn't like it basically; he didn't like work and he'd find any opportunity to get out of working. He had a temper which was unpredictable and also it was nasty. He could start off in a tantrum if something didn't suit him and on one occasion in particular I had a war of nerves with him where he refused to do something in class and I gave him lines for not doing it . . . then he refused to do the lines and it took a great deal of force on my part to make him do them. I'd to sit him in the chair at 4 o'clock and make him do them.

Mrs Jones, however, was slightly more sympathetic, identifying an 'aggressive *nature*' and a difficult home background. Mrs Jones was, of course, the most experienced of the four teachers, she had the most organised classroom and teaching style and she was the unit leader. She appeared to experience the fewest problems with order, and this may account for her generally more reflective accounts of the children.

Mrs Jones	Kevin had obviously learnt to defend himself at a
commenting	very early age because he was a very aggressive sort
on Kevin	of child . . . he was the cause of a lot of trouble and

got into trouble a lot himself. He was definitely in the bottom of the ability range and had this very aggressive nature. I'm sure his home background had a lot to do with it 'cos he lived with his mother and she had a terrible job controlling him. His parents had split up.

With such variations acknowledged, in most instances the children who were members of gang groups were the least favourably typed by the teachers. They were typically seen as difficult, irritating, lazy, disruptive or insolent.

In this section I have argued that teacher typifications of children can be incisively analysed by regarding them as an interpretive means of achieving the teacher's goal of coping in their classrooms. Each teacher, in my view, builds up a partial view of pupil attributes. This includes aspects which appear to serve a purpose in the teacher's concern with prediction and control, and it generally excludes those aspects which appear to have less pragmatic utility. The process of typification is thus firmly rooted in processes of interaction within the classroom and in the contextual conditions which structure them, although it is also the case that, as we saw in the case of gender expectations, the content of typifications also reflects the values of the wider culture.

The study of teacher knowledge is obviously important because of the significance of the teacher in classroom processes. However, it is only one of a large number of teacher factors which could be identified as influencing social differentiation in classrooms, for instance teacher language, classroom organisation, discipline structures and the curriculum. A second class of factors relate to children themselves and to their social world, with its own status systems, culture, hierarchy, peer groups, rules and 'currency'. Processes in this social system also lead to differentiation. We saw something of the factors involved in Chapters 3 and 4, and I cannot develop the points further here. However, the analysis which I do want to develop in more detail is one which attempts to relate the strategies of teachers and the strategies of children to each other—a necessity for an interactionist study.

THE MULTIPLICATION OF DIFFERENTIATION

The purpose of this section is to suggest some effects that teacher and pupil coping strategies may have when they mesh together. More specifically, I shall argue that, in classrooms where a working consensus exists, teachers and children interact to *mutually* reinforce classroom differentiation as a by-product of the mesh of their strategies.

As we have seen in earlier chapters, when a working consensus is established it represents a mutual accommodation for coping. Of course, such a truce cannot be taken for granted. The particular strategies which children develop when faced with their coping problem will vary depending on their biographies and on the particular nature of the cultural, institutional and classroom contexts which exist. Some may try to 'take on' the teacher and to challenge their authority, but I have suggested that it is far more common, among primary-school children at least, to find the type of acceptance of 'how things are' which supports the idea of a working consensus having been negotiated. Since the working consensus is a product of both teacher and child coping strategies having achieved some sort of balance vis-à-vis each other, it follows that in each case the particular coping strategies of the other represent a major factor to which their own strategies must have adapted. The result, as we saw in Chapter 8, is that over time the strategies of both the teacher and the children tend to become meshed together, with those of the children being the more adapted because of the teacher's greater power. One outcome of this is that, whatever the sociological significance of the teacher strategies may be, the children's coping strategies are likely to reinforce and 'multiply' this consequence.

I want now to try to substantiate and illustrate this suggestion by drawing on two classroom studies with six- and seven-year-olds. The classrooms were in different schools, Summerlands Infant School and Ashton First School, although the schools were themselves very similar, both being located on the edges of council estates in the inner suburbs of northern towns. They were also of similar age, construction and design. However, the forms of classroom organisation and the teachers themselves were very different. At Summerlands, Mrs Rothwell maintained what an adviser called a 'good formal régime', while the class at Ashton was run on what might have been called 'progressive' principles and was taught by Mr Harman. We can begin with Mrs Rothwell and her class.

Mrs Rothwell had a teaching certificate and was in her late thirties. She had taught for twelve years. She was married to a civil engineer, had two children and lived in a pleasant rural village outside the town. She had been brought up as, and was, a practising Christian.

A core aspect of Mrs Rothwell's perspective could be described as being 'familial'. As she explained to me:

A school should be like a good family, with discipline, love, and room to explore.

Mrs Rothwell felt a sincere, caring duty towards the children in her class, whom she believed came from generally poor and unstable home backgrounds. She felt that these homes failed to provide discipline, standards of behaviour and support for the children and, to compensate for this background, she emphasised 'developing an awareness of right and wrong'.

Mrs Rothwell frequently used personality constructs. Children were often described as 'extrovert' and 'lively' or as 'introverted'. Mrs Rothwell also identified those children who were 'immature' and those who were 'growing up'. From her experience with her own children she believed that she 'knew the stages that children go through'. Mrs Rothwell had a complex array of descriptions to describe the intelligence of children. These ranged from 'exceptionally bright, very bright, reasonably bright, intelligent, capable, great ability, very able, thoughtful' to 'poor, not very clever, needs help, backward'.

Mrs Rothwell had a clear image of her 'ideal pupil' but felt a type of resigned concern towards many of those who could not match up to this image. As she put it:

> It really is rewarding when you get a child who is bright, one who you can really talk to and rely on, but we don't get many of those . . . most of them here really do need a lot of help. We do what we can for them but some of them are very hard to help even when you want to do your best for them.

Regarding pedagogy, Mrs Rothwell felt that learning took place best when she transmitted the knowledge, usually in a discussion → blackboard → book-work sequence, and when the children had had enough practice. Thus there was frequent recitation of maths tables, practice of sums, reading and writing. In Mrs Rothwell's view, the children worked best when they had an incentive, and she provided this with a star reward system. Competition was encouraged so that children would 'get on quickly and carefully'. However, some children 'didn't try' and were 'careless', while others 'lacked concentration'. These children were regarded as unsettled, in contrast to those well adjusted to school.

Mrs Rothwell's perspective seemed internally consistent. She believed that the skills and the body of knowledge which it was her duty to teach were linear by nature, and she believed that learning occurs through practice and reinforcement. She therefore introduced work in a careful order and took her planning and preparation very seriously. She provided a fixed timetable in which there was plenty of time for work and practice, and awarded stars to stimulate competition and to provide reinforcement. In Mrs Rothwell's view the structured routines and timetables which she maintained provided the security the children needed. In turn she felt that security made it possible for the children to be happy, and as she said:

> They should be happy in school, even if they learn only a little, because they come from broken homes.

Mrs Rothwell's perspective was thus organised around what she saw as her two main duties: the compensation for poor home backgrounds by providing moral standards and security and the efficient imparting of knowledge and skills.

In Mrs Rothwell's classroom the tables were arranged in two rectangular blocks, with the blackboard and the teacher's desk at either end of the blocks. Seating places were officially allocated by Mrs Rothwell and were fixed. The 'brightest' and 'average' children each occupied the majority of a table block (the 'top' and 'middle' groups), with a group of 'less able' children split between the two blocks and clustered at the end of each nearest to the teacher's desk (the 'bottom' group).

Mrs Rothwell used classwork for almost everything: during craft activities everyone made a flower in the way they were shown; in writing practice everyone copied the patterns from the board; in number lessons everyone chanted their two-times, three-times, five-times and ten-times tables; in poetry times children spoke verses chorally; in creative English everyone wrote on the subject suggested using the words written on the blackboard. These examples occurred consistently and regularly.

The consistencies in Mrs Rothwell's image of her ideal pupil, her typifications and dominant constructs, and her formal pedagogy, classroom organisation and child-grouping methods are quite clear. They are all associated with the particular teaching strategies by which she sought to cope in the classroom. They were the means by which she reconciled her image of herself and her role with her daily practical situation.

From their close similarity to those found by Rist (1970), Mrs Rothwell's teaching strategies appeared likely to produce a social hierarchy within the class, and this was investigated by analysing the relationship between the friendship structure of the class and two indices of academic achievement.

A sociometric analysis showed that friendship groupings of girls and boys were distinct, and this was confirmed by observations of their play in the playground. The boys tended to be interested in Action Man, guns, fighting, chasing, Steve Austin, space, etc., while the girls tended to be more involved with skipping, dolls, and home games. This distinction was often reinforced by Mrs Rothwell; for instance, boys and girls lined up separately, were dismissed from the classroom separately, were given different types of classroom 'jobs' and were spoken to in qualitatively different ways. It was also found that the friendship groupings corresponded closely with the official academic ranking system used by Mrs Rothwell. Two indices of academic achievement were immediately available—official group seat places and reading-book levels—and the relationship between these and informal friendship groupings is shown in Table 9.1.

A pattern between informal friendship groups, group seat places and reading-book levels appears to be revealed here. For instance, in

Table 9.1   *Seat places and reading-book levels in Mrs Rothwell's class, by friendship groups.*

Friendship group		Seat places by table	Reading-book level
Group 1	Sandra	T	14
	Shirley	B	4
	Ann	M	12
	Andrea	M	12
	Denise	M	12
	Valerie	M	8
	Elaine	T	11
	Kathie	M	10
Group 2	Sarah	T	14
	Janet	T	14
	Jane	T	17
	Lee	T	16
Group 3	Clive	B	8
	Duncan	T	17
	Miles	T	17
	Roger	T	13
Group 4	Thomas	M	4
	Denis	M	8
	Charles	M	9
	Terry	M	4
	Peter	M	8
	Geoffrey	M	10
	Alan	T	10
Group 5	Raymond	B	6
	Catherine	B	4
Unplaced	Colin	B	—

the case of the girls, all of Group 2 sat on the top table and were on the fourteenth reading book in the scheme or beyond, while the other girls' group was made up mainly of children on the middle table and on or below the fourteenth reading book. The pattern was very similar for the boys, there being one group based on the top table and one group based on the middle table. Two children from the bottom table were shown by sociometric analysis as aspiring to join such groups, but their choice was not reciprocated. Two others, Raymond and Catherine, formed the only mixed-sex friendship group.

Mrs Rothwell's criteria for allocation of seat places were not designed to reinforce friendships. The seat places were fixed and maintained by Mrs Rothwell for occasional pedagogic convenience, and the social ranking of the children which resulted was validated by her perspective concerning the nature of children's abilities and by her view of the competitive spur which the possibility of 'moving to a higher table' or 'being on the highest table' might provide. There are thus good reasons for doubting that the friendships had developed independently of the seat-place pattern. My conclusion, then, is that, subject to the limitations of sociometric work, the children's friendships groups seemed to have been influenced by each child's degree of achievement and by their official identities in the classroom. This is a fairly unremarkable conclusion and appears to be a relatively simple consequence of Mrs Rothwell's perspective, classroom organisation and teaching strategies. One way of putting this is to say that, through her own coping strategies, she had created conditions for primary differentiation. She had a clear image of her 'ideal pupil' and a highly developed set of constructs and typifications. This was combined with forms of classroom organisation and pedagogy which derived from, and reinforced, her perspective.

I want now to focus on what could be termed 'secondary differentiation', which comes into play when the children and their coping strategies mesh in interaction with the teacher and his or hers.

An illustration of child strategies in Mrs Rothwell's class which can briefly be described as 'collaboration to produce' may make this argument clearer. First it should be said that a type of working consensus did appear to exist in the class, focused particularly on routinisation–drifting strategies. The majority of children appeared to accept the dominant definition of the situation, as initiated primarily by Mrs Rothwell, without demur. Indeed, in almost all their work, the majority tried to 'please teacher' by producing correct results; they wanted to win a star and, above all, they did not want to fail. As I have described, the most common setting requiring accomplishment in the class was when the children sat in their places. 'Number' was a typical lesson of this type, in which sums were put on the blackboard for everyone to do. Mrs Rothwell's movement pattern was then regular. After setting the lesson-task and checking that the children had begun, she went to her desk to hear readers. The result of Mrs Rothwell sitting at her desk, in combination with her class work and many children's determination to please her, was that the potential for collaboration to find the answers was enormous, and such collaboration was widespread. In fact the children appeared to have traded a degree of compliance with Mrs Rothwell's goals in exchange for her unwitting non-intervention with their strategies for attaining them. It was this trade-off that appeared to be the underlying basis of the working consensus.

The collaboration system was very interesting. On those occasions when there was general unease among the children about how to accomplish a set task, such as their sums, observations suggested that a few key children on each table actually did the work and that these answers then flowed through friendship groups in a 'ripple' of knowledge. In other circumstances, when the work set was familiar and most of the children felt confident, they could work alone. Of course, most commonly situations occurred somewhere between these alternatives and also varied within the class. However, collaboration was far from unusual and was an active process, as the following transcript of a conversation recorded on the top table shows.

Mrs Rothwell	Today we are going to try to do two sorts of sums at once; we'll try to do the take-away ones and the add-up ones, but I'm going to try and trick you by mixing them up [writes sums on board]. This is my day for tricking people.

The children work. A little later:

Janet	She hasn't caught me out yet.
Sandra	She hasn't caught me out yet.
Nigel	She hasn't caught me out yet—has she?
Janet	She has—you're caught—she's caught him out!
Nigel	Why?
Janet	He's got two 'ten take-aways'.
Nigel	I think she has caught me out.
Duncan	Nigel, I think you'd better copy off me, or you'll make a messy job. Ten take away nought makes ten.
Sandra	Ten take away nought makes ten?
Janet	You've done the second one wrong; you've done the second one wrong.
Nigel	I haven't.

Janet	You have—oh, there shouldn't be a four there, should there?
Duncan	There should.
Janet	Should there? [Janet alters the answer.]
Nigel	Yes, oh yes, that's right.
Sandra	You've done it wrong; there shouldn't be a four there, should there? [Children change answers.]
Duncan	Mine's right.
Nigel	So's mine.
Janet	Mine is.
Sandra	Mine is.
Janet	Everybody knows ten add ten makes twenty.
Nigel	Ten add ten makes twenty.
Nigel	What's ten add nothing?
Duncan	Nothing.
Sandra	Ten add nothing is nothing—it's nothing.
Nigel	Janet's done it wrong; she's done ten.
Sandra	Mine are right.
Duncan	They are tricky—oh, Sandra, you've done that one wrong, no, look. [Shows and Sandra alters.]
Duncan	That's it.

In effect these children were negotiating among themselves for the 'right' answer. As we have seen, academic criteria were important to the children's social system, and observations of 'negotiations for right answers' between children suggested that some children with a reputation for generally 'getting them right' had considerable prestige; for instance, the child who managed to get 'ten add nothing is nothing' accepted was the most chosen child on the sociomatrix.

A related strategy for accomplishing the seat-work lessons which was frequently observed was one of waiting for someone else to have their work marked and then checking and perhaps changing one's own answers. Some children seemed highly dependent on these collaborative strategies, and in these cases their timing was very important, because if they failed to collect enough answers early in the lesson, they ran a risk that some key children may finish, be marked and put their books away in drawers. In these circumstances the only possible strategy was to attempt to move seats, and some children were repeatedly told off for doing so, as well as subsequently receiving sanctions for 'not having tried'.

Hard evidence was available to support observations and cassette recordings of collaboration, in the form of analysis of 'errors in common' made by children in their sum books over half a term. This indicated high percentages of 'errors in common' between neighbouring children sitting at the top and middle tables. The top group tended to complete more sums than the middle group, and also to get more sums correct. The fact that they made relatively few mistakes means that the percentage of 'errors in common' was based on fewer items, but this in itself is interesting because observations suggested that they had a more efficient collaboration system than the other tables, in addition to being better able to work alone if necessary. In contrast, the bottom groups were seated apart. They tended to be shunned by other children and thus to have poor access to correct answers via the collaboration system. To make their difficulties worse, they were often given individual work cards when the class work was considered too hard for them. This meant that comparison of answers was impossible, and they tended to do only a small percentage of the work set.

The system of star rewards for 'good work' had the first unintended consequence of reinforcing the collaborative system as well as the work itself. Indeed, on several occasions a complete sequence of negotiation was witnessed, from getting answers from friends to receiving star reinforcement from Mrs Rothwell.

A second consequence of this was that it contributed to the self-fulfilling elements in the informal ranking system of the class. Mrs Rothwell evaluated the work that the children produced and presented, and she consequently assessed that some children were not capable of good work, and should be on the bottom table, and perhaps do special work cards, while others produced good work and therefore should be on the top or middle table and could do class work. Those judged not capable thus continued to be sealed off from the hidden means of accomplishing the lessons, while those judged capable were enabled to produce overt evidence.

Overall, the collaboration system functioned efficiently as a means of producing the explicit responses required, for it enabled the majority of the children to cope with the difficulties of a formal class-based lesson. Also important is the fact that from Mrs Rothwell's point of view, she also accomplished these seat-work lessons satisfactorily in terms of her educational perspective and structural position. The children were kept busy on educational tasks which gave them the practice she felt they needed; during this time there were no discipline problems, Mrs Rothwell was able to hear her readers, and at the end of the lessons their value was tangibly shown in neat rows of sums which in themselves legitimised her work. Thus the collaboration system rewarded the teacher, just as the teacher unwittingly reinforced the collaboration system. It was a stable process, with resources in the perspectives and commonsense knowledge of the participants which were mutually reinforcing. The classroom process, with its outcome of social differentiation, was a product of the mesh of the coping strategies of the participants.

Although the teacher clearly initiated and continued to structure such processes because of her power, the actions of the children significantly reinforced and multiplied the social consequence of differentiation.

Mrs Rothwell's was a rather formal classroom and, lest an impression is given that the multiplication phenomenon may be limited to classes of that type, we can now look at a second classroom, that of Mr Harman.

Of course we first met Mr Harman in Chapter 6 when his attempts to influence and 'subvert' the institutional bias at Ashton First School were discussed. As I suggested then, because of his relative isolation, Mr Harman valued his classroom autonomy which, being an accepted principle in the school, enabled him to implement his ideas despite the suspicion of them elsewhere. For instance, he was opposed to the head teacher's insistence on discipline and to her methods of punishment, and linked the issue to that of aims in the classroom:

> It doesn't matter if the children *think* they are in control, as long as the teacher is really controlling the teaching situation so that the results are in line with their broad aims.

Mr Harman thus encouraged children to initiate the activities and to follow their interests, and saw his role as 'asking the right questions. I ask, "What happens if . . . ?" '. This approach to learning was based on a belief in the value of intrinsic motivation, and Mr Harman was emphatic:

> I try to avoid all sorts of 'carrots'—even the unofficial ones like 'taking messages'.

Mr Harman used his ability at generating interest and his charisma as his main control and teaching technique. Frequently this would evolve spontaneously:

> It's my emotive response to situations in the classroom—it isn't analysable—I just happen to feel it is 'right' in the relationship between me and the kids.

This often took the form of humour or deliberately exaggerated acting. These attitudes were the main source of the constructs which Mr Harman used to describe the children, and particularly important to him was the degree of communicative rapport which he was able to develop with them. For instance, children were described as 'aware', 'has a good sense of humour', 'gets a joke' or for some children 'not very inspiring'.

There are several factors in the explanation of the prominence of such constructs. First, Mr Harman's control techniques were based on principles which forsook all physical sanctions and extrinsic inducements. This meant that the control techniques were highly verbal and depended upon children reasoning, 'getting the joke' or having enough awareness to sense teacher expectations. Second, because of his sense of isolation, Mr Harman derived a great deal of personal satisfaction from the rapport he was able to develop with the children. Those with quick-witted humour and verbal agility were rewarding to him. Third, Mr Harman interpreted his emphasis on 'thinking ability' in terms of conceptual development. He rejected the school's conventional wisdom that infant children had to learn basic three R skills before they could learn to 'think', and saw this as a communication problem, the solution to which was the use of:

> verbal language which can be a flexible tool even for young children, rather than trying to communicate on paper and get frustrated with failure—adults find it hard enough to think on paper so why should we expect kids to do it in schools?

Mr Harman therefore did not emphasise the formal skills of writing very much but used small-group work, discussions and 'asking the right questions' as his basic approach in most lesson periods.

At the start of the year the children in Mr Harman's class had not been entirely sure about his approach. Of course, in order to cope within the school Mr Harman could not entirely ignore the institutionalised definitions of standards, behaviour or pedagogy. However, to reconcile his ascribed role with his own beliefs he had to actively adapt and he had generated what might be characterised as a subversive 'subterranean value system' (Matza 1964) in his classroom. In particular, since he himself rejected many aspects of the institutionalised definition, he had considerable sympathy with children who shared his views. Thus descriptions of children such as 'a bit devious', 'clever enough to get away with things' and 'a bespectacled Dastardly Dick cartoon freak' contained implicit approval, since they indicated 'thinking' and divergence.

In Mr Harman's classroom the tables were arranged for children to work in small groups of five or six. Each child had an official seat at one of the six separate tables and this official seat was used for registration and for the first and most work-intensive lesson period of the day. These seat places were broadly based on ability criteria (two top tables, two middle, two bottom), which Mr Harman stated he disliked doing but found it convenient, since he could allocate work cards by table. These batches would include literacy and maths work, and when the quota was finished, 'choosing' and free movement were encouraged.

In other lesson periods work would be 'finished off' and Mr Harman would usually hear readers or take small groups of children for particular instruction on maths, reading or an interest topic, while the rest of the class dispersed to the activities of their choice. These included sand, painting, Wendy House, shop, Lego, bricks, plasticine, jigsaws, games, construction toys, crayons, 'sticky', interest tables, etc.

Thus, for the majority of the time, children would be involved individually or in freely chosen groups in their self-chosen activities or in their particular work cards.

Mr Harman's chosen form of classroom organisation and pedagogy represented his form of coping. They represented his resolution at the particular time of this study of the dilemmas and contradictions presented by his beliefs and views of himself with his role and the structural position within the school. The next link in the argument is to see if this particular form of coping was reflected in child strategies or had any social consequences.

In Mr Harman's class sociometric analysis showed six groups, three of girls and three of boys, and their table seat positions and official reading-book levels are shown in Table 9.2. Subject again to the limitations of sociometry, this provides some points of comparison with Mrs Rothwell's class.

Despite the more limited use of fixed seat positions in this class, some relationship between seat position and friendship group is apparent, particularly among the girls. In their case the three groups appeared to have been associated directly with their respective seat positions at the top, middle and bottom tables, and the data on reading-book level also broadly support the interpretation that the academic structuring of the classroom was significant for the girls' peer-group formation. The same is true of two of the three boys' groups, who formed particularly clear friendship groups based on the top and middle tables, but it is not the case for the third and largest group of boys, who had particularly diverse reading-book levels and also relatively diverse seat positions.

It appears from these data that, as in Mrs Rothwell's class, the children's social system was being affected by their official academic status—except, that is, for the large group of boys. Focused observations of this group of boys showed that they were frequently involved in deviant activities but that many of them had a close rapport with Mr Harman (see the example of Matthew which was discussed in Chapter 8). These findings were somewhat unexpected, but some possible explanations are provided by considering the early

Table 9.2 *Seat places and reading-book levels in Mr Harman's class, by friendship groups.*

Friendship group		Seat places by table	Reading-book level
Group 1	Stuart	M	7
	William	T	24
	Len	M	4
	Marcus	B	1
	Keith	T	16
	Adam	T	19
	Matthew	M	5
	Joe	M	7
	Simon	T	8
	Malcolm	T	7
Group 2	Dick	M	3
	Julian	M	6
	Philip	M	3
	Patrick	B	3
	Peter	M	7
	Sam	M	5
	Edward	M	9
Group 3	Sandra	M	3
	Linda	M	5
	Christine	B	2
	Jill	M	7
Group 4	Paula	T	19
	Maria	M	6
	Susan	T	11
	Janet	T	9
	Carol	T	16
Group 5	Kathleen	B	3
	Barbara	M	6
	Tessa	B	4
Group 6	Gregory	T	27
	Jeremy	T	16
Unplaced	Stephen	B	3
	Gareth	T	15
	Martin	M	3

process of establishment of understandings in Mr Harman's class at the start of the year.

In their previous, and their first, school year, the children in Mr Harman's class had been taught by the deputy head of the school. She and Mr Harman did not share perspectives, and in fact probably provided the greatest contrast of teaching styles existing in the school. In their reception class the children had been used to a daily routine of 'work' in the morning and 'activities' in the afternoon. Mr Harman initially aimed to integrate the two:

> I tried to establish not 'work' and 'play' time but just 'in class' time—but I totally failed. This distinction between work time and choosing time was forced on me, early on, when I realised they *expected* to do work in the morning. They couldn't cope with the idea of someone 'playing' (in their terms) whilst they were 'working' . . . I had groups in sand, water, painting, maths, writing, etc. . . . they kept asking 'What are those children doing?'. They got confused and didn't know what they were meant to do. I found myself policing all the time, checking on what they had and hadn't done. So I've established this system of 'work periods', which they found acceptable and I found productive, and also 'choosing periods', in which I am able to have groups, and gradually I'm getting this idea that some kids can be working when others are choosing.

Thus in the process of establishment the children had forced Mr Harman to compromise on his intentions. When he was asked to recall the names of those children who had been most confused by his attempt to change their anticipated definition of the classroom situation, he mentioned ten names; six were girls, and the four boys were all members of the average group. None of the academically diverse group of boys was mentioned. From this it appears that a sizeable proportion of Mr Harman's class, including all the girls and the academically average boys, continued to maintain something of the overall definition of the classroom situation which had been established in their first year of schooling and had been maintained by the general institutional bias, conventions and expectations thereafter.

However, the ambivalence of Mr Harman's structural position and personal perspectives was manifested in the formation of the large group of boys of diverse ability. These children related directly to Mr Harman's subterranean value system. They were regarded as good communicators and they could get a joke. Mr Harman thus developed a particularly good rapport with these children—they provided his consociates—while for the more conformist, 'less inspiring' remainder of the class a greater 'distance' existed in their relationship. Thus, in a very real sense, this boys' group was sponsored by Mr Harman and his personal value system. This sponsorship included the relabelling of deviant acts. Not only did Mr Harman sympathise with bored children and thus allow peripheral inattention, but some acts which were deviant within the institutionalised definition were regarded within the classroom as indicating creative thinking and thus 'learning how to learn'. As Mr Harman said on several occasions:

> Some of them are clever enough to get away with it, and anyway, I don't blame them.

Thus at the primary stage of differentiation Mr Harman favoured divergent, creative 'jokers', and at the secondary stage those children took advantage of the scope which he allowed. It is perhaps indicative of external cultural forces that no girls' group took similar advantage, and it could well be that Mr Harman's joky style particularly fitted masculine cultural forms and presented the girls with just another instance of the 'Catch 22' described by Clarricoates (1978).

It appears that there was a close relationship between the coping strategies of Mr Harman and those of his class. Many of the children derived their strategies from the institutionalised child role and definitions which Mr Harman also felt constrained to sustain, but a significant group of boys developed alternative strategies which Mr Harman's values and coping strategies also made possible, and this was reflected in the structure of friendship groups within the class.

What we have here, then, is a classroom process in which the coping strategies of the pupils mesh into the coping strategies of the teacher as a mediated product of whatever working consensus has been negotiated within the class. The result of this is that social effects of teacher strategies tend to be reinforced and multiplied.

CONCLUSION

In this chapter I have argued first that the way teachers perceive children is often related to their particular concerns and interests as they seek to cope both personally and professionally in their classroom. This argument provides a situational element which could complement those analyses which see teacher expectations as being based largely on cultural assumptions derived from society at large.

It thus provides an explanation for the initial, or primary, phase of the differentiation of children in a class by a teacher. Teachers like and favour children who help them to cope and who reinforce their interests. They dislike those who provide threat and provocation.

The expectations that teachers develop may have a *self*-fulfilling effect to the extent that they influence a child's sense of identity directly, but the second main section of the chapter has drawn attention to a *socially* fulfilling process which comes into play when child strategies mesh into teacher strategies. The result of this is a type of secondary differentiation in which the social consequence of teacher strategies tends to be multiplied in its effect by the children themselves.

This discussion completes the three central and analytical parts of the book, which have been concerned with *perspectives, social context* and *interaction*. However, the book began with a preliminary chapter on *teaching and learning* and it is therefore to the issues which were raised there that we now return.

CONCLUSION

10
Teaching and Learning Revisited

INTRODUCTION

The presentation in this book of an interactionist model for reflecting on everyday processes in primary-school classrooms has probably opened up many more issues than it has resolved. Perhaps this is inevitable given the subjective and qualitative nature of the data which have been the focus of the analysis. Nevertheless, the attempt to generate grounded theory has been derived from established ethnographic procedures and is thus offered as a relatively systematic attempt to identify patterns in the perspectives and routine actions of teachers and children.

Of course it is sometimes felt that even those aspects of classroom life with which we may be very familiar appear rather strange when expressed like this in an analytical form, and this feeling can easily be misunderstood. I must immediately suggest, therefore, that this sense of strangeness and distancing is necessary if the type of incisive reflection which many people argue is required in teaching today is to be achieved. Having adequate practical experience is certainly the only way, at one level, to achieve a capacity to reach quick and sure classroom decisions, but there are other circumstances in which a more structural, long-term type of reflective thinking is also necessary. The present analysis may thus be of most use to teachers who are attempting to theorise about their own classroom practice. Such practical theorising has been usefully defined by Reid (1978) as:

> an intricate and skilled intellectual and social process whereby, individually or collectively, we identify the questions to which we must respond, establish grounds for deciding on answers, and then choose among the available solutions. (Reid 1978, p.43)

An ethnographic analysis of schools, classroom interaction and teacher–child relationships can, in my view, offer one way of getting beneath the surface phenomenon of school life to help identify what Reid calls the underlying 'questions to which we must respond'.

Although this type of teacher inquiry will always be classroom based and derive its impetus from its direct relationship with practice, it seems likely to become increasingly important in other educational spheres in the future. For instance, there are signs of a marked lack of confidence among some educational researchers who have been trying to develop a body of explicit theoretical knowledge about teaching from studies of classroom behaviour. McIntyre (1980), for example, acknowledges many difficulties with research based on 'systematic observation' and suggests that we should look to 'interpretive and action research designed to elucidate, examine, explain and extend teachers' working knowledge' (McIntyre 1980, p.293). The present book is an interpretive account of the sort which McIntyre possibly had in mind, but I make only modest claims for it in research terms. The real potential for an increase in our research-based knowledge of classroom processes must, in my view, come from new types of research design which *combine* interpretive and systematic observation methodologies, qualitative and quantitative data, and studies of meaning and of behaviour. Ethnography could clearly make an important contribution to such research in the future if balanced research teams can be brought together.

There are also interesting developments in teacher education. The conventional idea of a 'teaching practice' has been that students are taught skills and acquire knowledge in the training institution and are then sent to 'practise' them in school. In a sense this model simply institutionalised the theory–practice divide and adopted it as an implicit principle of course design. However, some of the most recent new courses are based on 'school-based study' or 'a school experience model' of teacher education (Alexander 1984). According to Alexander the school experience model regards schools '. . . not only as a place to practise teaching, to demonstrate what one can do and to be assessed, but also as a place to learn, to observe, to study and to experiment' (Alexander 1984, p.97). It is expected that closer relationships and new partnerships between schools and training institutions will be developed to underpin these increasingly inquiry-oriented activities, and the hope, of course, is that each student will develop a new type of practically based theory of teaching/learning processes from the more actively analytical posture which they are encouraged to adopt towards their work in school. If ethnographic studies are to contribute to these developments, as some have suggested (e.g. Woods 1985), then a clear appreciation of their practical relevance is necessary. I therefore now want to return to some of the issues which were raised in Chapter 1 concerning relationships, teaching and learning. In doing so I shall both review salient features of the ethnographic model which I have introduced in the book and demonstrate some aspects of it which I think have particular implications for practice.

RELATIONSHIPS, TEACHING AND LEARNING

The existence of order and a good relationship in a classroom is not something which can be assumed. As has been pointed out on many occasions, an inherent conflict exists between teachers and pupils as a result of the respective positions which they occupy.

To understand the nature of these potential clashes of interest is, in my view, a vital step towards understanding the nature of classroom relationships. Thus, in Chapters 2 and 4 I identified the particular interests which teachers and children appear to be most concerned about in the immediacy of their classroom lives.

The most important point which was implied in this analysis was that both parties maintain a primary concern with their 'self'—a concept used in the symbolic interactionist sense to represent an essential quality of being a person with an identity in society.

A basic problem which was also identified is that classrooms tend to be potentially threatening to the self-image of teachers and children because of their very structures and purposes. In simple terms, the teacher faces relatively large numbers of children and is expected to educate them, while each child faces the evaluative power of the teacher and is expected to learn.

The threat to the self-image of both parties is thus inherently high and is reciprocally applied so that teachers and children put considerable efforts into developing ways of coping with the situation. These represent a means to their primary goal. In the case of teachers, instructing the children and keeping order can be seen partly as being significant enabling interests to that end, while for children peer-group membership and learning fulfil a similar function.

How, then, is order achieved? If we accept that there is a basic conflict of interests, there are only two basic possibilities: either order is imposed by teachers using their power or there is negotiation between each teacher and class so that sets of social understandings which define order are constructed. In fact the developmental tradition and the child-centred ideology which are endorsed by most primary-school teachers have always placed great emphasis on establishing good relationships with children, so that consciously coercive teachers are rare. However, it is not unusual for teachers who lack negotiative skills and who feel their interests to be threatened in particular situations to fall back on coercion. Tension, anxiety and frustration often accompany this response.

Although the strategy may work in the short term, it has unfortunate side-effects, and these are caused essentially because the coercive strategy can be made to succeed only at the expense of the children's interests. When teachers 'become angry', 'go mad' or 'get eggy' they are likely to act in ways which will be seen by children as being unfair. Children then report being 'picked on', 'shown up', 'done over' and humiliated. Children, throughout the primary age range, are quick to discern when the expectations of them and the sense of order in the classroom begin to be based more on the use of teacher power than on a sense of fairness or justice.

Justice is perhaps rather a high-flown word to use here, but I think that is essentially what is under consideration. I suggest this because a shared sense of the moral order of the classroom, with social conventions, expectations and tacit rules, and thus a sense of what is 'right', is the normal outcome of a successfully conducted round of negotiations. Such negotiations are particularly significant at the start of a school year and they last until understandings about the parameters of behaviour for teacher and children are established and accepted. I have called the result of these understandings a working consensus, which is an agreement based, in a sense, on a mutual exchange of dignity. Such an accommodation between the teacher and the children is essential if the potential conflict in classroom life is to remain latent.

The implicit point which is worth making clear here is that teacher and child strategies tend to mesh together. Thus the particular actions of a teacher will yield reactions from the children which they deem to be appropriate, given their subjective perceptions of the situation and their interests in it. The same applies in reverse, with teachers reacting to child acts in ways which they perceive to be appropriate.

The stabilisation of relationships which is brought about as strategies mesh together can be very productive educationally. For instance, consider the model of a positive cycle of teaching and learning in Fig. 10.1—a model seen from the child perspective. In this model it is first suggested that teacher initiatives lead to children

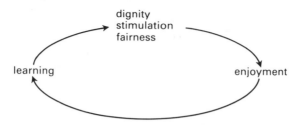

Figure 10.1 *A positive cycle of teaching and learning.*

enjoying a sense of their own dignity and value. Second, it is postulated that children are stimulated by the curriculum or learning activities provided for them by the teacher. These are judged to be interesting and appear likely to satisfy children's interest-at-hand in learning. Third, the situation is regarded as being fair. There are two aspects of fairness here, relating to the way the children are ordered and controlled and to the nature of the tasks which they are presented with. Regarding the first, let us assume that the children and teacher are operating within established organisational and social frameworks and that thus they have both negotiated and both understand the parameters of permissible action. Order thus has a secure base. The other aspect of fairness concerns the appropriateness of the match between the task which the children are faced with and their ability and motivation to do it. If the task is well matched and attractively presented, then the children are likely to accept its challenges and attempt to grapple with them vigorously.

The result of the existence of this sense of dignity, stimulation and fairness is postulated in the model as being children's enjoyment and their learning. This is brought about essentially because the children's interests-at-hand are satisfied by teacher provision and action from the start. The further, and crucial, result of this child enjoyment and learning is that *teacher* interests-at-hand are thereby satisfied. Order is maintained, instruction is effective and teacher self-esteem can flourish, with the likely result that the teacher will feel able to inject further energy and care with which to again project the dignity, stimulation and fairness to fuel another cycle. A cyclical process of reinforcement is created which can then spiral upwards into a higher and higher quality of learning experiences. Sometimes teaching in primary schools goes just like this.

On the other hand, we must also recognise the existence of negative cycles which, instead of spiralling upwards, can lead to a decline into suspicion, hostility and unpleasantness. Again this can be represented by a model seen from the child perspective (Fig. 10.2).

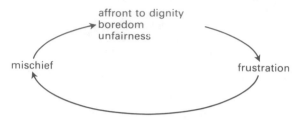

Figure 10.2 *A negative cycle of teaching and learning.*

In this model it is suggested that teacher initiatives threaten children's interests-at-hand on three counts. First, they represent an affront to children's dignity as people. Teacher actions may be seen as being dismissive, high-handed or even aggressive. Second, the learning activities provided for the children are seen as being boring. In other words, they are badly matched to the ability and concerns of the children. They are too hard, too easy or too disconnected from children's interests to provide any significant motivational attraction. Third, teachers may be seen to be acting unfairly. In other words, they do not abide by negotiated understandings about their behaviour or that of the children. They use their power to act unilaterally.

The children will, in a situation of this sort, feel and express a great deal of frustration. Their interests-at-hand, far from being satisfied, are being ignored or threatened while at the same time they are relatively powerless to defend themselves. And yet they do have a degree of defensive power which comes from their numbers, friendships and peer-group membership, and this collective solidarity is likely to be used to neutralise the damage done by their teacher (with a shrug of the shoulders or a wink to 'mates') or to respond in kind with forms of resistance such as mischief, mucking about and having a laugh at the teacher's expense. Work evasion, rather than learning, is a probable outcome.

Ironically, the further result of this, which completes the cycle, is likely to be *damage* to the teacher's interests-at-hand. Order in the classroom will constantly be challenged if it is essentially oppressive. Attempts at instruction will not be matched by quality in learning if children have not been offered an appropriate motivation to learn. The children's deviant responses will constantly threaten the teacher's self-esteem and autonomy. Such resistance is likely to further reduce the teacher's enjoyment but increase the stress and the potential workload which that teacher faces.

Fortunately there are not many classrooms where this situation endures, but regrettably, if we are to believe HMI and other reports, there are not many where the positive cycle is consistently at its peak either. However, teachers are able to sense movements over time in their teaching and in their relationship with the children, and perhaps these movements may be seen as variations in the area between the two models.

I hope that this discussion has illustrated the way in which ethnographic analysis can contribute to the development of our understanding of the educational significance of social relationships between teachers and children. In my view it is a fundamental issue which determines not only the nature of the environment in which it is hoped that children will learn but also the qualitative feel of the whole experience of schooling.

As I argued in Chapter 1, the fact that such qualitative issues are rather intangible and difficult to analyse compared with more measurable aspects of behaviour or learning should not be allowed to reduce our concern for them. Indeed, since the essential character of much modern primary education is founded on the quality of the interpersonal relationships and experiences which are offered to children, we should perhaps put what energy we can into the further development of our understanding of the issue.

One aspect of this issue is of outstanding importance from the sociological point of view. I refer, of course, to the topic of social differentiation—a topic which I also raised in Chapters 1, 5 and 9.

SOCIAL DIFFERENTIATION

As we have now seen, there are many ways in which teacher strategies, child strategies and their interaction together create and amplify social differences between children. The processes which create these divisions are not often overt or final in primary schools, but they are present none the less. Perhaps they can best be seen as having their effect on the layers of experience that go to make up a child's sense of identity.

In its sociological use the concept of identity derives from Mead's (1934) work, and in many ways it can be seen as the socialised element of the self. In other words, it is the image of self which any individual holds as a result of the ways in which other people relate to them. As Berger and Berger (1972) put it, 'identity is the product of an interplay of identification and self-identification' (Berger and Berger 1972, p.73). The prime situation in which this interplay of identification and self-identification takes place is that of interaction.

Of course the most significant period in the formation of identity is that of very early childhood, before formal schooling begins. However, the sense of identity which is produced by such early socialisation will continue to be developed by other experiences, and clearly the younger the child the more significant these are likely to be. This is why teachers in primary schools have such a particular responsibility to maximise the quality of their pupils' experience so that balanced and positive identities are developed.

In a secondary-school context Woods (1979) has suggested that:

> pupils are engaged in a continual battle for who they are and who they are to become, while the forces of institutionalisation work to deprive them of their individuality and [to press them] into a mould that accords with teachers' ideal models.
>
> (Woods 1979, p.248)

The class-based and child-oriented system of most primary schools should, in theory, make it easier to avoid such battles. However, in practice we have seen that primary-school teachers have serious practical concerns themselves, so that such avoidance is not always possible. In fact, I would go further and say that the pressures and constraints of many situations in primary schools are such that the question of how classroom experiences may be influencing child identities comes very low on our agendas.

In my view this matters a great deal because of the way in which their sense of identity is likely to contribute to the ultimate life chances of the children.

This link between identity and life chances comes about through the interaction of two sets of factors as each child's educational and occupational 'career' develops. The first and most obvious is an externalised and social set of factors. For example, the 'typification' of each child within teacher knowledge will affect the way the teacher interacts with him or her and thus will condition the learning opportunities which are presented. The teacher's perception of the child's identity may be disseminated further through staffroom conversation or through record systems, so that future opportunities may also be affected. Change may come through 'critical incidents' or experiences of 'status passage' (Glaser and Strauss 1971) when children move between classes or institutions, but the identity which is ascribed in any particular context can never be entirely thrown off. One reason for this relates to the second set of factors—those which are internalised and personal.

The point here is that the way in which a child's or any individual's identity develops in interaction with others directly influences their self-confidence and self-respect. This in turn influences their competence and performance in new situations and is sequentially reflected in the type of 'identification' which others then make of them.

I would postulate that predictable career trajectories exist for many children in our schools, with some being offered and developing positive identities which progressively lead to higher levels of success in educational, occupational and personal terms as they grow older. At the same time the school experience of other children may ultimately yield negative identities, feelings of alienation and poor life chances. In primary education we tend to think that the problems of disaffected pupils are essentially a secondary-school issue. Perhaps those of us who work in primary education also have a responsibility. This responsibility must, however, be put in context. In this respect I have argued that the issues and social processes which have been identified are the product of teachers and children being active, creative and purposeful as they seek to cope with the situations which they face each day in their schools and classrooms. Such situations are strongly framed by constraints—legal structures, resources, ratios, buildings, conventions, hegemony—and by a variety of pressures to give priority to particular educational objectives. These constraints and pressures are not, by and large, the responsibility of teachers. Meanwhile practical, workable decisions have to be made at speed in the classroom.

This is not an easy situation, but it seems to me that there are two things which can constructively be done about it. The first is to develop a social policy for one's own classroom which is in a sense as 'socially progressive' as one can make it. The second is to remain aware of the influence of the wider social structure and seek to influence it where one can. I shall discuss these suggestions in turn.

SOCIAL POLICIES FOR THE CLASSROOM

The development of long-term classroom social policies is one possible outcome of the type of practical theorising discussed earlier in this chapter, especially when it is applied to relationships. The need for them is perhaps particularly clear with regard to discipline, and can be contrasted with a mechanistic, technical and tip-based solution to incidents and difficulties which may arise. Such responses may well be skilled, but they will always constitute a relatively superficial treatment of surface phenomena unless the underlying issues influencing teacher–child relationships are exposed. Not only is coping in such a way on a day-to-day basis exhausting, but it offers little hope, just as treating the symptoms of an illness but failing to investigate its cause is unlikely to produce very satisfactory results.

It is arguable that it is the complexity of classrooms itself which often creates such day-to-day strategies. There are always a lot of things going on involving many people. Such events normally occur simultaneously, and there are numerous dimensions and issues to be considered. Fast, decisive and appropriate initiatives and responses are required, and one of the things which teachers thus have to do is simplify the complexity. The main point that I want to make is that if a social policy has been thought out it enables that simplification to be made in a positive, constructive and consistent way because it is based not on instant pressured response but on considered analysis and reflection. It also makes it possible for teachers to take the initiative more confidently and more coherently; they know where they are going. As a result, children are offered a relatively stable and consistent pattern of actions from their teachers and are likely to be more able to identify and to adjust to them. This can then produce the beginning of a more positive mesh of teacher–child strategies, with the enormous benefit that the creativity and energy of the children are used in ways which are supportive of educational concerns and of teacher interests rather than against them.

So what policy issues might be considered by a classroom teacher? I have already suggested that children's sense of identity is a very important issue and argued that teachers should do what they can to support each child in the development of a positive self-image. However, the facts that teachers have a complex job to do and that within our society people are routinely classified and valued in different ways seem to mean that classification is also common in classrooms in both overt and tacit ways. Sexist practices are often particularly obvious—boys to carry heavy things, girls to do teachers' jobs, sex used as an organisational device for lining up, being dismissed, competitions, etc.—but social class, race, ability and age also tend to be used unconsciously as the basis for convenient divisions.

Such divisions, particularly where they are institutionalised by such organisational devices as ability-based group work, almost inevitably create a sense of superiority in some and a sense of inferiority in others, and have results which can only be divisive. Those whose dignity is affronted must either accept the reduction in the esteem in which they are held or defend themselves by developing alternative valuation systems. The latter course may well mean that, by rejecting the dominant set of values, they act in ways which are regarded as being disruptive. A crucial policy question which we face when teaching thus concerns the way in which we protect and foster the self-image of *all* the children in the class. Likely directions for finding solutions lie in the systematic search for and celebration of children's success, in carefully thought out organisational structures and routines and in a conscious self-monitoring of what one does and says when in the classroom.

I am well aware that many of these suggestions are likely to be difficult to implement; after all, much of our teaching is constrained, habituated, personal and simply has to 'work'. The exchange of ideas between socially aware teachers in staffrooms, meetings, networks, in-service courses and conferences would obviously help, as might further research to identify viable but 'socially progressive' coping strategies. A precondition of any development, though, is conscious-ness of its importance, and in that respect I am simply making a bid for more consideration of an issue which seems to me to be of enormous consequence.

Another area of policy-making which I would identify as being important, particularly to children's learning, is that which relates to children's peer-group membership, culture and friendship patterns. As Opie and Opie (1959) reminded us, children's culture is their own, and adults know relatively little about it. We are gradually learning more about it, but we still have a limited understanding at the present time. Two points which are clear, however, are first that child culture and child friendship groups generate norms, values, rules, under-standings and a sense of social structure which is extremely complex and sophisticated, and second that these provide a means by which children make sense of and cope with the adult world when it impinges on them. There are thus a lot of things about children and the ways in which they think that we simply do not understand, and the social side of this is as important as the cognitive. Some of the things that children do in class may be regarded as being totally senseless and obtuse behaviour by a teacher, but by children they may be thought of as being entirely rational, appropriate and justified. They will almost certainly be socially structured by child understandings about behaviour.

There are, in other words, two major and discrete social systems and sets of perspectives which come together within the social world of a primary school: those of the teachers and those of the children. In my view wise teachers will do everything they can to understand the children's culture and social structure. If this is done policy decisions can be made which will make it possible to work *with* the children and to harness their energy and enthusiasm to educational and social goals.

This discussion of classroom social policy constitutes the first of the two responses which I have suggested could be made by teachers to the situation in which they work. It has looked inwards, to the classroom over which teachers have some autonomy and control. The second possible response looks outwards to the wider society.

TEACHING AND THE SOCIAL STRUCTURE

Political rhetoric claims that the modern education system has been designed to provide 'equality of opportunity' for children so that they can realise their creative and cognitive potential. I have argued, however, that once in the classroom, the pressure of innumerable other aims and the constraint of structures and resources produce in most schools a situation which is so difficult for the participants to cope with that educational purposes are likely to be subverted by pragmatism of various sorts. To put one example of this in its simplest form, I have suggested that, with class sizes in the order of 25 to 30, differentiation processes of a fairly crude type become almost inevitable. With such large numbers of children teachers have a need to simplify and they thus tend to classify. Children then have to protect their self-image in the best way they can vis-à-vis their peers. There can never be enough teacher attention to go round; the quality of the relationship between the teacher and each child is almost bound to vary considerably unless a conscious effort is made to equalise it, and the teaching–learning process appears to have a tendency to lurch towards a transmission mode when classroom pressures mount.

It is salutary to remember the history of the development of the public education system. The fact is that it was developed in the nineteenth century to increase levels of basic skills and to provide a 'moral' education for working-class children at a time when greater industrial production was required and when there was increasing pressure for an extension of the franchise. Legal and administrative structures and the resourcing levels were established to achieve those ends as efficiently and cost-effectively as possible. It could be argued that, while conditions have undoubtedly improved, the underlying assumption that the education system should provide for cheap and efficient socialisation and skill development remains much the same.

Improvements in structures and resources to increase efficiency in the attainment of such ends are quite different from those which would really make it possible to develop the needs and interests of children as unique individuals.

Meanwhile teachers are caught up in a type of hegemonic bind. Cultural values such as the work ethic and deference to authority have a double articulation. First they are projected by the government and industrial interest groups in ways which tend to be reinforced by the media and confirmed by evidence of the benefits of materialism. Such societal values then find their second level of articulation in the classroom, where they make direct sense to teachers because of the way in which the work ethic relates to their enabling interest in instruction and because of the way in which deference relates to their ever-present concern with order. Dominant social values are thus reinforced by the practical commonsense knowledge which teachers' interests-at-hand in the classroom represent.

We appear to have a system which is extremely coherent. Macro-level factors influence micro-level processes and these tend to reproduce the macro-level structures again. I would suggest that understanding this continuously evolving dialectical process is vital for concerned educationists. The philosophy of primary-school teachers is often idealistic, and this is something to be proud of. However, such ideals will not be achieved, other than by quite exceptionally dedicated members of the profession, without attention to structural, material and practical realities. The fact that fundamental control of such factors lies largely outside teachers', pupils' and parents' hands points inexorably to the need for action to achieve a reappraisal of the relationship between the aims, structure and funding of primary education. Without this it seems doubtful that caring, high-quality and socially equitable educational experiences can consistently be provided for our young children.

So what are teachers to do? Obviously there are limitations to what is possible, but perhaps the first necessity is to develop an increased degree of consciousness about the issues among the profession as a whole. Unfortunately, classroom experience can sometimes reduce such consciousness at the same time as it increases practical skills. This can be seen in a condensed form in teacher-education programmes where students on teaching practice often develop pragmatic, utilitarian perspectives which separate teaching from its 'ethical, political and moral roots' (Zeichner and Teitelbaum 1982).

In my view the most hopeful way forward here lies in the further development of the capacity to generate 'practical theory'. Such developments will have to move beyond technical or practical issues to become incisive and 'critical' of many of the existing assumptions and taken-for-granted understandings which make up the educational status quo (Van Manen 1977). The foundations of a sustained campaign for the reappraisal of such assumptions in the minds of politicians, policy-makers and the public at large would then have been laid.

Social arrangements, whether in schools or in society as a whole, are the product of constraint *and* action, of material forces *and* creative idealism. There is every reason to expect that existing arrangements will change over time, and in my opinion the underlying commitment and philosophy of many primary-school teachers present a real opportunity to influence such changes in socially progressive ways.

Notes for Further Reading

These notes are intended to provide the interested reader with suggestions for various 'points of entry' for further study of the issues and approaches which have been discussed or applied in this book.

REFLECTIVE TEACHING

A number of books are available which advocate that teachers should adopt a self-critical posture in their teaching or engage in 'action research' focused on their classroom practice. It should be remembered, though, that such work has been heavily criticised for encouraging introspection, for having a weak theoretical framework and for ignoring the need to develop a 'social awareness' of issues outside the classroom which affect practice within it. I focus on such work here because, despite the criticisms, I believe it has great strengths in terms of increasing reflection on taken-for-granted practice and also because I believe that symbolic interactionist and ethnographic studies could help to overcome some of the weaknesses that have been identified.

Two important books which focus on curriculum development from practical action are:

Reid, W.A. (1978) *Thinking about the Curriculum*. London: Routledge and Kegan Paul.
Stenhouse, L. (1975) *An Introduction to Curriculum Research and Development*. London: Heinemann.

A more recent book which discusses the idea of 'reflection in action' in a number of professions is:

Schon, D.A. (1983) *The Reflective Practitioner*. Hounslow: Maurice Temple-Smith.

Examples of classroom-based action research are provided by:

Armstrong, M. (1980) *Closely Observed Children*. London: Writers and Readers.
Nixon, J. (1981) *A Teacher's Guide to Action Research*. London: Grant McIntyre.
Rowlands, S. (1984) *The Enquiring School*. Lewes: Falmer Press.

Examples of reflexive studies which are more contextualised than most British work are contained in an American collection:

Grant, K.A. (ed.) (1984) *Preparing for Reflective Teaching*. Boston: Allyn and Bacon.

SYMBOLIC INTERACTIONIST THEORY

The classic source of symbolic interactionism and a book which remains influential is:

Mead, G.H. (1934) *Mind, Self, and Society*. Chicago: University of Chicago.

There are a number of more modern expositions and developments of the approach, for instance:

Blumer, H. (1969) *Symbolic Interactionism*. Englewood Cliffs, NJ: Prentice-Hall.
Rock, P. (1979) *The Making of Symbolic Interactionism*. London: Macmillan.

For an introductory book which provides an overview see:

Meltzer, B.N., Petras, J.W. and Reynolds, L.T. (1975) *Symbolic Interactionism; genesis, variations and criticism*. London: Routledge and Kegan Paul.

ETHNOGRAPHIC METHODOLOGY

A direct and interesting introductory guide to field methods is:

Schatzman, L. and Strauss, A. (1973) *Field Research: Strategies for a Natural Sociology*. Englewood Cliffs, NJ: Prentice-Hall.

For a classic book which established the ideal of generating grounded theory see:

> Glaser, B.G. and Strauss, A.L. (1967) *The Discovery of Grounded Theory*. London: Weidenfeld and Nicolson.

Two recent books by British ethnographers which provide very full discussion and guidance on the various stages of ethnographic fieldwork are:

> Burgess, R.G. (1984) *In the Field: An Introduction to Field Research*. London: George Allen and Unwin.
> Hammersley, M. and Atkinson, P. (1983) *Ethnography: Principles in Practice*. London: Methuen.

For a very useful and clearly structured collection of US and British papers on fieldwork see:

> Burgess, R.G. (ed.) (1982) *Field Research: A Sourcebook and Field Manual*. London: George Allen and Unwin.

ETHNOGRAPHIC STUDIES OF SCHOOLING

For two excellent introductory overviews of the best work of the last ten years see:

> Delamont, S. (1983) *Interaction in the Classroom* (2nd edition). London: Methuen.
> Woods, P. (1983) *Sociology and the School*. London: Routledge and Kegan Paul.

Two review papers provide a concise source of references regarding classroom-focused work:

> Hammersley, M. (1980) Classroom ethnography, *Educational Analysis*, **2**(2).
> Hammersley, M. (1982) The sociology of classrooms, in Hartnett, A. (ed.) *The Social Sciences in Educational Studies*. London: Heinemann.

A great many reports of ethnographic studies have been given at conferences or have been published in journals. The following are among a number of collections of papers which are very useful:

> Delamont, S. (ed.) (1984) *Readings on Interaction in the Classroom*. London: Methuen.
> Hammersley, M. (ed.) (1983) *The Ethnography of Schooling*. Driffield: Nafferton.
> Hammersley, M. and Woods, P. (ed.) (1976) *The Process of Schooling*. London: Routledge and Kegan Paul.

Hammersley, M. and Woods, P. (ed.) (1984) *Life in School: The Sociology of Pupil Culture*. Milton Keynes: Open University Press.
Hargreaves, A. and Woods, P. (ed.) (1984) *Classrooms and Staffrooms: The Sociology of Teachers and Teaching*. Milton Keynes: Open University Press.
Woods, P. (ed.) (1980) *Pupil Strategies*. Beckenham: Croom Helm.
Woods, P. (ed.) (1980) *Teacher Strategies*. Beckenham: Croom Helm.

There are an increasing number of monographs reporting ethnographic case studies of school settings, though still very few of primary schools. One notable exception is:

King, R. (1978) *All Things Bright and Beautiful? A sociological study of infants' classrooms*. Chichester: Wiley.

Other important recent studies of secondary schools are:

Ball, S. (1981) *Beachside Comprehensive*. Cambridge: Cambridge University Press.
Burgess, R.G. (1983) *Experiencing Comprehensive Education*. London: Methuen.
Macpherson, J. (1983) *The Feral Classroom: High School Students' Constructions of Reality*. London: Routledge and Kegan Paul.
Woods, P. (1979) *The Divided School*. London: Routledge and Kegan Paul.

Rather different types of study which explicitly attempt the important task of relating their case study to the wider social structure include one other study of an infant school:

Corrigan, P. (1979) *Schooling the Smash Street Kids*. London: Macmillan.
Sharp, R. and Green, A. (1975) *Education and Social Control: A study in progressive primary education*. London: Routledge and Kegan Paul.
Willis, P. (1977) *Learning to Labour: How working class kids get working class jobs*. Aldershot: Saxon House.

EDUCATION AND SOCIETY

For the most recent statistical study of the bare facts about education and social differentiation in Britain see:

Halsey, A.H., Heath, A.F. and Ridge, J.M. (1980) *Origins and Destinations*. Oxford: Oxford University Press.

My efforts to explain how primary-school processes influence such statistics can, in a sense, be seen as an attempt to grasp the 'sociological imagination'—an inspirational phrase coined by C.W. Mills to describe the task of documenting the relationship of individuals to society and of biography to history. His book remains readable and challenging:

> Mills, C.W. (1959) *The Sociological Imagination*. New York: Oxford University Press.

A more recent work which also attempts to make macro–micro links is:

> Apple, M. (1982) *Education and Power*. London: Routledge and Kegan Paul.

For three excellent studies which place people and school processes within their social context in a fascinating and powerful way see:

> Connell, R.W., Ashenden, D.J., Kessler, S. and Dowsett, G.W. (1982) *Making the Difference: Schools, families and social division*. Sydney: Allen and Unwin.
> Grace, G. (1978) *Teachers, Ideology and Control: A study in urban education*. London: Routledge and Kegan Paul.
> Humphries, S. (1981) *Hooligans or Rebels? An oral history of working class childhood and youth 1889–1939*. Oxford: Blackwell.

References

Alexander, R. (1984) *Primary Teaching*. Eastbourne: Holt, Rinehart and Winston.

Apple, M. (1982) *Education and Power*. London: Routledge and Kegan Paul.

Aries, P. (1962) *Centuries of Childhood*. Harmondsworth: Penguin.

Armstrong, M. (1980) *Closely Observed Children*. London: Writers and Readers.

Ashton, P.M. (1981) Primary teachers' aims 1969–77, in Simon, B. and Willcocks, J. *Research and Practice in the Primary Classroom*. London: Routledge and Kegan Paul.

Ashton, P.M., Kneen, P., Davies, F. and Holley, B.J. (1975) *The Aims of Primary Education*. London: Macmillan.

Bachrach, P. and Baratz, M.S. (1962) Two faces of power, *American Political Science Review*, **56**(4).

Bagley, J.J. and Bagley, A.J. (1969) *The State and Education in England and Wales*. London: Macmillan.

Ball, S. (1980) Initial encounters in the classroom and the process of establishment, in Woods, P. (ed.) *Pupil Strategies*. Beckenham: Croom Helm.

Ball, S. (1981) *Beachside Comprehensive*. Cambridge: Cambridge University Press.

Ball, S.J. and Lacey, C. (1980) Subject disciplines as the opportunity for group action, a measured critique of subject subcultures, in Woods, P. *Teacher Strategies*. Beckenham: Croom Helm.

Barker, R. and Gump, P.V. (1964) *Big School, Small School*. Stanford, California: Stanford University Press.

Barnes, D. (1969) *Language, the Learner and the School*. Harmondsworth: Penguin.

Baron, G. (1956) Some aspects of the 'Headmaster Tradition', *Leeds Researches and Studies*, **14**, 7–16.

Bassey, M. (1978) *900 Primary Teachers*. Slough: NFER.

Bealing, D. (1972) The organisation of junior school classrooms, *Educational Research*, **14**(4), 231–3.

Becker, H.S. (1952) Social-class variations in the teacher–pupil relationship, *Journal of Educational Sociology*, **25**, 451–65.

Bennett, N. (1976) *Teaching Styles and Pupil Progress*. Shepton Mallet: Open Books.

Bennett, N., Desforges, C., Cockburn, A. and Wilkinson, B. (1984) *The Quality of Pupil Learning Experiences*. London: Lawrence Erlbaum.

Berger, P.L. and Berger, B. (1972) *Sociology: A Biographical Approach*. Harmondsworth: Penguin.

Berlak, H. and Berlak, A. (1981) *Dilemmas of Schooling*. London: Methuen.

Bernstein, B. (1971) On the classification and framing of educational knowledge, in Young, M.F.D. (ed.) *Knowledge and Control*. West Drayton: Collier Macmillan.

Bidwell, C.E. (1965) The school as a formal organisation, in March, J.G. (ed.) *Handbook of Organisations*. Chicago: Rand McNally.

Blishen, E. (1969) *The School that I'd Like*. Harmondsworth: Penguin.

Blumer, H. (1969) *Symbolic Interactionism*. Englewood Cliffs, NJ: Prentice-Hall.

Blumer, H. (1971) Sociological implications of the thought of G.H. Mead, in Cosin, B.R. et al. (ed.) *School and Society*. London: Routledge and Kegan Paul.

Blyth, W.A.L. (1965) *English Primary Education*, Volumes I and II. London: Routledge and Kegan Paul.

Board of Education (1931) *Report of the Consultative Committee on the Primary School* (Hadow Report). London: HMSO.

Bone, T. (1983) Exercising leadership, in Paisey, A. (ed.) *The Effective Teacher*. London: Ward Lock Educational.

Bossert, S.T. (1979) *Tasks and Social Relationships in Classrooms*. Cambridge: Cambridge University Press.

Boudon, R. (1974) *Education, Opportunity and Social Inequality*. New York: Wiley.

Boydell, D. (1978) *The Primary Teacher in Action*. Shepton Mallet: Open Books.

Boydell, D. (1981) Classroom organisation, 1970–7, in Simon, B. and Willcocks, J. (ed.) *Research and Practice in the Primary Classroom*. London: Routledge and Kegan Paul.

Burgess, R.G. (ed.) (1982) *Field Research: A Sourcebook and Field Manual*. London: George Allen and Unwin.

Burgess, R.G. (1983) *Experiencing Comprehensive Education*. London: Methuen.

Burgess, R.G. (1984) *In the Field: An Introduction to Field Research*. London: George Allen and Unwin.

Calvert, B. (1975) *The Role of the Pupil*. London: Routledge and Kegan Paul.

Central Advisory Council for Education (1967) *Children and their Primary Schools* (The Plowden Report). London: HMSO.

Clarricoates, K. (1978) Dinosaurs in the classroom—a re-examination of some aspects of the 'hidden' curriculum in primary schools, *Women's Studies International Quarterly*, **1**, 353–64.

Clarricoates, K. (1981) The experience of patriarchal schooling, *Interchange*, **12**(2–3), 185–205.

Connell, R.W., Ashenden, D.J., Kessler, S. and Dowsett, G.W. (1982) *Making the Difference: Schools, families and social division*. Sydney: Allen and Unwin.

Corrigan, P. (1979) *Schooling the Smash Street Kids*. London: Macmillan.

Cox, C.B. and Boyson, R. (ed.) (1975) *Black Paper 1975*. London: Dent.

Cox, C.B. and Dyson, A.E. (ed.) (1969) *Fight for Education: A Black Paper*. London: Critical Quarterly Society.

Cox, C.B. and Dyson, A.E. (ed.) (1970) *Black Paper Two*. London: Critical Quarterly Society.

Davies, B. (1979) Children's perceptions of social interaction in school, *Collected Original Resources in Education*, **3**(1).

Davies, B. (1982) *Life in Classroom and Playground*. London: Routledge and Kegan Paul.

Davies, L. (1983) Gender, resistance and power, in Walker, S. and Barton, L. *Gender, Class and Education*. Lewes: Falmer Press.

Delamont, S. (1983) *Interaction in the Classroom* (2nd edition). London: Methuen.

Delamont, S. (ed.) (1984) *Readings on Interaction in The Classroom*. London: Methuen.

Denscombe, M. (1980a) 'Keeping 'em quiet': the significance of noise for the practical activity of teaching, in Woods, P. (ed.) *Teacher Strategies*. Beckenham: Croom Helm.

Denscombe, M. (1980b) Pupil strategies and the open classroom, in Woods, P. *Pupil Strategies*. Beckenham: Croom Helm.

Department of Education and Science (1977) *Education in Schools: a consultative document*, Cmnd 6869. London: HMSO.

Department of Education and Science (1978) *Primary Education in England*. London: HMSO.

Department of Education and Science: Welsh Office (1980) *A Framework for the School Curriculum*. London: DES.

Department of Education and Science: Welsh Office (1981) *The School Curriculum*. London: HMSO.

Department of Education and Science (1983) *Teaching Quality*, Cmnd 8836. London: HMSO.

Diamond, J. (1979) *Royal Commission on the Distribution of Income and Wealth*, Report No. 7, Cmnd 7596. London: HMSO.

Esland, G.M. (1971) Teaching and learning as the organisation of knowledge, in Young, M. (ed.) *Knowledge and Control*. West Drayton: Collier Macmillan.

Evans, T. (1979) Creativity, sex-role, socialisation and pupil–teacher interactions in early schooling, *Sociological Review*, **27**(1), 139–55.

Galton, M., Simon, B. and Croll, P. (1980) *Inside the Primary Classroom*. London: Routledge and Kegan Paul.

Garner, J. and Bing, M. (1973) Inequalities of teacher–pupil contacts, *British Journal of Educational Psychology*, **43**, 234–43.

Gerth, H.H. and Mills, C.W. (1948) *From Max Weber*. London: Routledge and Kegan Paul.

Glaser, B.G. and Strauss, A.L. (1967) *The Discovery of Grounded Theory*. London: Weidenfeld and Nicolson.

Glaser, B.G. and Strauss, A.L. (1971) *Status Passage*. New York: Aldine.

Goffman, E. (1959) *Presentation of Self in Everyday Life*. New York: Doubleday.

Grace, G. (1978) *Teachers, Ideology and Control: A study in urban education.* London: Routledge and Kegan Paul.

Gramsci, A. (1978) *Selections from Political Writings*, Volumes 1 and 2. London: Lawrence and Wishart.

Grant, K.A. (ed.) (1984) *Preparing for Reflective Teaching.* Boston: Allyn and Bacon.

Gray, H. (1982) Organisation development and the primary school, in Richards, C. (ed.) *New Directions in Primary Education.* Lewes: Falmer Press.

Halpin, A.W. (1966) The organisational climate of schools, in Halpin, A.W. (ed.) *Theory and Research in Administration.* New York: Macmillan.

Halsey, A.H., Heath, A.F. and Ridge, J.M. (1980) *Origins and Destinations.* Oxford: Oxford University Press.

Hammersley, M. (1980) Classroom ethnography, *Educational Analysis*, 2(2), 47–74.

Hammersley, M. (1982) The sociology of classrooms, in Hartnett, A. (ed.) *The Social Sciences in Educational Studies.* London: Heinemann.

Hammersley, M. (ed.) (1983) *The Ethnography of Schooling.* Driffield: Nafferton.

Hammersley, M. and Atkinson, P. (1983) *Ethnography: Principles in Practice.* London: Methuen.

Hammersley, M. and Woods, P. (ed.) (1976) *The Process of Schooling.* London: Routledge and Kegan Paul.

Hammersley, M. and Woods, P. (1984) *Life in School: The Sociology of Pupil Culture.* Milton Keynes: Open University Press.

Hargreaves, A. (1978) The significance of classroom coping strategies, in Barton, L. and Meighan, R. (ed.) *Sociological Interpretation of Schooling and Classrooms.* Driffield: Nafferton.

Hargreaves, A. (1979) Strategies, decisions and control: interaction in a middle school classroom, in Eggleston, J. (ed.) *Teacher Decision-Making in the Classroom.* London: Routledge and Kegan Paul.

Hargreaves, A. (1981) Contrastive rhetoric and extremist talk: teachers, hegemony and the educationist context, in Barton, L. and Walker, S. (ed.) *Schools, Teachers and Teaching.* Lewes: Falmer Press.

Hargreaves, A. and Woods, P. (ed.) (1984) *Classrooms and Staffrooms: The Sociology of Teachers and Teaching.* Milton Keynes: Open University Press.

Hargreaves, D.H. (1967) *Social Relations in a Secondary School.* London: Routledge and Kegan Paul.

Hargreaves, D.H. (1972) *Interpersonal Relationships and Education.* London: Routledge and Kegan Paul.

Hargreaves, D.H. (1978) Whatever happened to symbolic interactionism? in Barton, L. and Meighan, R. (ed.) *Sociological Interpretations of Schooling and Classrooms.* Driffield: Nafferton.

Hargreaves, D.H., Hestor, S.K. and Mellor, F.J. (1975) *Deviance in Classrooms.* London: Routledge and Kegan Paul.

Harré, R. (1974) Rule as a scientific concept, in Mischel, T. (ed.) *Understanding Other Persons.* Oxford: Blackwell.

Henry, J. (1955) Docility: or giving teacher what she wants, *Journal of Social Issues*, 2, 33–41.

Humphries, S. (1981) *Hooligans or Rebels? An oral history of working class childhood and youth 1889–1939.* Oxford: Blackwell.

Isaacs, S. (1933) *Social Development in Young Children: A Study of Beginnings*. London: Routledge and Kegan Paul.

Jackson, B. (1964) *Streaming: An Educational System in Miniature*. London: Routledge and Kegan Paul.

Jackson, P.W. (1968) *Life in Classrooms*. New York: Holt, Rinehart and Winston.

Johnson, R. (1970) Educational policy and social control in early Victorian England, *Past and Present*, **49**, 96–119.

Jones, B. (1984) *Beyond a Laugh*. Unpublished BEd. Honours Dissertation, Oxford Polytechnic.

Jones, R. (1980) *Fostering Femininity in Middle School Girls*, Paper given at the Middle Schools Research Group Conference, Woburn.

Keddie, N. (1971) Classroom knowledge, in Young, M. (ed.) *Knowledge and Control*. London: Macmillan.

Kessen, W. (1965) *The Child*. New York: Wiley.

King, R. (1973) *School Organisation and Pupil Involvement: a study of secondary schools*. London: Routledge and Kegan Paul.

King, R. (1978) *All Things Bright and Beautiful? A sociological study of infants' classrooms*. Chichester: Wiley.

King, R. (1984) *The Sociology of School Organisation*. London: Methuen.

Kirby, N. (1981) *Personal Values in Primary Education*. London: Harper and Row.

Kogan, M. (1971) *The Government of Education*. London: Macmillan.

Kogan, M. (1978) *The Politics of Educational Change*. Manchester: Manchester University Press.

Kogan, M., Johnson, D., Packwood, T. and Whitaker, T. (1984) *School Governing Bodies*. London: Heinemann.

Kyriacou, C. (1980) Coping actions and occupational stress among school teachers, *Research in Education*, **24**, 57–61.

Lacey, C. (1970) *Hightown Grammar*. Manchester: Manchester University Press.

Lambart, A.M. (1976) The sisterhood, in Hammersley, M. and Woods, P. *The Process of Schooling*. London: Routledge and Kegan Paul.

Leiter, K.C.W. (1974) Ad hocing in the schools, in Cicouvel, A.V. (ed.) *Language Use and School Performance*. New York: Academic Press.

Lukes, S. (1974) *Power: A Radical View*. London: Macmillan.

McCann, P. (ed.) (1977) *Popular Education and Socialisation in the Nineteenth Century*. London: Methuen.

McIntyre, D. (1980) The contribution of research to quality in teacher education, in Hoyle, E. (ed.) *The World Yearbook of Education*. London: Kogan Page.

Macpherson, J. (1983) *The Feral Classroom: High School Students' Constructions of Reality*. London: Routledge and Kegan Paul.

Manning, M., Heron, J. and Marshall, T. (1978) Styles of hostility and interactions at nursery, at school and at home, in Hersov, L.A., Berger, M. and Shaffer, D. (ed.) *Aggression and Anti-social Behaviour in Childhood and Adolescence*, Monograph of the *Journal of Child Psychology and Psychiatry*, **1**. Oxford: Pergamon.

Marsh, P., Rosser, E. and Harré, R. (1978) *The Rules of Disorder*. London: Routledge and Kegan Paul.

Matza, D. (1964) *Delinquency and Drift*. New York: Wiley.

Mead, G.H. (1934) *Mind, Self, and Society*. Chicago: University of Chicago.
Meighan, R. (1978) The learner's viewpoint, *Educational Review*, **30**(2).
Meltzer, B.N., Petras, J.W. and Reynolds, L.T. (1975) *Symbolic Interactionism: genesis, variations and criticism*. London: Routledge and Kegan Paul.
Meyenn, R.J. (1980) School girls' peer groups, in Woods, P. *Pupil Strategies*. Beckenham: Croom Helm.
Mills, C.W. (1959) *The Sociological Imagination*. New York: Oxford University Press.
Mishan, E.J. (1967) *The Costs of Economic Growth*. London: Staples Press.
Montagner, H. (1978) *L'enfant et La Communication*. Paris: Pernoud/Stock.
Moran, P.R. (1971) The integrated day, *Educational Research*, **14**(1), 65–9.
Morgan, J., O'Neill, C. and Harré, R. (1979) *Names and Nicknames*. London: Routledge and Kegan Paul.
NAS and UWT (1976) *Stress in School*. Hemel Hempstead: NAS/UWT.
Nash, R. (1973) *Classrooms Observed*. London: Routledge and Kegan Paul.
Nash, R. (1976) *Teacher Expectations and Pupil Learning*. London: Routledge and Kegan Paul.
National Union of Teachers (1982) *Schools Speak Out*. London: National Union of Teachers.
Nixon, J. (1981) *A Teacher's Guide to Action Research*. London: Grant McIntyre.
Norwood, C. and Hope, A.H. (1909) *The Higher Education of Boys in England*. London: John Murray.
O'Leary, K.D. and O'Leary, S.G. (1972) *Classroom Management*. New York: Pergamon.
Opie, I. and Opie, P. (1959) *The Lore and Language of School Children*. Oxford: Oxford University Press.
Opie, I. and Opie, P. (1969) *Children's Games in Street and Playground*. Oxford: Oxford University Press.
Piaget, J. (1959) *The Language and Thought of the Child*. London: Routledge and Kegan Paul.
Pollard, A. (1976) *Classroom Interaction Processes: Towards a grounded sociological model of cultural, structural and experiential factors*, Unpublished MEd. dissertation, University of Sheffield.
Pollard, A. (1979) Negotiating deviance and 'getting done' in primary school classrooms, in Barton, L. and Meighan, R. (ed.) *Schools, Pupils and Deviance*. Driffield: Nafferton.
Pollard, A. (1980) Teacher interests and changing situations of survival threat in primary school classrooms, in Woods, P. (ed.) *Teacher Strategies*. Beckenham: Croom Helm.
Pollard, A. (1981) *Coping with Deviance: School processes and their implications for social reproduction*, Unpublished PhD. thesis, University of Sheffield.
Pollard, A. (1982) A model of coping strategies, *British Journal of Sociology of Education*, **3**(1), 19–37.
Pollard, A. (1983) Coping strategies and the multiplication of social differentiation in infant classrooms, *British Journal of Educational Research*, **10**(1).
Pollard, A. (1984) Ethnography and social policy for classroom practice, in Barton, L. and Walker, S. (ed.) *Social Crisis and Educational Research*. Beckenham: Croom Helm.

Pollard, A. (1985) Opportunities and difficulties of a teacher–ethnographer: a personal account, in Burgess, R. (ed.) *Field Methods in the Study of Education: Issue and Problems*. Lewes: Falmer Press.

Postman, N. and Weingartner, C. (1969) *Teaching as Subversive Activity*. New York: Delacorte Press.

Reid, W.A. (1978) *Thinking about the Curriculum*. London: Routledge and Kegan Paul.

Rist, R.C. (1970) Student social class and teacher expectations: the self-fulfilling prophecy in ghetto education, *Harvard Education Review*, **40**, 411–51.

Rock, P. (1979) *The Making of Symbolic Interactionism*. London: Macmillan.

Rosenthal, R. and Jacobson, L. (1968) *Pygmalion in the Classroom*. New York: Holt, Rinehart and Winston.

Rosser, E. (1976) And if they can turn nasty we can turn nasty too, *Self and Society*, **4**(6), 19–25.

Rousseau, J.J. (1972) *Emile*. London: Dent.

Rowlands, S. (1984) *The Enquiring School*. Lewes: Falmer Press.

Roy, W. (1983) *Teaching Under Attack*. Beckenham: Croom Helm.

Rubin, Z. (1980) *Children's Friendships*. London: Fontana.

Rutter, M., Maughan, B., Mortimore, P. and Ouston, J. (1979) *Fifteen Thousand Hours*. Shepton Mallet: Open Books.

Salter, B. and Tapper, T. (1981) *Education, Politics and the State*. London: McIntyre.

Schatzman, L. and Strauss, A. (1973) *Field Research: Strategies for a Natural Sociology*. Englewood Cliffs, NJ: Prentice-Hall.

Schon, D.A. (1983) *The Reflective Practitioner*, Hounslow: Maurice Temple Smith.

Schutz, A. (1964) *Collected Papers* (ed. Natanson, M.). The Hague: Nijhoff.

Schutz, A. (1970) *On Phenomenology and Social Relations: selected writings* (ed. Wagner, H.R.). Chicago: Chicago University Press.

Sharp, R. and Green, A. (1975) *Education and Social Control: A study in progressive primary education*. London: Routledge and Kegan Paul.

Sluckin, A. (1981) *Growing up in the Playground*. London: Routledge and Kegan Paul.

Snyder, B.R. (1971) *The Hidden Curriculum*. New York: Knopf.

Spender, D. (1980) *Man Made Language*. London: Routledge and Kegan Paul.

Spender, D. and Sarah, E. (ed.) (1980) *Learning to Lose: Sexism and Education*. London: Women's Press.

Stebbins, R.A. (1980) The role of humour in teaching: strategy and self expression, in Woods, P. (ed.) *Teacher Strategies*. Beckenham: Croom Helm.

Stenhouse, L. (1975) *An Introduction to Curriculum Research and Development*. London: Heinemann.

Strauss, A.M. (1978) *Negotiations: Varieties, Contexts, Processes and Social Order*. London: Jossey-Bass.

Tawney, R.H. (1931) *Equality*. London: George Allen and Unwin.

Turner, G. (1983) *The Social World of the Comprehensive School*. Beckenham: Croom Helm.

Van Manen, M. (1977) Linking ways of knowing with ways of being practical, *Curriculum Enquiry*, **6**.

References 261

Walker, R. and Adelman, C. (1976) Strawberries, in Stubbs, M. and Delamont, S. *Explorations in Classroom Observation*. Chichester: Wiley.

Waller, W. (1932) *The Sociology of Teaching*. New York: Russell and Russell.

Weber, M. (1976) *The Protestant Ethic and the Spirit of Capitalism*. London: George Allen and Unwin.

Westwood, L.J. (1967) The role of the teacher, *Educational Research*, Part I, 9(2), 122–34; Part II, 10(1), 21–37.

Whitbread, N. (1972) *The Evolution of the Nursery-Infant School*. London: Routledge and Kegan Paul.

Willis, P. (1977) *Learning to Labour: How working class kids get working class jobs*. Aldershot: Saxon House.

Wilson, B. (1962) The teachers' role—a sociological analysis, *British Journal of Sociology*, 13(1), 15–32.

Woods, P. (1975) Showing them up in secondary school, in Chaman, G. and Delamont, S. (ed.) *Frontiers of Classroom Research*. Slough: NFER.

Woods, P. (1976) Having a laugh, an antidote to schooling, in Hammersley, M. and Woods, P.E. (ed.) *The Process of Schooling*. London: Routledge and Kegan Paul.

Woods, P. (1977) Teaching for survival, in Woods, P. and Hammersley, M. (ed.) *School Experience*. Beckenham: Croom Helm.

Woods, P. (1979) *The Divided School*. London: Routledge and Kegan Paul.

Woods, P. (ed.) (1980a) *Teacher Strategies*. Beckenham: Croom Helm.

Woods, P. (ed.) (1980b) *Pupil Strategies*. Beckenham: Croom Helm.

Woods, P. (1983) *Sociology and the School*. London: Routledge and Kegan Paul.

Woods, P. (1985) Sociology, ethnography and teacher practice, *Teaching and Teacher Education*, 1(1).

Yardley, A. (1976) *The Organisation of the Infant School*. London: Evans.

Zeichner, K. and Teitelbaum, K. (1982) Personalised and inquiry-oriented teacher education: an analysis of two approaches to the development of curriculum for field-based courses, *Journal of Education for Teaching*, 8(2), 95–117.

Name Index

Adelman, C. 84
Alexander, R. 236
Apple, M. 112
Aries, P. 38
Armstrong, M. 8
Ashton, P.M. 18, 19, 39

Bachrach, P. 122
Bagley, A.J. 98–9
Bagley, J.J. 98–9
Ball, S. 134, 159, 194
Baratz, M.S. 122
Barker, R. 162
Barnes, D. 43
Baron, G. 119
Bassey, M. 19
Bealing, D. 18, 19
Becker, H.S. 202–3
Bennett, N. 6, 19, 102
Berger, B. 241
Berger, P.L. 241
Berlak, A. 23, 121
Berlak, H. 23, 121
Bernstein, B. 162
Bidwell, C.E. 122
Bing, M. 41
Blackie, J. 18
Blishen, E. 86
Blumer, H. 155
Bone, T. 120
Bossert, S.T. 50

Boudon, R. 97
Boydell, D. 18
Boyson, R. 101
Burgess, R.G. 123, 138

Callaghan, J. 102
Calvert, B. 39, 42
Clarricoates, K. 195, 196, 199, 231
Clegg, Sir A. 7, 18
Cockburn, A. 6
Coe, J. 7
Cox, C.B. 101
Croll, P. 19, 41, 110, 193

Davies, B. 45, 47, 48, 84, 88
Davies, F. 18
Davies, L. 196
Desforges, C. 6
Dewey, J. 101
Dyson, A.E. 101

Esland, G.M. 43
Evans, T. 41

Froebel, F. 98, 101

Galton, M. 19, 41, 110, 193
Garner, J. 41

Gerth, H.H. 120
Glaser, B.G. xi, 242
Goffman, E. 154
Grace, G. 99–100, 112, 138, 140
Gramsci, A. 107
Gray, H. 120
Green, A. 10, 122, 135–6, 199
Gump, P.V. 162

Halpin, A.W. 115
Halsey, A.H. 97
Hammersley, M. 155
Hargreaves, A. 141, 152, 189
Hargreaves, D.H. xi, 33, 42, 49, 161, 194, 200–1
Harre, R. 48, 86, 155, 193
Heath, A.F. 97
Henry, J. 187
Heron, J. 91
Hestor, S.K. 161, 200–1
Hope, A.H. 119
Humphries, S. 195–6

Isaacs, S. 98, 101

Jackson, B. 17
Jackson, P.W. 41, 42

Jacobson, L. 199
Johnson, R. 99
Jones, B. 196
Jones, R. 209

Keddie, N. 15
Kessen, W. 38
King, R. 10, 124–5,
134, 142
Kirby, N. 7, 103
Kogan, M. 105, 144
Kyriacou, C. 27

Lacey, C. 134, 194
Lambart, A.M. 195
Leiter, K.C.W. 202
Lowe, R. 99, 100
Lukes, S. 187

McCann, P. 99
McIntyre, D. 236
Manning, M. 91
Marsh, L. 7, 18
Marsh, P. 48, 193
Marshall, T. 91
Martin, T. 38
Matza, D. 227
Maugham, B. 115
Mead, G.H. 152–3
Meighan, R. 86, 90
Mellor, F.J. 161,
200–1
Meyenn, R.J. 49, 83,
195
Mills, C.W. 120
Montagner, H. 91
Moran, P.R. 19
Morgan, J. 86

Nash, R. 86, 90
Norwood, C. 119

O'Leary, K.D. 42
O'Leary, S.G. 42
O'Neill, C. 86
Opie, I. 44, 45, 48,
49
Opie, P. 44, 45, 48,
49
Owen, R. 98, 100,
101

Pestalozzi, J.H. 98
Piaget, J. 5, 98
Pluckrose, H. 18
Pollard, A. ix, xii,
56, 57, 133
Postman, N. 138

Reid, W.A. ix, 233
Ridge, J.M. 97
Rist, R.C. 199, 220
Rosenthal, R. 199
Rosser, E. 48, 86,
193
Rousseau, J.J. 38
Rowlands, S. 7, 8
Roy, W. 103
Rubin, Z. 46
Rutter, M. 115

Salter, B. 104
Sarah, E. 119
Schutz, A. 116, 201,
209
Sharp, R. 10, 122,
135–6, 199

Simon, B. 19, 41,
110, 193
Sluckin, A. 47, 49,
87, 89, 91
Snyder, B.R. 164
Spender, D. 119, 142
Stebbins, R.A. 84
Strauss, A.M. xi,
122, 242

Tapper, T. 104
Tawney, R.H. 101
Teitelbaum, K. ix,
247
Thomas, W.I. 155
Turner, G. 88, 194

Van Manen, M. 248

Walker, R. 84
Waller, W. 22, 37, 40,
156–8
Weber, M. 108,
121–2
Weingartner, C. 138
Westwood, L.J. 33
Whitbread, N. 100–1
Wilkinson, B. 6
Willis, P. 194
Wilson, N. 33
Woods, P. 46, 47, 49,
83, 152, 154, 185,
187, 194, 237, 242

Yardley, A. 7, 18

Zeichner, K. ix, 247

Subject Index

Adaptation 3, 113
Ashton First School xii
  head teacher 28
  institutional bias 138
  rule-frame phases 164–71
  subversive teacher 138–40,
    226–31
    classroom organisation 227–8
    control and teaching
      technique 226–31
    friendship groups 228, 229
    subterranean value
      system 227, 230
Assemblies 125, 127–9
Australian friendship groups 45, 88

Bishop McGregor Comprehensive
  School 138
Black Papers 101–2
Board of Education 17, 101
Burnley Road Infant School 124
Burns Road Infant School xii
  bypassing by staff 137–8
  commitment of staff 31
  parents and staff 28
  staffroom conversation at 21
  structure 120
  support staff 143–4

Central Advisory Council for
  Education 5, 16
Child-centred teaching
  methods 16–17, 19–20, 35

Child culture 44, 150
  social conventions 48
Children
  adult views of 39–40
  biographical factors 153
  'child as evil' 38, 150
  'child as good' 38, 150
  competence 47–8
  in crowds 41–2
  and curriculum 43–4
  dignity 86–7, 239–40, 244–5
  enjoyment at school 83–5,
    191
  evaluation of lessons 89
  evaluation of teachers 159
  gang rivalry 51–2
  gangs 51–5
  interests-at-hand 81–90, 155,
    156, 179, 240
  learning 89–90, 239, 240
  peer-group membership 87
  praise of 42–3
  pressures on 40, 150
  reference groups 81
  relationships 46–8, 50
  role factors 151, 153
  and school institutional bias 142
  self-image 42–3, 82–3, 154, 237,
    241
    development of 199
    formation of 242, 244
    in secondary schools 242
    and self-confidence 242–3

Children (*Cont.*)
  sexual awareness 79–80
  social expectations of adults 39,
    150
  social system 81, 89
  status 49–50
  stress 85–6
  and teachers' attitudes 86, 164,
    173, 175, 238
  and teachers' expectations 86,
    90, 231
  and teachers' power 43, 156,
    159–61, 187–8, 237–8
  work-evasion skills 181–3
  see also Child culture, Classroom
    strategies, Groups of
    children, Typification
Classroom strategies 157
  appeal strategies 173, 177, 178
  at Ashton First School 226–31
  behavioural structuring 178–9
  biographical factors 152–4
  child strategies 184–94, 218
    collaboration to
      produce 222–6
    drifting 187, 190–2, 204, 222
    evasion 181–3, 188–92
    open negotiation 185–6, 190,
      237–9
    parameters 193–4
    rebellion 189, 192
    withdrawal 189
  and children's interests 174
  classification 90–3, 191
  conflict 156–8, 180
  counter-strategies 181–3
  gender differences 195–7
  imbalances 180
  inherited practices 155, 229–30
  interaction between teachers and
    children 172–9, 184, 237
  and joker groups 194, 218
  meshing 218–9, 225–6, 238, 244
  and power 184, 190
  routine 173, 230
  routine deviance 190–2
  strategic action 155
  at Summerlands Infant
    School 218–22
  teacher reactions 192
  teacher strategies 184–93, 204

Classroom strategies (*Cont.*)
  teacher strategies (*Cont.*)
    domination 189–90, 192, 237
    manipulation 187–9, 190, 192
    open negotiation 185–6, 190,
      237–9
    routinisation 186–7, 190, 192
    timing 178
    see also Groups of children,
      Working consensus
Cognition 5
Cognitive matching 6
  see also Matching of knowledge
    and tasks
Coping 149–56
  see also Classroom strategies
Countesthorpe College 141
Crowds, children in 41–2
Crowther Report 107
Curriculum 43–4
  'common core' 102
  government pressure on 105

Department of Education and
  Science 5, 15, 20, 102, 104–5,
  117
Deviance
  girls' 195–6
  routine 190–2, 194, 208
  typification of boys' 214–7
  typification of girls' 213

Economic system, British 107–8,
  110
Education Act 1870 98
Education Act 1902 103
Education Act 1944 125
Education as political issue 102,
  105
  centralised control 102
  efficiency as criterion 102
  and teachers' autonomy 103
Education system, British 103–7
  decentralisation 103–4
  effect on individual
    schools 106–7
  resistance to established
    values 112
  role of government 104–5

Elementary schools
  aims of Victorian era   99–100,
    111, 246
  financing   98–9, 101
  influence of Dewey on   98–101
Ethnography   x–xi, 200, 236

Finance   2, 9, 118
Formal authority   121
Friendships, children's   46–50,
    220–1, 228–9, 245
  see also Groups of children
Functional authority   121, 134–5

Gangs
  see Groups of children
Girls
  deviance   196
  standard of teaching of   199
  strategies   195–7
  typification   199, 211
Governing bodies   104–6
Government role in
    education   104–5
Governors and school institutional
    bias   144
Groups of children   51–5, 57–89,
    193–4
  academic success   78–9
  attitudes to teachers   72–8
  gang groups   60–2, 71–8, 88, 180
    activities   65–8
    disturbance in lessons   70–1,
      84
    learning   89
    open negotiation and   185
    strategies   91
    and teachers' strategies   194
    typification   213–7
  gender factors   195
  good groups   59–61, 68–9, 72–3,
    76–7, 84
    activities   62–3
    learning   89
    open negotiation and   185
    strategies   91
    and teachers' strategies   194
    typification   209–13
  housing types   78
  intergroup rivalry   66–7, 87

Groups of children (*Cont.*)
  joker groups   60–1, 69–70, 73–5,
    84, 180
    activities   63–5
    learning   89
    open negotiation and   185
    and teachers' strategies   194
    typification   205–9
    and working consensus   194,
      206
  maths and English scores   79
  reference groups on lessons   81
  school involvement   79
  social class   78
  within school system   89

Hadow Report   17, 101
Hawthorn Junior and Infant
    Schools   xii
Head teachers   27–8, 133
  autonomy   103–4, 119
  influence on schools   123–4,
    133–4
  Mapledene   135–7
  Moorfields   127–33
    teachers' views of   130–2
  and parents   124
  Summerlands   125–7
Her Majesty's Inspectors   104, 240
Humour in classrooms   21, 84, 186,
    191, 226
  'having a laugh'   68–71, 73–5, 83,
    187, 191

Individualistic purpose of primary
    education   18–39
Infant school movement   100
Institutional bias, school   150
  and children   142–3
  and class teachers   133–42
  and head teachers   123–33
  and parents and governors   144
  and support staff   143–4

Janine's Terrors   51–5
  and teacher authority   53
Joker groups
  see Groups of children

Langley Infant School   124
Learning, child's control of   8

Local education authorities   101,
    105
  expenditure   106
  and governing bodies   106

Macro factors in school life   95–6,
    97–8, 247
Manpower Services
    Commission   105
Mapledene Infant School   10,
    135–7, 199
Matching of knowledge and
    tasks   5, 6
Mixed ability classes   17–18
Moorside Middle School   xii
  autonomy of teachers   27
  characteristics of ideal
      pupil   206–17
  deviation from ideal   213–17
  child interviewers   57
  children's status   49
  children's views of teachers   72–6
  classroom strategy   157
  commitment of teachers   25–6
  discipline at   32–4
  drifting strategy   204
  enjoyment of teaching at   24
  evaluation of lessons   89
  friendship groups   51–5, 58–80
  'having a laugh' at   68–71, 83
  head teacher   27, 73, 127–33
    staff views of   130–2
  health of teachers   26–7
  Janine's Terrors   51–5
  learning   89–90
  Moorside Investigation
      Department   57
  parents   28, 144
  practicalities of teaching at   31–3
  rule frame   162
  school institutional bias   127–33,
      142–3
    bypassing by staff   137–8
    challenge to by staff   140–2
  self-image of children   82–3
  self-image of teachers   29–33
  social cleavages   57–8
  social structure   56
  staffroom conversation   21
  support staff   143
  teachers on neatness   111

Moorside Middle School (*Cont.*)
  teachers on respect for staff   111
  teachers' stress   27
  typification at   203–5
  units   131–2
Moral standards, deterioration
    of   102
Motivation in the classroom   5–6

National Association for Primary
    Education   103
National Association of
    Schoolmasters and Union of
    Women Teachers   27
National Union of Teachers   103,
    113
Netherdyke Primary School   xii

Parents
  and school institutional bias   144
  and teachers   28
Playground games   45–8
Plowden Report   5, 101, 105
  and child-centred teaching
      methods   16–17, 19, 149
  and open-plan school design   18
  and streaming   17
Praise and evaluation   42–3
Primary schooling
  developmental tradition   100–1,
      103, 121
  history   98–103
Primary schools   115–18
  assemblies   125
  democracy in   120
  finance   118
  governing structure   104
  head teachers   119–20, 122–33
  numbers of pupils   117
  parental involvement   124, 144
  school institutional bias   122–33
  size   117
  staff   117–18
    career stucture   121
  see also Teachers
Priorities, educational   1
Progressive movement in primary
    education   18–19

Quality of classroom life   4

Reflective teaching   ix, 235
Relationships, teacher–pupil   7–9,
    41, 72–6, 86–7, 149–71, 237–41
    see also Classroom strategies,
       Working consensus
Riverdale Middle School   141,
    142
Role, children's   39, 151, 156
Role, teachers'   2, 151, 156
    expectations   149
Royal Commission on the
    Distribution of Income and
    Wealth   96–7
Rule frame
    at Ashton First School   164–71
    categories
       activity 162–3
       people 163–4
       place 162
       time   161–2
    changes 179–80, 181–3
    children's exploitation of   181–3
    during lesson   173, 176, 179
    at Moorside Middle School   204
    and teachers' interests   180

Schooling system and social
    inequality   97–8
Schools Council   105
Social atmosphere   5–6, 241
Social context of classroom   151
Social differentiation   9–10, 97–8,
    198
    and child's sense of identity   241
    cleavages   57–8
Societal purpose of primary
    education   18, 39, 247
Staffroom   20–3, 150
Status of children   49–50
Streaming   17–18
Summerlands Infant School
    children's backgrounds   219–20
    children's strategies   222–5
    familial atmosphere   218–9
    friendship groups   220–1
    gender differentiation   220–2
    head teacher   125–7
    hierarchy of children   220–6
    incentives   219, 222
    playground games   45–6
    school birthday party   126–7

Summerlands Infant School (*Cont.*)
    school institutional bias   125–7
    teaching strategies   220, 222–5
Support staff   143–4
Symbolic interactionism   x, 95, 122,
    155, 237

Taylor Report   106
Teacher–child interaction   x,
    xiv-xv, 3, 10, 215–7
Teacher–pupil ratios   40, 41
    nineteenth-century   101
    1983–84   106
Teacher–pupil relationships   7–9,
    41, 72–6, 86–7, 149–71
    and child-centred ideology   238
    conflicts of interest   22, 237
    size of classes and   246
Teachers, primary-school
    acceptance of school institutional
       bias by   136–7
    autonomy   27–35, 53, 103, 134
    biographical factors   153
    bypassing of institutional bias
       by   137–8
    categorisation of pupils   see
       Typification
    challenge of classroom work   152
    challenges to institutional
       bias   140–2
    commitment   2, 5, 25, 30–1
    competence   33
    and curriculum   43–4
    discipline   32–5
    in educationist context   15–16
    enjoyment of work   24–5
    functional authority   134–5
    and head teachers   27, 124,
       130–3
    health   26–7
    interests-at-hand   24–35, 155,
       156, 179–80
    knowledge of pupils   200–17
    numbers   119
    and parents   28
    payment by results   100, 101
    and playground games   45–6
    power   43, 156, 159–61, 187–8,
       237–8
    practical realism   23
    pressures on   6, 10, 23, 124, 150, 243

Teachers, primary-school (*Cont.*)
  and progressive movement   19
  promotion   118, 121
  role factors   151, 153
  and school institutional
    bias   133–40
  self-image   28–33, 154, 237
  social values   108–11
  and streaming   17–18
  stress   27, 240
  subversion   138–40
  in teacher context   15–16
  view of children   39
  workload   25–6, 240
  see also Classroom strategies,
    Head teachers
Teaching
  negative cycle   240
  positive cycle   240
  social policies in 243–6
  theory of 235–6

Teaching practice   189–90, 236, 247
Teaching style, longer-term   186
Teenage culture   52
Theory–practice problem   3–4
Typification   199–217, 242, 244,
    246
  gender   199, 208–9, 211–13
  ideal pupil   205–17
  reasons for typing   201
  social class   199, 202

Wealth, distribution of   97, 198
William Tyndale Primary
    School   102
Working-class children
    under-achievement   10, 199
Working-class education in the
    nineteenth century   99–100
Working consensus   158–61, 174,
    185, 191, 193